THE ROMANTIC CONFLICT

'Thomas Chatterton taking the Bowl of Poison from the Spirit of Despair' by John Flaxman (1755–1826)

The
Romantic Conflict

By

ALLAN RODWAY

Senior Lecturer in the Department of English
University of Nottingham

1963

CHATTO & WINDUS

LONDON

Published by
Chatto & Windus Ltd
London
★
Clarke, Irwin & Co Ltd
Toronto

Printed in Great Britain by
Spottiswoode, Ballantyne & Co Ltd
London and Colchester

CONTENTS

ACKNOWLEDGMENTS

THANKS are due to The Royal Institute of Cornwall, Truro, for permission to reproduce the drawing by G. Romney on the dustcover, and to the late Iolo Williams for the picture by Flaxman reproduced as Frontispiece; to Penguin Books for permission to print extracts from *The Pelican Guide to English Literature* (5); to Nicholas Kaye for permission to use pieces from Alfred Cobban's collection of documents; and to the Oxford University Press for permission to quote from W. W. Robson's *Byron as Poet*.

A debt of gratitude is also owed to the writers of all those works which have contributed, under conscious or unconscious levying, to this one.

Finally, especial thanks must be given to my colleague Dr. J. T. Boulton, whose thoroughness in checking proofs has prevented many errors, to my wife and daughters for their patient aid in the labour of indexing, and to Emeritus Professor Pinto for his counsel during the initial stage of compilation.

PREFACE

THE present study of English romantic poetry argues that romanticism is more profitably approached as the product of a particular period than as the product of a particular kind of personality. Such an approach is inevitably somewhat sociological, but it does not thereby reduce romanticism, in this work, to the outworn fashion of a buried age. On the contrary, it turns out to emphasise the fact that, no matter how sociological some of the causes may have been, the main insights of the romantic movement were deeply psychological, and therefore comparatively permanent.

Two consequences follow from this approach. Firstly, any *simple* definition of 'romanticism' is precluded, because the reaction against 'Reason' is taken to be really not against reasoning but against a type of society–but it did have non-rational, psychological consequences. So 'romanticism' becomes a complex rather than a creed. The 'Romantic Conflict' of the title must be taken to have both an outward and an inward aspect; to indicate conflict between the poets and their society as well as conflict within the poets themselves. Secondly, the book moves from very general background studies to detailed discussion of individual poets and poems.

Part I, then, attempts to assign romanticism to a time and place–on grounds of critical utility; to show why English romanticism should have come when it did and been what it was; to give evidence of social pressures not existing before or after the romantic period (thus accounting for the outward aspect of the conflict); and finally to indicate the creative dilemma (the inward aspect) which this situation put the English romantics into.

Part II, the main body of the book, contains analyses of the work of the most notable romantic poets writing before the French Revolution, and those–subject to greater pressures–who wrote, and wrote better, during and after it. The predicament of these later writers is profitably, if crudely, conceivable as a conflict between material realities and spiritual ideals. And this seems generally, as one would expect, to lead to confusion between the imaginary and the real, to wishfulfilment, or to morbid fantasy-faults less evident in the earlier and lesser poets. But occasionally in the major poets it leads to new and valid revelation. Their metaphysics may be wrong but their human insights are right-and greatly expressed. Much of their work, then, may be rhetorical propaganda on behalf of a suspect system of belief, but some turns out to be a poetry of shared experience: experience previously neglected as unimportant or non-existent, or, if not neglected, inadequately expressed. It is the achievement of the great romantics in this small field that makes them still relevant and still worth study. All conflicts have their casualties, but the romantic conflict has its victories too.

NOTE ON CRITICAL VOCABULARY

SINCE the romantics themselves made extravagant claims for poetry, and indeed so defined it as to include almost anything highly approved, it seems necessary to make a disclaimer here and say that the word 'poetry', in this book, is not intended to carry any laudatory overtones. 'Poetry' will simply refer to the content of verse, and a 'poem' will indicate any complete set of verses, good, bad, or indifferent (verse being any writing in which line-length is part of the expressive form). This seems to have at least the negative merits of not prejudging any critical issues, of not requiring the reader to remember yet another complicated evaluative definition, and of according with popular usage.

Again, much attention has been given recently to imagery-some of it excellent-but no conclusive formulation has emerged, and many of the ingenious definitions are so inclusive that they hinder critical discrimination. Here, then, 'image' will just refer to any verbal (but not necessarily visual) model of something usually expressed less figuratively, whether idea or entity. In fact, it will be a general word covering metaphor, simile, metonymy, personification and synecdoche, when particularising is not required. But what are often loosely styled 'images' of touch, muscular tension and so on will be spoken of as 'references to' or 'evocations of' to mark their difference of kind. The word 'symbol' will refer to an image used as a sign-the model plus a message, as it were-having, that is to say, an intellectual reference of some generality. Different sorts of symbolism may then be distinguished by the use of qualifying words or phrases.

On a pitch now so queered by the subtleties of experts, such homespun usage, like the village slogger, may plead effectiveness as an excuse. It forces one to make any further discriminations, not theoretically, but instance by particular instance, it does not distract one from the texts by requiring any difficult mnemo-technic, and it avoids subtle traps, such as confusing English romantic symbol-users with the French Symbolists-a confusion which has led several recent writers to take the further step of implying that Eliot and Pound are really romantics because they were influenced by the Symbolists. This needlessly blurs distinctions, for these two poets are so different from those of the romantic period as obviously to require another name if criticism is not to make confusion worse confounded.

Part One

INTRODUCTION

ROMANTICISM is a vague term[1] and a vast subject, yet whatever it may be it is very important, for the European mind has probably been altered more by romanticism than by anything else save the development of scientific method. It could almost be defined as the development of unscientific method–almost, but not quite, as the romantic movement was much too complicated to be summed-up in a phrase. Still, from one point of view, it was a wilful narrowing of art. Coming in with the great rise of science and industry in the late eighteenth century, it rejected that truth and that aspect of human endeavour and discovery–save when it could be turned to partisan purpose. On the other hand, it revealed aspects that science and industry tended to suppress. In particular, it enfranchised psychological states, including some sub-conscious ones, by giving them thenceforward the status of fact.

Fortunately, the subject delimits itself, and by doing so it automatically renders the idea of 'romanticism' less vague and more useful, for it ties it, not loosely to the spirit of a type of personality, but to the spirit of an age as expressed through certain personalities who would have been otherwise than they were (though probably never 'augustan') in another period. There is, in fact, a Romantic Period: very roughly the period from 1750 to 1850. Before and after that period many works show romantic tendencies, but they are not central, not close to the vital issues of their age. They are literally eccentric. Indeed, the *main* romantic period can be reduced to the first fifty years of the nineteenth century. The preceding half-century is better styled pre-romantic, for though there is much work similar in kind to that produced after 1800, it tends to be less forceful and assertive. Moreover, it is subordinate to the mode of the Enlightenment, that reasonable reformism which is the best product of the

---

[1] Vague enough, for example, to have opposite opposites: classicism and realism.

dominant augustanism of the eighteenth century. At any rate, there is certainly little point in extending the term 'romanticism' beyond the period 1750–1850, since even within that period essential common characteristics become rather disguised as soon as you attempt to cross national boundaries.

If, then, this is *when* romanticism is, *what* is it that it is? As it happens, the when and the what cannot really be separated, because if it had not happened when it did it would have been other than it was. It has proved temptingly easy to give a superficial account of romanticism by defining it as a psychological disposition (roughly that of the intuitive introvert) or a metaphysical inclination (towards transcendental idealism). What is wrong with this is that there is nothing in it to prevent the assumption that men with such propensities existed in every age and produced characteristic works of art. But even if all romantic artists were of such disposition or inclination–and they weren't–it would not do, since it does not account for the tremendous outburst of one type of art in this particular period, particularly the latter half of it. Moreover, it entirely ignores the fact that human beings are more adaptable to their environment than any other animal, largely because they *make* a good deal of that environment. In short, it ignores the fact that characteristics in the romantics which would have been diminished in another period could have been, and indeed were, exaggerated in this. Chance could hardly ordain that in England all those coming to maturity between 1789 and 1830, and possessed of poetic genius, should have been born with a romantic temperament while the genius of, say, 1689 to 1730 was born augustan. We are forced to the conclusion that the milieu probably encouraged one type of genius and inhibited another. The art-form is inseparable from the circumstances of the age.

Renaissance humanism in Europe had gradually developed into the augustanism of the late seventeenth and early eighteenth centuries. That augustanism found its ideal in the Rome of Augustus and the court of Louis XIV. Basically, the ideal was one of Good Sense. After an age of fanatical religious and civil wars, men wanted stability. Consequently, writers aimed at moderation in both style and matter. At its best, this was the age of the Enlightenment. At its worst, however, it was the age of Corruption, since its devotion to the status quo rendered it deliberately unprogressive, and in such ages any abuse that can establish itself tends to become traditional and sacrosanct.

Romanticism grew as reform came to seem more desirable than stability. It was not, of course, the only reform movement-witness the Encyclopedists and Utilitarians. It was that reform movement which was sufficiently passionate to react against a whole civilisation, the best and the worst of it-in intention, if not quite in fact. This was not so much because the romantics had no good sense as because Good Sense had been brought into disrepute by concurrent corruption. The negative augustan characteristics of indifference, complacency, prudence and cynicism had been matched by such positive characteristics as sense, science, tolerance and wit. But all were indiscriminately labelled 'Reason' and reacted against by the more extreme romantics. This 'Reason' came to mean something like 'calculation', and was thus very different from the 'reason' sometimes evoked (with only seeming inconsistency) by the romantics themselves. That 'reason' implied something like 'judging by principle', rather than by convention. Romantic characteristics tended to be, negatively, fanaticism, crankiness, mysticism and egotism; and positively, insight, daring, grandeur, exploration and independence.

Romantics, then, are as much made as born. They are not to be assessed solely in physiological or psychological terms, and they need the right environment. Not all are sensual or introverted or mystical. Wordsworth (in Shelley's phrase) was a 'solemn and unsexual man', and there is little mysticism in Byron or introversion in Keats. As for the right environment-it seems to have been an unfavourable one. The romantics throve on opposition and neglect. Their works tended to be characterised by emotional intensity and disregard for formal rules, in contradistinction to works of the preceding era. This is not to say, of course, that their works lack form; only that they are not formed by rule.

Where augustan writers believed in an equilibrium of the faculties, with Reason as chairman with casting vote, romantic writers believed with Wilde that nothing succeeds like excess. However, there are different degrees of excess in different periods, and different kinds of excess in different places and people.

One thing is strikingly clear: in England, France and Germany, the period of pre-romanticism (c.1750–1800) coincides not only with the rise of science but also with the rise to dominance of the middle-class, the bourgeoisie; while the period of romanticism proper coincides with the French Revolution, the Napoleonic Wars, and their aftermath of reaction and respectability. Aesthetically speaking, the earlier period tends (despite a number of exceptions) to be more muted, registering discontent with old forms and ideas rather than blasting and bombardiering for new ones.

Since art is an expression of society, or of various parties within society, this is what might have been expected. Pre-romanticism tended to be the expression of bourgeois dissatisfaction with the aristocratic culture of the landowning class. On the Continent, it tended to be anti-clerical as well, because the hand of the Church lay heavier there than in England. But when a violent revolution broke out, devoted not to reforming but to sweeping away the old society, all attitudes naturally became more extreme.

In England most romantics became more radical and revolutionary–Burke and Scott, and the post-romantic Newman and Carlyle being the only exceptions–but in Germany many became partisans of absolute monarchy and often Roman Catholics as well. Possibly English Protestantism had much to do with this difference. Englishmen associated the French Revolution with the Glorious Revolution of 1688, whereas the Germans had been 'liberated' by French armies and were less keen on liberty thereafter. This seems to have had the disastrous effect of leading to an abdication of political responsibility by German intellectuals. Romanticism became the dominant form but was unhealthily associated with a disdainful aristocratic transcendentalism. In France, there was an interregnum during the Napoleonic period, mainly because writers were not allowed to be romantic under Napoleon (all necessary changes having been inaugurated and everyone liberated and ordered). Moreover, despite the fact that he is said to have slept with Macpherson's *Fingal* under his pillow, Napoleon was essentially augustan; his coming to power marks a partial return to augustanism after the Revolution. Consequently, the only likely exceptions are Chateaubriand, who exalted Throne and Altar, and Madame de Staël, who was wise enough to go abroad to be romantic. And even these two are better considered, with Rousseau, as marking a late end to pre-romanticism in France. As Van Tieghem puts it in his great work *Romantisme dans la littérature Européenne:* 'Vers mille huit cent quinze ces deux écrivains avaient accompli leur tâche; le romantisme français pouvait naître.' After 1830, French romanticism, in contrast to pre-romanticism, becomes very *anti*-bourgeois.

In all three countries, however, romantic work shows common features, though not all writers have all of them. There is, for instance, a general tendency to prefer potentiality to actuality. There is the interest in one's emotional self, an interest which can develop into narcissism. There is the tendency to ecstatic worship of Man, Nature, God or Woman–four ways of idealising the self–and a corresponding tendency to retire into ideal worlds. These worlds may take a psychological form, in the shape of admitted fantasies, 'Dreams' or 'Visions'; they may take a geographical form, in the shape of stories of noble savages in warm countries (Soft Primitivism) or sturdy peasants in chilly ones (Hard Primitivism), until they are driven into the Future by anthropologists and explorers. Finally, they may take historical form, in the shape of reconstructions of some Golden Age–usually medieval, but sometimes Greek-pagan with the emphasis rather on Dionysian than Apollonian features.

In sharp contrast to this idealising tendency, is the tendency to insist on minute particulars and actual localities–partly because the augustans had been interested in generalities, and partly, it would seem, because of the growing nationalism provoked by Napoleon's conquests and the extra-national repressiveness of the Holy Alliance which succeeded him.

Again, there is the tendency to justify aspirations condemned by law or prejudice less by argument than by calling in Nature, or the World Spirit, or the Deity as witness. Should the Church say that the Deity (or Nature) is in fact on the side of law or prejudice, that usually tends to confirm a feeling that the Church is satanic.

Here, however, the matter of there being different kinds of excess comes sharply to notice. For certain romantics–particularly on the Continent–are highly clerical and monarchical. Chateaubriand has already been instanced. And in Germany most of the people who call themselves romantics seem to be of this type (while the others who would be romantics according to the English model call themselves something different).

In accordance with the principle of linking romanticism to a time and place, therefore, it seems necessary to distinguish two kinds: *Romantic Radicals* and *Romantic Reactionaries*. But in the following chapters the word 'Radical' may usually be understood, since all our best romantic creative literature is in verse and all our best poets in their best periods are of this comparatively beneficial kind. Indeed, only Scott–a poet of secondary merit–is of mildly reactionary type. Even if prose were to be taken into greater account than it need be, the position would be unchanged, for Burke, and the Victorian Newman and Carlyle were not, or at any rate did not suppose themselves to be, writing imaginative fictions. So far as works of creative imagination are concerned, England's romanticism is essentially that of its poets.

What radical and reactionary romantics have in common–in addition to their anti-rationalism–is the feeling that they are Outsiders–and feeling an outsider in your own society naturally leads to the characteristics indicated: subjectivism, utopianism and extremism. The difference is that reactionaries think society is, or rather *was*, natural, and therefore they want to be insiders, but in a society of an older type. Hence their support of feudalism or an authoritarian monarch and Church. The radicals think society is and was *un*natural and therefore do not wish to be insiders. They would be at one only with the universe–and directly so, not through a Church.

8

The cause of this startling difference is fundamentally simple. Reacting against reason-as-calculation, romantics naturally emphasised 'reasons of the heart', and such reasons can lead to very different beliefs: that, for instance, personal sentiment should play a major part in moral decisions, *or* that morality consists in abandoning one's own judgement and will to something Higher.

To put it another way, there are two ways of reacting against an age of common-sense and rather corrupt compromise-or rather three ways that look like two. Firstly, uncompromising rationalism, which assumes men to be entirely guided by selfish calculation. This is the most exaggerated form of utilitarianism, which became, in fact, more obviously triumphant than romanticism. The Victorians seem, at any rate, to have acted in a utilitarian way and felt in a romantic one-a split that may well account for much that is unsatisfactory in their literature. The second way of reaction is that of uncompromising passion. But this is really two ways, for you can be tyrannous and conservative on principles of passion just as easily as you can be rebellious and humanistic. If you are going to bring in Nature or God to justify your own rebellion, why not bring them in to repress other people's? If 'reasons of the heart' justify revolt on behalf of Liberty or the small nation, why should they not justify any repression supposed to be needed to preserve the nation? After all, reasons of the heart are not really reasons at all; they are superstitions and prejudices in disguise.

A further cause of difference within romanticism is the way in which one human outlook can pass by apparently logical steps into its opposite as soon as the habit of empirical compromise is abandoned. The Middle Ages ended with Catholics burning people at the stake in the name of Love, and our own age has seen Communists killing the workers in the name of the proletariat.

Suppose, after the Revolution, certain awkward people do not want to be free, natural and equal. Why then, they must be forced to be free, and disciplined into naturalness! Suppose you are a worshipper of Universal Nature, but also (on equally intuitive grounds) a Nationalist. Then you show that the dialectic of the World Spirit is working for the supremacy of your nation, so that your duty bids you subdue other nations to amend their unnatural state. Suppose, freed from the tyranny of priests and kings, you find people still behaving improperly. It is obvious they are now enslaved by their own passions. So you demonstrate that 'true' freedom consists in submerging the self in some larger metaphysical entity – the State, the Race or (why not?) the old Church. It is then only one step to 1984: 'Freedom is Slavery'.

Admittedly, this is caricature. But it is not so far from the truth of the romantic period as it sounds. Bertrand Russell points out in his *History of Western Philosophy* that Hegel came close to defining freedom as the right to obey the police. The Frenchman, de Maistre, thought that the foundation of society was and ought to be the State-torturer. And England had Cardinal Newman, who said in 'The Religion of the Day' (*Parochial and Plain Sermons*):

> I will not shrink from uttering my firm conviction that it would be a gain to this country were it vastly more superstitious, more bigoted, more gloomy, more fierce in its religion that at present it shows itself to be. . . .(This is) more promising than a heathen obduracy and a cold self-sufficient, self-wise tranquillity.

In his *Apologia* he reiterated the view that he would rather the whole human race should perish in the utmost agony than that one person should commit a single venial sin.

This major difference between the two main branches of romanticism is only the most striking of many. Subjectivism naturally leads to independence and individuality. This accounts for the fact that romanticism led to so many things: to realism and surrealism, symbolism and decadence. It accounts, too, for its inconsistent effects. Its major achievement, probably, is that it helped to bring about the open society and established the artist's freedom to choose almost any matter or manner. Yet it also helped the movement back to totalitarianism and the use of art as propaganda.

Similarly, the dislike of reason, because it had come to be identified with the preservation of a disliked *status quo*, led to a vast enrichment of vocabulary and technique to express a side of human nature that had been previously rather inhibited: namely the realms of feeling, sensation and the subconscious. But, on the other hand, it also led to fanaticism, and, through the cult of the image, to obscurity.

Dislike of the Church led to a great and beneficial enlargement of the idea of morality, doing justice to vital elements of life that had been repressed or guilt-ridden. But it also led to approval of a *more* dogmatic Church-the idea of freedom from selfhood leading to the romanticism of pain, asceticism and renunciation.

Again, the approval of feeling because it was *not* reason or dogma easily passed into approval of feeling that *was* unreasonable or satanic-thus opening a way to the Decadence. This latter was no doubt partly a reaction to the rigid bourgeois respectability of the period after 1830. Another possible reaction to such middle-class respectability, however, is to be passionately feudal and royalist. In each case, there is a divergence from the middle way-but on different sides of it.

The worship of Nature, likewise, had mixed effects. For traditionalist Christians, God had been a benevolent despot (personal and authoritative); for the augustan Deists, a First Cause (impersonal and uninterfering, a logical postulate); for the romantics there was Nature (impersonal but vital). This was more in keeping with observed scientific facts than traditional Christianity, but less so than Deism. Not surprisingly, therefore, it had less influence on material development in the nineteenth century than the utilitarian and positivist successors to Deism; but because it satisfied new emotional needs it had much effect on spiritual development.

Of course, to bring in Nature-or for that matter a deity-does not *in fact* justify any attitude whatever. For no fact or entity, even if it exists and is all it is alleged to be, can logically warrant any value. It is always logically possible, for example, for an opponent to argue that morality consists in fighting against nature (as many Christians did), or the universe, or the deity (as many romantics did). Romantics do in fact seem to be subconsciously aware of this logical weakness, for they commonly mingle with their poetry of shared experience a high proportion, not of discursive argument, but of rhetoric.

In part, to be sure, this tendency towards rhetoric may be due to *the fear of having no spontaneous feelings*. When there is no cult of feeling, men experience feelings but do not think about them. But when they start examining their feelings are they *really* feeling? Of course, if the feelings are very passionate or very strange. . . . Hence much extravagance and eccentricity in romanticism – but hence, also, much discovery. They really do put on the map previously unexplored emotional territory – in language made memorable, sometimes, by the conflict behind it.

SOCIAL AND HISTORICAL
BACKGROUND

In England, all the best romantic poetry is to be found between 1789, when Blake began his *Songs of Experience*, and 1824, when Byron died. This is commonly styled the period of the Romantic Revolt. For two reasons, however, that style is unsatisfactory: it has come to suggest a purely literary reaction against the forms and content of previous literature, and it ignores the factor of internal conflict within the writers themselves. What now needs stressing is that the literary revolt was symptomatic of a widespread social conflict and a deep-seated psychological one connected with it. Since this chapter is concerned mainly with the outward aspect of the romantic conflict, it may properly begin by noting that 1789 is also the date of the outbreak of the French Revolution and 1824 the date of the repeal of the Combination Acts, a repeal which marked the end of the English Repression. These coincidences of date are not the result of mere chance—Blake was tried for treason and Byron died while struggling for Liberty in Greece.

There is poetry written before the French Revolution which is sufficiently similar in kind to that of the great romantic radicals (Blake, Wordsworth, Coleridge; Shelley, Byron, Keats) to be considered of the same genus. It is written by men not obviously of inferior abilities (men such as Smart, Chatterton and Cowper). Yet its quality is undoubtedly less impressive on the whole. Such similarity in kind and difference in degree, together with the coincidence of dates, argues for a mutation in the evolution of English romanticism, at about the time of the French Revolution, and justifies the assumption of two species, pre-romantic and romantic. In short, a sudden increase in social pressures seems to have resulted in a corresponding increase of force in the poetry of the period.

The earlier romantic writers were unhappy about many aspects of their situation, cultural and political, but they were not rebellious. The later romantic writers revolted radically against their society because they were revolted by it, and this provoked a daring, a heart-searching, a struggle both deeper and more directed than anything their predecessors got into their poetry.

Both groups were dissatisfied with what they felt to be an inadequate, unrepresentative, upstairs 'Order', but the earlier lacked theory and passion, the two requisites of successful rebellion. To them governmental inadequacy was at worst a matter of corruption or unconstitutional behaviour (as in the Wilkes affair), and their reaction tended to be personal and escapist. Their political discontent expressed itself in Whiggery, which was not radical. The later writers, on the other hand, felt the oppression of their period as a tyranny over mankind as well as themselves. Besides this passion, they had principles, derived in part from previous thinkers whose ideas had lain latent, and in part from the great debate on the French Revolution[1] which raged in England.

Furthermore, the position of the later poets caused more serious conflict. They were for the French Revolution yet, as romantics, against French rationalism. Against utilitarianism yet, like the utilitarians, for reform. Against the Church, as a propagandist for the repressors, but for transcendentalism. This considerably over-simplifies, but it does indicate a genuine reason for the ambiguity, tension and guilt so common in the English romantic radicals. In the wartime poets, Blake, Wordsworth and Coleridge, it is increased by the Revolution's progress from Liberty, Equality and Fraternity to Terror, Conquest and Dictatorship. In the post-war poets, Shelley, Byron and Keats, it is increased by exile and a sense of betrayal–betrayal by the wartime group who had gone over to the Right, and by the Government which did not grant either the reform the fighting had allegedly made impracticable earlier or the liberty allegedly

---

[1] Alfred Cobban has made an excellent selection of documents illustrating this controversy: *The Debate on the French Revolution*, (1950) p. 496. Passages quoted in this chapter will be given the reference, 'Cobban p. . . . .'

fought for. Wordsworth's lines in Book X of *The Prelude* give some idea of the depth to which he and his like were stirred. Read in conjunction with the lines in the same Book on the beginning of the Revolution ('Bliss was it in that dawn . . .') they give the romantic gamut from ecstasy to despair:

> I scarcely had one night of quiet sleep
> Such ghastly visions had I of despair
> And tyranny, and implements of death,
> And long orations which in dreams I pleaded
> Before unjust Tribunals, with a voice
> Labouring, a brain confounded and a sense
> Of treachery and desertion in the place
> The holiest I knew of, my own soul.
>
> (374/381. 1805 version)

Possibly the sense of guilt so vividly rendered here may be due to Wordsworth's treatment of Annette Vallon or to repressed incestuous feelings for his sister. Or it may not. In any case, the literary critic is properly concerned at most with the 'psychology' of the poem not with what he may suppose that of the author to have been. And what is significant here is that the intense mental conflict revealed in the verse is expressed in political terms—as immediate today, incidentally, as they were then.

The following passage from Byron's journal sufficiently indicates a mood common amongst the post-war romantics:

> 'And all our *yesterdays* have lighted fools
> The way to dusty death.'

I will keep no further journal of that same hesternal torchlight; and to prevent me from returning, like a dog, to the vomit of memory I tear out the remaining leaves of this volume, and write, in *Ipecacuanha*, –'that the Bourbons are restored! ! !–'Hang up philosophy.' To be sure, I have long despised myself and man, but I never spat in the face of my species before–'O fool! I shall go mad'

(April 19, 1814. Byron, *A Self-Portrait* (1950), ed. Quennell, vol. 1,
p. 258)

Such conflict, though distressing for the poet, is valuable for poetry; at least for romantic poetry. Augustan poetry, broadly speaking, is conformist. True, Swift and Pope were not free from the tension which results from conflict, but theirs could be discharged through socially accepted channels, for in the long run they felt at one with the fundamental values of their age. They are angered by their age because of discrepancies between theory and practice, not because they do not accept the theory. Both Tories, they look back to a Golden Age whose values the dominant class accepts as a criterion (Defoe's *Essay on Projects*, typical of the forward-looking nonconformity which later became dominant, is precisely the sort of thing Swift satirised in *Gulliver's Travels*). For the romantics the Golden Age tends to be looked for in the future–or, if in the past, only because its values are very different from the orthodoxy of their own age.

Romantic poetry of both species, tending to enthusiasm, relies less on proportion than on opposing strains and tensions. Its association with Gothic architecture is not accidental. Moreover, the religious associations of 'enthusiasm' are significant; for romanticism, with its fervour, its emphasis on sudden illumination, slowly overshadows augustanism in much the same way as 'reasonable' nonconformist sects and moralistic Anglicanism came to be overshadowed by inspirational sects and Evangelicalism.

For such poetry, conflict is doubly valuable: it opens a way to the subconscious, the storehouse of new images for the new themes and attitudes, and it forces the whole personality to make an immense effort to discriminate between values of principle and values of habit, or to synthesise conflicting feelings. Allowing little to orthodoxy, it makes possible an unhackneyed poetry. Again Book X of *The Prelude* provides a convenient illustration of an effort and anguish that are rarely to be found in pre-romantic poetry and, when found, are found unrelated to matters of principle and forms of justice as they are here:

> Thus I fared
> Dragging all passions, notions, shapes of faith,
> Like culprits to the bar, suspiciously
> Calling the mind to establish in plain day
> Her titles and her honours, now believing,
> Now disbelieving, endlessly perplexed

> With impulse, motive, right and wrong, the ground
> Of moral obligation, what the rule
> And what the sanction. . . .
>
> (889/897. 1805)

It is obvious that a man forced to such probing is likely to come to a better knowledge not only of the subjects he is scrutinising but also of himself, and his self-discovery is likely to be set in a wider context than that of a man not forced to such probing. Certainly this seems to be true of the romantics. Indeed, though they may be pushed into 'passion' by 'notions and shapes of faith', their directly political writing is usually a good deal worse than more personal work. Partly, no doubt, that is because political poetry inevitably becomes propagandist whereas psychological poetry may well be exploratory. But probably more important is the fact that 'Nature', ambiguously conceived, can more aptly be made to embody intangible psycho-somatic states than political or metaphysical notions.

The development of this ambiguous concept of 'Nature' is a matter for the next chapter, but it does bear on the social history of the period 1760–1830: the reigns of those utterly unromantic monarchs, George III and George IV. For the augustans, Nature tended to go with Reason; for the romantics, with Inspiration. For the augustans, it was stable and orderly, as Newton had shown, and it seemed to support the *status quo*; for the romantics, it was progressive and vital, as various evolutionists maintained, and it seemed to support ideas of reform.

The augustan age, we have said, was an age of compromise, devoted to preserving the *status quo*. At the beginning of the eighteenth century, Englishmen felt they had arrived in a safe haven after the storms of two revolutions. Consequently, neither Reason nor Feeling was pushed so far as to provoke action and alteration. That is to say, it was not an age of principle, and was therefore susceptible to both rationalistic and romantic attack as soon as the *status quo* should seem less preferable than some alternative.

Since compromise is an inherently unstable relationship, needing constant adjustment, augustan culture was bound to disintegrate, for this was a period which insisted on freedom of person, thought, commerce, and invention, and at the same time insisted on the immutability of those institutions which James II had attempted to tamper with at the cost of his throne. Inevitably, then, the country outgrew its institutions; indeed it could hardly have avoided doing so, for an institution become sacrosanct does not merely cease to develop; it becomes corrupt and decays. Those not profiting by the corruption sooner or later cease to find the age's complacency agreeable. Pope's famous, and fatuous, lines in the *Essay on Man* (Bk. I) indicate by their content how complacent the age could be; by their form, how urbane:

> Submit.–In this, or any other sphere,
> Secure to be as blest as thou canst bear:
> Safe in the hand of one disposing power,
> Or in the natal, or the mortal hour.
> All nature is but art, unknown to thee;
> All chance, direction which thou canst not see;
> All discord, harmony not understood;
> All partial evil, universal good:
> And, spite of pride, in erring reason's spite,
> One truth is clear, WHATEVER IS, IS RIGHT.

This view, that things should be left alone because they are really all right as they are, clearly has something in common with utilitarian *laissez-faire*, the view that if things were left alone they would work out all right. But the difference of emphasis is fundamental. Pope feels that what is, is right, and does not want the people to interfere with the Government–to put it crudely–while Bentham at the other end of the century feels that what is, is wrong, and wishes the Government wouldn't interfere with the people. Thus in certain ways he has more in common with the romantic individualists who feel not that they have arrived but that they are setting out. Indeed there are many more links between reason and feeling to be found in the work of the later romantic radicals than in that of the pre-romantics, despite their greater hostility to eighteenth century 'Reason'.

Probably the most fundamental difference between romanticism proper and pre- and post-romanticism is that the former really grapples with problems while the latter are escapist. The great romantics are great not by reason of any superior verbal technique (none had more of that than Tennyson), but rather by reason of their ability to come to grips with their experience. Since they are mainly personal and psychological discoverers, they are not predominantly concerned to frame a metaphysic or expound a programme, though they sometimes do so. Their main concern is simply to *make sense* of their experience. But their experience was such that making sense of it meant not only making it graspable by externalising in concrete imagery what was inarticulate and intangible, but also setting it in a wider, less personal context– and this latter necessarily involved thinking, since rebels fall back on orthodoxy. For the pre-romantics however, such a course was still possible. . . .

When George III came to the throne in 1760 to hasten the inevitable disintegration of the augustan stasis by his determination to reign as an active king, the point of no return had already been reached. In addition, the Seven Years' War left a heavy burden of taxation. Enclosures, needed for the new large-scale farming techniques, the beginnings of the Industrial Revolution, and a Scots Prime Minister, Lord Bute, who was a mere tool of the King– these things caused much dissatisfaction. Diminishing complacency brought sharply to notice the corruption of Parliament and Church–without the compensation of high quality in either sphere. Walpole's accounts of 'the burlesque Duke of Newcastle' are sufficient indication of the qualities of that master of political 'management'; while of Dr Blackbourne, the Archbishop of York, he wrote: '(he) had the manners of a man of quality, and though he had been a buccaneer and was a clergyman, he retained nothing of his former profession except his seraglio'.

Reform was perceived to be badly needed. The slave trade shocked even so frivolous a man as Horace Walpole; Coke, a great landlord convinced of the need for enclosures in order to improve farming, was horrified at their effect on the country labourer; and Cowper, an uncommonly patriotic and unpolitical Whig, was moved to write (in a letter to Lady Hesketh), 'God grant that we may have no revolution here, but unless we have a reform we certainly shall'. Book IV of Cowper's long poem *The Task* gives what seems a sober picture of the labourer's life:

> Poor, yet industrious, modest, quiet, neat,
> Such claim compassion in a night like this,
> And have a friend in every feeling heart.
> Warmed, while it lasts, by labour all day long
> They brave the season, and yet find at eve
> Ill clad and fed but sparely, time to cool.
> The frugal housewife trembles when she lights
> Her scanty stock of brushwood, blazing clear,
> But dying soon, like all terrestrial joys;
> The few small embers left she nurses well.
> And while her infant race with outspread hands
> And crowded knees sit cowering o'er the sparks,
> Retires, content to quake, so they be warmed....
> The taper soon extinguished, which I saw
> Dangled along at the cold finger's end
> Just when the day declined, and the brown loaf
> Lodged on the shelf, half eaten, without sauce
> Of savoury cheese, or butter costlier still,
> Sleep seems their only refuge.

The law, already chaotic and sanguinary, became increasingly severe as discontent and rising prices caused an increased lawlessness. In the second half of the century capital offences increased from 160 to 253, death being the penalty for thefts over five shillings (or one shilling for pocket picking). The *Table Talk* of Samuel Rogers gives a vivid glimpse of this side of the century, and suggests its effect on humane men:

When I was a lad, I recollected seeing a whole cartful of young girls, in dresses of various colours, on their way to be executed at Tyburn. They had all been condemned on one indictment, for having been concerned in (that is, perhaps, for having been spectators of) the burning of some houses during Lord George Gordon's riots. It was quite horrible.

Greville was present at one of the trials consequent on those riots and heard several boys condemned, to their own excessive amazement, to be hanged.

'Never,' said Greville, with great *naïveté*, 'did I see boys *cry* so.'

Gibbon's description of eighteenth-century Oxford reveals why dissatisfaction should extend to orthodox education, and why many gentlemen who were not themselves Dissenters should send their sons to the Dissenting academies, which were originally set up to provide for those legally excluded from Oxford and Cambridge as nonconformists:

> The fellows or monks of my time were decent easy men, who supinely enjoyed the gifts of the founder; their days were filled by a series of uniform employments; the chapel and the hall, the coffee-house and the common-room, till they retired, weary and well satisfied, to a long slumber. From the toil of reading, or thinking, or writing, they had absolved their conscience; and the first shoots of learning or ingenuity withered on the ground, without yielding any fruits to the owners or the public.

(Autobiography, p. 44. Everyman's, 1948)

Even Smart, a disgraceful don, prayed 'for the professors of the University of Cambridge to attend and amend..., (for God to) make the professorship of fossils in Cambridge a useful thing' (*Jubilate Agno*). And Gibbon's 'fat slumbers' seemed a fair comment on the Church.

That so much cause for complaint gave rise to no rebellion and little rebellious literature seems to be due to several things. Firstly, reform was expected–and in mild sort came about just when dissatisfaction with the King's government reached its height: when the idea of relieving England by taxing America had led to a further expensive and unsuccessful war. In 1782 Parliament became more independent, and under the Whig control of Rockingham, and later Pitt, made much improvement. Corruption was reduced, the Cabinet system established, finances reconstituted and a new empire founded on the ruins of the old. Secondly, the Whig movement for reform—which had started as soon as George III and the Tories began exploiting old Whig abuses for their own ends–was not directed at the Church, for the Church was unlikely to affect party power, and in any event was slowly beginning to reform itself under the influence of Wesley. In the countryside, the tithe-paying farmer regarded the parson as his natural ally against the unrest of his miserably-paid workers. In the new towns, a lack of new churches left the worker to enthusiastic Methodism, undisturbed by ecclesiastical corruption. Until the period of the French Revolution, therefore, there was no great pressure on poets to become antagonistic to religion or to make a religion of 'Nature'. They could, indeed, still find comfort in the Church.

More important than these reasons, however, is the fact that the poets have no theory, and therefore, so to speak, don't know they are romantic. And the reason they have no theory is that, even before the reforms of the eighties, the causes of complaint are all negative ones; the government is not positively and actively oppressive.

Thus, in this period, various pre-romantic tendencies develop but they are eccentric rather than radical; there is no depth to them. It is the period of such enthusiasts as Thomas Day, who met his death applying the educational principles of Rousseau's *Emile* to unbroken horses.

In religion, Methodism becomes the most active force; in art, the Picturesque (the quaint, rough, or irregular) is added to the categories of the Sublime and the Beautiful; in literature, the period sees the rise of primitivism (admiration for the simple life- a form of escapism from a 'polite' civilisation). It sees, too, the rise of Sensibility (unpurposive pity, which seems, psychologically speaking, to be a sign of guilt and a substitute for reformism), and of Horror (largely as a change from decorum).

With the outbreak of the French Revolution in 1789- or at any rate shortly afterwards- the reform movement came to a full stop. The monopoly of power by landowners had not been broken, and a scared Tory government used it rigorously, though not unnaturally, to defend the *status quo* against any encroachment of democracy, against anything which might disturb the inoperative balance of the constitution between King, Lords and Commons. Thomas Hardy, the Secretary of the London Corresponding

Society, was tried for treason in 1794, having advocated 'representative government, the direct opposite of that which is established
here'. When the reform movement stopped, the movement of
ideas accelerated. The Revolution crystallised Radical discontent,
giving it a theory and an example of action. The reaction of the
Tory party aggravated the social and economic ills attendant on
the remorselessly proceeding Industrial Revolution. Romantic,
rationalist, and dissenting radicals joined in demanding a new
order. On the other hand, the Tories acquired for the first time a
justification for reaction–formulated mainly by Burke, who had
moved to the right as the threat to the *status quo* changed from
Jacobite to Jacobin:

> We fear God; we look up with awe to kings; with affection to
> parliaments; with duty to magistrates; with reverence to priests; and
> with respect to nobility. Why ? Because when such ideas are brought
> before our minds, it is *natural* to be so affected; because all other
> feelings are false and spurious, and tend to corrupt our minds, to
> vitiate our primary morals, to render us unfit for rational liberty; . . .

> You see, Sir, that in this enlightened age I am bold enough to
> confess, that we are generally men of untaught feelings; that instead of
> casting away all our old prejudices, we cherish them to a very con-
> siderable degree, and, to take more shame to ourselves, we cherish
> them because they are prejudices; and the longer they have lasted, and
> the more generally they have prevailed, the more we cherish them.
> We are afraid to put men to live and trade each on his own private
> stock of reason; because we suspect that this stock in each man is small,
> and that the individuals would do better to avail themselves of the
> general bank and capital of nations and of ages.

> (*Reflections on the Revolution in France* (1790). Cobban, p. 247)

In his rejection of good sense and his appeal to *natural* passions,
Burke is a romantic, though of the reactionary type, very rare in
England. So, too, in his intemperance:

> Our present danger from the example of a people whose character
> knows no medium, is, with regard to government, a danger from
> anarchy; a danger of being led through an admiration of successful
> fraud and violence, to an imitation of the excesses of an irrational, un-
> principled, proscribing, confiscating, plundering, ferocious, bloody and
> tyrannical democracy. On the side of religion, the danger of their

example is no longer from intolerance, but from atheism; a foul, un-natural vice, foe to all the dignity and consolation of mankind.

> (*Debate on the Army Estimates* (1790). Cobban, p. 67)

Compare Shelley writing from a contrary romantic standpoint (in an introductory passage prudently omitted by his publisher from *Hellas*):

> This is the age of the war of the oppressed against the oppressors, and every one of those ringleaders of the privileged gangs of murderers and swindlers, called Sovereigns, look to each other for aid against the common enemy, and suspend their mutual jealousies in the presence of a mightier fear. . . . But a new race has risen throughout Europe nursed in the abhorrence of the opinions which are its chains, and she will continue to produce fresh generations to accomplish that destiny which tyrants foresee and dread.

It is interesting to note that when Mary Wollstonecraft vindicated the Rights of Men, against Burke, in 1790, she used words and images distinctly resembling much in Shelley's poetry. As the wife of William Godwin – whose *Political Justice* Shelley read at least six times – and the mother of Shelley's wife, Mary, she is a good example of the many intermediaries who linked rationalist and romantic radicals together despite their temperamental differences and thus enabled the romanticism of that time to be far less purely emotive and irrational than anything that has gone by that name since:

> Surveying civilized life, and seeing, with undazzled eye, the polished vices of the rich, their insincerity, want of natural affections, with all the specious train that luxury introduces, I have turned impatiently to the poor, to look for man undebauched by riches or power – but alas! what did I see? a being scarcely above the brutes, over which he tyrannized; a broken spirit, worn-out body and all those gross vices which the example of the rich, rudely copied, could produce. Envy built a wall of separation, that made the poor hate, whilst they bent to their superiors; who, on their part, stepped aside to avoid the loathsome sight of human misery.
>
> What were the outrages of a day to these continual miseries? Let those sorrows hide their diminished head before the mountain of woe that thus defaces our globe! Man preys on man; and you mourn for

the idle tapestry that decorated a gothic pile, and the dronish bell that summoned the fat priest to prayer. You mourn for the empty pageant of a name when slavery flaps her wing, and the sick heart retires to dwell in lonely wilds, far from the abodes of men. Did the pangs you felt for insulted nobility, the anguish that rent your heart when the gorgeous robes were torn off the idol human weakness had set up, deserve to be compared with the long-drawn sigh of melancholy reflection, when misery and vice are thus seen to haunt our steps, and swim on the top of every cheering prospect? Why is our fancy to be appalled by terrific perspectives of a hell beyond the grave?–Hell stalks abroad;–the lash resounds on the slave's naked sides; and the sick wretch, who can no longer earn the sour bread of unremitting labour, steals to a ditch to bid the world a long good-night–or, neglected in some ostentatious hospital, breathes his last amidst the laugh of mercenary attendants.

Such misery demands more than tears–I pause to recollect myself; and smother the contempt I feel rising for your rhetorical flourishes and infantine sensibility.

(Cobban, pp. 84/5)

Innumerable links such as this are to be found, indicating some- times a direct fertilising influence from one group to the other, but more often just fierce ideas at large. Thus Godwin, in *Caleb Williams*, praises 'Energy... of all qualities the most valuable', almost as if he had read Blake's *Marriage of Heaven and Hell* which was being written at the same time (he did, of course, know Blake personally). His Bethlem Gabor, in *St Leon*, is a typical Byronic hero–villain. In *The Rights of Man* (1791/2)–the great book which challenged Burke's ethic–occur numerous passages reminiscent of romantic poems, including one which reads as if it might have prompted Wordsworth:

The scene which that country (America) presents to the eye of a spectator has something in it which generates and encourages great ideas. Nature appears to him in magnitude. The mighty objects he beholds act upon his mind by enlarging it, and he partakes of the greatness he contemplates.

(Everyman's, (1944) p. 152.)

It was Wordsworth, of course, who told a young student to burn his books of chemistry and read Godwin. But the most apt symbol of the awkward alliance of rationalists and romantics is that warning by Blake which enabled Paine to flee the country just in time. Equally symbolical was the death sentence passed on him in his absence (for writing *The Rights of Man*). England was no longer a land of freedom, nor was there room to hope for reform through mildness by the one side and tolerance by the other.

Repression was the inevitable governmental reaction to the wave of romantic and radical delight which swept over England, setting Coleridge and Southey writing revolutionary poetry while planning a Pantisocracy, impelling Blake to join a treasonable society, and making Wordsworth, in France, a fervent revolutionary. As Hazlitt wrote later:

> Scenes lovely as hope can paint dawned on the imagination; visions of unsullied bliss lulled the senses, and hid the darkness of surrounding objects, rising in bright succession and endless gradations, like the steps of a ladder which was once set up on earth and whose top reached to heaven. Nothing was too mighty for this newbegotten hope; and the path that led to human progress seemed as plain as the pictures in the Pilgrim's Progress leading to Paradise.
>
> (*Complete Works* (1932), ed. Howe, vol. III
> p. 155)

Contemporary writings, however, lacked that sardonic, disillusioned note. Witness Mrs Barbauld, typical of many:

> The genius of Philosophy is walking abroad, and with the touch of Ithuriel's spear is trying the establishments of the earth.[1] The various forms of Prejudice, Superstition and Servility start up in their true shapes, which had long imposed upon the world under the revered semblances of Honour, Faith and Loyalty. Whatever is loose must be shaken, whatever is corrupted must be lopt away; whatever is not built on the broad basis of public utility must be thrown to the ground.
>
> (*Address to the Opposers of the Repeal of the Corporation and Test Acts*
> (1790). Cobban, pp. 49/50)

On the other side, Pitt was opposing in Parliament even reform he admitted to be desirable, 'rather than afford an inlet to

---

[1] A passage to be borne in mind when considering the ambiguity of Keats's *Lamia*: v, p. 233.

principles with which no compromise can be made' (Cobban, p.115). And Burke, in his *Reflections on the Revolution in France*, was advancing an almost Hegelian concept of human 'rights':

> Government is a contrivance of human wisdom to provide for human *wants*. Men have a right that these wants should be provided for by this wisdom. Among these wants is to be reckoned the want, out of civil society, of a sufficient restraint upon their passions. Society requires not only that the passions of the individual should be subjected, but that even in the mass and body, as well as in the individuals, the inclinations of men should frequently be thwarted, their will controlled and their passions brought into subjection. This can only be done by a *power out of themselves;* and not, in the exercise of its function, subject to that will and to those passions which it is its office to bridle and subdue. In this sense the restraints on men, as well as their liberties, are to be reckoned among their rights.
>
> (*Reflections on the Revolution in France*. Cobban, p. 184)

The 'subjection' advocated by Burke was thoroughly effected by the Government with which he was associated.

For a long time England had been becoming divided into Disraeli's 'two nations'–a division that was psychological as well as economic. Now the two nations were at war: a cold war embittered by thwarted hopes, by repression, and by the heavy taxation which followed the outbreak of hostilities with France in 1793. The upper classes throve on enhanced rents, but indirect taxation on articles of consumption–by which the bulk of the national income was still found, despite some adjustments by Pitt–pressed very heavily on the poor. The poor were at a considerable disadvantage because the constant rise in population gave a surplus of labour, the movement of population to the new industrial towns disenfranchised them, and a ruthless economic philosophy prevailed (strongly supported by religion). Benthamite utilitarianism was much censured in the nineteenth century for its heartlessness, but this is not Bentham:

> And, first, I premise that labour is, as I have intimated, a commodity, and, as such, an article of trade. If I am right in this notion, then labour must be subject to all the laws and principles of trade, and not to regulations foreign to them, and that may be totally inconsistent with

those principles and those laws. When any commodity is carried to market, it is not the necessity of the vender, but the necessity of the purchaser that raises the price. . . .The impossibility of the subsistence of a man, who carries his labour to the market, is totally beside the question in this way of viewing it. The only question is, what is it worth to the buyer?. . . . (We must) resist the very first idea, speculative or practical, that it is within the competence of government, taken as government, or even of the rich, as rich, to supply to the poor those necessaries which it has pleased the Divine Providence for a while to withold from them. We, the people, ought to be made sensible that it is not in breaking the laws of commerce, which are the laws of nature, and consequently the laws of God, that we are to place our hope of softening the Divine displeasure to remove any calamity under which we suffer, or which hangs over us.

(Burke, *Thoughts and Details on Scarcity* (1795). Cobban, pp. 409/10)

(Malthus, too, denied the right of the poor to any assistance, even parish assistance; and, being as a clergyman averse from birth-control, stoically resigned himself to their starvation, as a solution of the problem: 'A man born into a world already possessed. . . has no claim of right to the smallest portion of food and in fact has no business to be where he is. At nature's mighty feast there is no vacant cover for him.)

Such deterministic views, however, did not prevent the government from passing legislation against trade unions in order to stop workers getting corresponding wage increases as prices rose. And in 1811-12, when starving Luddite rioters demanded that the old laws fixing wages should be put into operation, Parliament's answer was to *repeal* the Elizabeth statutes which gave magistrates power to enforce a minimum wage. Byron was one of the only two dissentients in the Lords from a Bill to inflict the death penalty on the rioters. All this, of course, was of a piece with the repressive measures of the 1790s (strengthened in 1817 and 1819): the repeal of Habeas Corpus, the banning of public meetings, the prohibition on anonymous publication, the severe restrictions on freedom of the press.

In contrast, considerable deference towards religion was shown, particularly to the less nonconformist varieties. Penal laws against Catholics were allowed to lapse or were repealed, and freedom of religious association was respected. In 1798 the Lord Chancellor refused to hold any further dinners on the Sabbath; in 1805 Wilberforce (a leader of the *Society for the Suppression of Vice*) persuaded Parliament to stop Sunday drilling; and in 1809 Spenser Perceval, the new Prime Minister, ceased to call Parliament on Monday, so that new members should not be tempted to travel on the Sabbath. In 1818, Parliament voted £1,000,000 for church-building. Religion, of all varieties, could be assumed to be opposed to the atheistic jacobinism of the *Philosophes* and their English followers, rationalist or romantic. Hannah More tells of the astonishment of simple folk at seeing the approaches to the churches crowded with carriages. Irreligion was no longer finding favour with the upper classes, since it seemed to encourage insubordination; and the lower classes found escape from earthly infelicity in the compensations of fervent nonconformity or evangelicalism. As Archdeacon Paley said in *Reasons for Contentment* (1792): 'Religion smoothes all inequalities, because it unfolds a prospect which makes all earthly distinctions nothing.'

This use of religion to justify ruthlessness, inequality and privilege, or to compensate earthly infelicity and thus avoid reform, was widespread, and largely accounts for the hostility shown to it by romantic radicals who might have been supposed to be temperamentally predisposed to favour it. Dr Horseley's sermon to the Lords spiritual and temporal (1793), and Hannah More's exhortation to the women of the Shipham Club (1801) represent a typical outlook:

Let us remember that a conscientious submission to the Sovereign Powers is, no less than brotherly love, a distinctive badge of Christ's disciples. Blessed be God, in the Church of England both those marks of genuine Christianity have ever been conspicuous.

(Cobban, p. 427)

Yet let me remind you that probably that very scarcity has been permitted by an all-wise and gracious Providence to *unite* all ranks of people *together*, to show the *poor* how immediately they are dependent on the *rich*, and to shew both *rich* and *poor* that they are all dependent on *Himself*. . . . We trust the poor in general, especially those that are well instructed, have received what has been done for them as a matter of *favour*, not of *right*.

In the light of such propaganda, the high proportion of counter-propagandist rhetoric in romantic poetry, as compared with poetry of shared experience, is not surprising.

The anti-religious propaganda of wealthy and respectable radicals like Bentham and Owen was tolerated, though attacked and misrepresented, but that of poorer pamphleteers such as Hone (whose *Sinecurist's Creed* and *Political Liturgy* were at once parodies of the Anglican liturgy and satires on the government) was severely punished. Carlile, the deist bookseller, publisher of Paine's works and Shelley's *Queen Mab*, spent in all nine years and three months in jail, a martyr to the cause of free expression. The romantic poets, who were fairly well off though not respectable, suffered rather from the force of public opinion, though Shelley was deprived of the custody of two of his children on the grounds that an atheist and radical was unfit to bring them up. Byron writes:

> The man who is exiled by a faction has the consolation of thinking that he is a martyr; he is upheld by the hope and the dignity of his cause, real or imaginary; he who retires from the pressure of debt may indulge in the thought that time and prudence will retrieve his circumstances; he who is condemned by the law has a term to his banishment, or a dream of its abbreviation, or, it may be, the knowledge or the belief of some injustice of the law, or of its administration in his own particular; but he who is outlawed by general opinion, without the intervention of hostile politics, illegal judgement or embarrassed circumstances, whether he be innocent or guilty, must undergo all the bitterness of exile without hope, without pride, without alleviation. This case was mine.
> (*Some Observations upon an Article in Blackwoods Magazine No.* 39, *August* 1815. *Letters and Journals* (1898/1901), ed. Prothero, vol. IV,
> p. 478)

In his *Autobiography and Memoirs*, Haydon recalls Keats

> . . . at Hampstead lying in a white bed with a book, hectic and on his back, irritable at his weakness and wounded at the way he had been

used. He seemed to be going out of life with a contempt for this world
and no hopes for the other.

(Vol. 1, p. 302. 1922 edn.)

The slashing criticism which the *Anti-Jacobin*, the *Quarterly*,
Blackwood's and lesser organs directed at the romantics was often
religious, political or ethical, rather than literary criticism[1].
Blake, Wordsworth, Coleridge, Keats, Shelley and Byron were
all manhandled on such grounds, while a *Poetical Introduction to
the study of Botany*, by Frances Arabella Rowden (*Anti-Jacobin*
1801), and other lesser works were praised. Shelley put the case in
a nutshell:

As to *Endymion*, was it a poem, whatever might be its defects, to be
treated contemptuously by those who had celebrated with various
degrees of complacency and panegyric, 'Paris', and 'Woman', and a
'Syrian Tale', and Mrs Lefanu, and Mr Barret, and Mr Howard Payne,
and a long list of the illustrious obscure?

(Preface to *Adonais*)

These, and earlier quotations, are little enough, perhaps, to
give an idea of the ferment of the period. But they sufficiently
indicate how much more anachronistic an augustan style or
content would have seemed to a poet connected, however
loosely, with the opposition side in the debate on the French
Revolution, than it would have seemed to his Whiggish predecessors. If the abuses were of long standing, the temper of
opinion towards them had changed sharply with the advent of
the Revolution. The Age of Compromise was no longer merely
unsatisfactory, vaguely unfulfilling. It had turned into its opposite,
an Age of Extremism, and poetry had changed accordingly.

In general, then, the period from 1760 to 1790 is pre-romantic.
This does not mean that less augustan work is produced, but that
more and more romantic work is. The period makes romanticism
a psychological necessity, but does not otherwise further its
expression. Discontent has no political policy apart from that of
the Whig aristocracy angered at the third George's taking back

[1] *v.* W. S. Ward: 'Some Aspects of the Conservative attitude toward Poetry
in English Criticism 1798–1820'. PMLA, (1945) vol. 60, p. 393 *et seq.*

from them powers the first two had relinquished. The theory that property not people should be represented in Parliament is, therefore, hardly challenged, and the pre-romantic poets comparatively rarely soil their romanticism with politics or advanced speculation. Significantly, Cowper, Chatterton and Smart all tend to adopt a distinctly augustan idiom for the occasions on which they *are* political. On the whole, poets of this period express a vague malaise and ennui rather than a revolt. Lacking the stimulus of hope and theory, they have nothing to give their discontent force and direction. Consequently, they tend to attack the individual oppressor not the system, if they attack at all. More usually they escape in fantasy or withdrawal, finding an outlet in products of Fancy: the Picturesque or the Sentimental. They work off on themselves (to use Lawrence's phrase) feelings they 'haven't really got', because they lack a sufficient stimulus to develop the feelings they really have, if only in embryo.

Hogarth's last picture, *The Bathos* (1764), graphically characterises the period. The augustan age lies in ruins; and until the American and French Revolts there is nothing to take its place. Lacking a 'philosophy' of rebellion the pre-romantic is not proud, but ashamed of feeling anti-social: so that when his conflict becomes severe it has no outlet, and he tends to crack under the strain. That Smart and Cowper go mad, and Chatterton kills himself before his eighteenth birthday, may be allowed a symbolic significance.

In contrast, the later romantics are able to glory in their defiance (and when, like Wordsworth and Coleridge, they cease to defy, the glory departs from their poetry). The feeling that they speak for great causes allows them to abandon themselves without shame (though not without guilt), without loss of sanity, and without losing the capacity to develop. The forces that inspire their poetry, they believe, are the forces of Nature which govern both the spiritual and physical world. Godwin, who was immensely influential on the romantics[1], well conveys the effect of the change:

[1]Further detail is to be found in Rodway, *Godwin and the Age of Transition* (1951).

Study is cold if it be not enlivened with the idea of the happiness to arise to mankind from the cultivation and improvement of the sciences. The sublime and pathetic are barren, unless it be the sublime of true virtue, and the pathos of true sympathy. The pleasures of the mere man of taste and refinement 'play round the head, but come not to the heart.' There is no true joy, but in the spectacle and contemplation of happiness. There is no delightful melancholy but in pitying distress. (*Political Justice* (1798 version). Bk. IV, chap. x)

Where the pre-romantics tend to escape by forgery, fantasy, or pastoral, the radical romantics are forced to explore reality–at least sometimes–by the spirit of their time.

Four periods, however, need to be distinguished in this later time, if the feeling (and indeed mere factual reference) of their poetry is to be appreciated.

Firstly, there is the period of idealism described by Hazlitt. Secondly, there is the period of gradual disillusion, produced by the successive shocks of the Terror (1793), Napoleon's invasion of the free Swiss Republic (1798)–difficult to reconcile with his role of Liberator–and his acceptance of a crown (1804). In this period Wordsworth and Coleridge after years of bitter internal strife become conservative in politics and orthodox in religion. (In the eyes of the post-war romantics, that is to say, they rat on their principles.) Blake turns from France to America for his ideal republic, and moves somewhat nearer to orthodoxy under the cover of rapidly thickening obscurity.

Thirdly there is the period from 1804 till the end of the war in 1815, the year of Waterloo. In this period conditions were still bad, prices high and wages low. Slavery had been abolished abroad but not at home, for children from four to ten (often collected from the parish authorities by contractors and farmed out) still worked from twelve to eighteen hours a day, whipped into wakefulness. But in wartime, feeling tends to be directed outward at the enemy; moreover, the repression was fairly efficient; and then, the religious revival was conservative in effect; above all, hope gave patience. A long war fought for liberty must surely lead to reform? This is the period of the pseudo-romantics, Campbell and Moore, and the traditionalist Scott.

The fourth period, from 1815 up to the repeal of the Combination Acts in 1824 or the achievement of the first Reform Bill in 1832, is marked by a long and bitter struggle for that unattained liberty. This is the period of the poets of European vision. To Wordsworth and Coleridge in the 1790s *England* seemed in need of Freedom; to Byron and Shelley, all *Europe* seemed enslaved. Both at home and abroad, the end of the war signalised renewed repression; and repression provoked a renewed rebellion in which literature shared.

Abroad, the restoration of Louis XVIII and the signing of the Holy Alliance in 1816, revealed that liberty had been lost, not won during the war. And the idea of foreign powers (Russia, Austria and Prussia) suppressing nationalist and popular-reformist movements, guided by 'the principles of Christian ethics', seemed significant of the relationship of Church and State-at home as well as abroad, since to the anger of Byron and Shelley England did nothing to aid the revolutions which broke out in Spain, Naples, Portugal and Greece, and a great deal to repress any such tendencies in this country.

Only after Byron's death in the War of Greek Independence did Canning (after the death of Castlereagh) aid the independence of the Spanish colonies, in the cause of trade (1825) and, by the accidental battle of Navarino, that of Greece (1827). By that time the repression in England was easing, the first Reform Bill was in sight, and Romanticism was entering its Victorian decline.

In England, a similar state of severity and revolt had reigned, though at a lesser intensity. In a land believed to be on the verge of violent revolution, the Government-without police, and almost without an army-could not afford to be mild. On the other hand, it was physically unable to be fully repressive. So, though increased repression no doubt helped to make the post-war poets rather more rebellious than the wartime group, it is arguable that Byron and Shelley, having personal grievances against England, did, in fact, project on to her an image of the more efficient, iron repression they knew abroad. Keats, who did not live abroad, was less extreme (though this may be due in part to his not belonging to the ruling class and therefore not seeing

34

its corruption from inside). Spasmodic physical repression, however, had a constant ally–anathema to the poets–in religious and ethical cant, the agent of mental conformity.

None the less, physical oppression and physical suffering were real enough. Despite unemployment and low wages, a Tory government of landowners passed the Corn Laws designed to keep out cheap foreign corn. Five 'rogues who roar'd for bread', in Byron's phrase, were hanged in Cambridgeshire, and the struggle began that was to culminate in Peterloo.

Since Whig and Tory seemed to have become names of factions rather than policies, a new radical people's party grew up, led by the Hampden Club, of which Byron was a member. In reaction, the government attempted a reign of terror. Publicans who allowed (perfectly legal) petitions to be signed in their bars were threatened with the withdrawal of their licences; Castlereagh employed German mercenaries at the public flogging of English peasants; in 1820 *The Examiner* tells of the execution of six people for sacrilege (i.e. breaking open a church)–a curious parallel to the case of the Italian whom Shelley and Byron planned to rescue from being burnt alive for a similar crime in Italy (an attempt dropped when the sentence was commuted to imprisonment for life). In 1817, the Coercion Acts reinforced all the prohibitions of the 1790s. The Seditious Meetings Bill drove the Hampden Club underground; no more public meetings were permitted, and even scientific societies were forbidden. Halévy instances a magistrate's refusing to sanction a mineralogical society on the grounds that mineralogy led to atheism.

After a brief respite of comparative prosperity, in which both sides prepared, renewed economic hardship brought about the bitter struggle of 1819, when Lancashire was on the verge of a general strike and great mass meetings demanded reform of the franchise and repeal of the Corn Laws. The struggle culminated in the Six Acts and that 'massacre' of Peterloo which brought forth a letter of congratulation to the magistrates from Lord Sidmouth, and Shelley's greatest poem *The Masque of Anarchy*.

Yet despite these measures, the battle was lost. For with an improvement in trade, the royalist direction taken by popular feeling at the Queen's grotesque trial for adultery (the subject of Shelley's comedy *Swellfoot the Tyrant*), and the replacement of Castlereagh, revolutionary fervour waned, and therefore the Tory repression lost its point. The Whigs were able to accuse Wellington of dreams of military dictatorship; against his policy of repression they put forward that of the utilitarians, a policy in harmony with the country's growing industrial and commercial bent.

Consequently the Tory Cabinet had to make concessions to stay in power. Reluctant penal reform was followed by equally reluctant repeal of the Navigation Acts and the Combination Acts, and so inevitably on towards the Reform Bill. The battle had been won – but not for romanticism. The Reform Bill ushered in, not Shelley's millenium, a Coleridgian pantisocracy, Byron's cantfree republic, or Keatsian paganism, but that reign of economists and calculators gloomily prophesied by Burke.

THE GROWTH AND NATURE OF
ENGLISH ROMANTICISM

ROMANTICISM, then, seems to be related, at least indirectly, to social change- to the movement from the comparative harmony of the era of Queen Anne to the Regency's discord. But how precisely does this operate? By no means all those dissatisfied are romantics; and in the pre-revolutionary period when they are, their dissatisfaction is usually found to be muddled. They cannot clearly be distinguished as either romantic radicals or reactionaries, or indeed as indisputable romantics at all, since their writing is not of one kind. It is such facts, of course, as well as the matter of lesser intensity, which justify their separate classification as 'pre-romantics'. Moreover, their dissatisfaction with politics is not only expressed as a rule in augustan verse but is also usually unconnected with their dissatisfaction with the main current of ideas, which summed up Nature as a Newtonian machine and made Reason a law of nature acting in the moral world as Newton's law of gravity acted in the physical world. Can 'romanticism', then, be given any meaning which will at once isolate its essential nature and comprehend its variety?

A too inclusive definition is as useless as one too selective. By confounding essentially different modes because of superficial similarities, it becomes useless as a tool of thought. Thus it would be misguided to count Thomson as a romantic, though *The Seasons*, by making the changing appearance of the countryside a self-sufficient subject for poetry, certainly prepared the way for romanticism. But Thomson is in no other way explorative, or rash, or innovatory, so that his is essentially a new *augustan* nature poetry: it tones in with the dominant mood of his age. The mild Collins is a more difficult case, sharing on the one hand the calculated, melancholic indistinctness of the landscape painters which is a muted form of the unifying imaginative tone of later romantics, and sharing on the other hand the stiff allegorical

37

personifications of the opposite school. Any definition obviously ought to be flexible enough to accommodate the idea of a spectrum shading from infra-roused to ultra-violent.

It is probably impossible to frame a satisfactory definition of European romanticism, (even when anchored to a limited period) of any greater precision than that given in the Introduction. Even for English romanticism alone, limited to the same period (1750-1850), it is not easy to go much further without omitting what ought to be in or including what ought to be out. But we may extend and particularise the general notion by first considering how, in its outward aspect, it subdues the prime difficulty of definition, romantic *variety*-accounting for it as a multifarious reaction against 'Reason' (a label for a society) rather than reason (a mode of thought)-and then considering how, in its inward aspect, it accounts for romantic *quality*.

Certainly most current definitions of English romanticism are open to objection. We cannot sum it up as liberal Idealism[1] since the romantics are different from other liberal idealists, particularly the utilitarians. On the other hand, it is not merely a literary reaction to previous literature, since it takes non-literary forms (especially in the earlier stage). Those tend to have a similar course of evolution. Witness, for example, landscape gardening and architecture.

Definition by enumeration will not do, for doubts immediately arise. Smart, Chatterton, Cowper; Beckford, Lewis, Macpherson, Maturin; Blake, Wordsworth, Coleridge; Keats, Shelley, Byron; all these must be included, but what of Sterne, Boswell, Goldsmith, Godwin and Burns? And what do writers so different possess in common to distinguish them from such contemporaries as Sheridan, Johnson, Churchill or Jane Austen?

'Similarity of opinions'[2] cannot be a determinant, since their opinions are not similar. Smart's religious outlook, for instance, is far nearer to Johnson's than to Shelley's. Sheridan's politics

[1] E.g. W. Graham, "The Politics of the Greater Romantic Poets" PMLA (1921), vol. 36, pp. 60-78.
[2] Fairchild, *Religious Trends in English Poetry* (1942/9), vol, III, p. 4, quotes various definitions based on common belief (particularly quasi-religious).

are nearer to those of Byron than those of Johnson–and so on. Yet to anyone with a feeling for literature it is evident that the later romantics were right in feeling for Smart, Chatterton and Cowper an affinity they did not feel for Sheridan and Johnson.

'Two different conceptions of Nature'[1] seems at first sight more promising. The idea of Nature as the Spontaneous supplanting the idea of Nature as Law could account for the romantics' inclination to wild scenery where the augustans preferred pastoral, and their approval of passion before prudence. But it is open to two objections. Firstly, some romantics, particularly Shelley, saw Nature as Law, for a time, and secondly, certain aspects of romanticism are not connected with scenic nature at all. Hazlitt was not being essentially unromantic in speaking of his indifference to the peasant and his dislike of the country, when he reviewed *The Excursion*. Nor was Lamb when he firmly declined Wordsworth's invitation to visit the Lakes in these words:

Separate from the pleasure of your company, I don't much care if I never see a mountain in my life . . . . I should pity you did I not know that the Mind will make friends of anything. . . . Your sun and moon and skies and hills and lakes affect me no more than as a gilded room.

(*Letters* (1897), ed. Ainger, vol. I, p. 165)

The closely related idea of a simple opposition of emotion and reason[2] is more helpful, though not in the end as helpful as it seems. It accounts for the romantic elevation of the imagination, and for the belief in an organic rather than a mechanistic universe. For what is organic can be supposed neither dead nor static but in a state of Becoming, and therefore amenable to evolutionary and reformist doctrines. Moreover, it can be conceived to possess or be informed by a Soul–at any rate if you don't enquire too closely into the meaning of the word when transferred from its normal habitat. In such a universe, the whole of nature will be felt as a 'Presence' in every part, concepts of value can be introduced, and the poet can feel that his own mind is not different from but integral with nature. If the integration is

[1] E.g. Stopford Brooke, *Naturalism in English Poetry* (1920), p. 1.
[2] E.g. Bush, *Science and English Poetry* (1950), chap. IV, 'The Romantic Revolt against Rationalism'.

complete (not marred by the effect of growing up in civilised society), he may then feel himself the prophet, bard, or un-acknowledged legislator for mankind; for the worshipper of nature, like the worshipper of a deity, imagines in defiance of logic–and indeed morality–that the rightness of his views is guaranteed if they are backed by a big power. Augustan 'Reason', however, (whether taken favourably as Good Sense or unfavour-ably as Calculation) gives no inkling of such integration, and must concern itself with practical material morality. Imagination, seemingly independent of space and time, appears fitted to transcend the material. 'A repetition in the finite mind of the eternal act of creation in the infinite I AM' (as Coleridge inflated it), the imagination comes to be thought of as *creating*, not depending on, reality. The finite reality which forms its material becomes a ladder to an infinite spiritual reality.

The development of this viewpoint, incidentally, gives a good instance of the way in which romantic extravagance did on occasion lead to profound truth–in this instance rather obliquely. For in emphasising the creative element in man in opposition to current theories of mechanical association of ideas arising auto-matically from sensation, Coleridge anticipated Freud's greatest achievement, the demonstration that man is a drive-directed being, who explores and reorganises reality (sometimes with disastrous inefficiency, of course) under the pressure of psycho-somatic needs. Put like this, though, it sounds less gratifying. That the romantics should prefer the more inflated formulation indicates one reason for conflict and baffled despair: their aspira-tions were rationally unrealisable without being psychologically incredible.

This same definition, opposing heart to head, also allows for the increasing importance of Primitivism, geographical or chronological. In a place or period sufficiently remote from polite civilisation the spontaneous prompting of the heart may reasonably be supposed to be translated into a mode of life. Primitivism, in turn, brings in most of the other romantic or pre-romantic escapes from an unsatisfactory present: Chinoiserie, the Gothic, the Celtic, and the Greek (valued not for 'classical' but 'pagan' associations). In like manner, this theory can assimilate the Celtic and Norse revivals, associated with Macpherson and Gray, the renewed interest in the ballad, associated with Percy's *Reliques* (1765), the approach to Shakespeare as the 'Child of Nature', and the less condescending approach to Spenser and others of his time, signalised by Hurd's *Letters on Chivalry and Romance* (1762).

This approach, in short, has the merit of subsuming various aspects of that shift of sensibility which slowly accelerates after 1760 and goes into top gear after 1790. But it is much better for the later romantics, and even so, it fails to account for their considerable theorising, for Byron's advocacy of Pope, for Shelley's rationalism, or for the fact that romanticism becomes dominant only under certain conditions. Moreover, it would include Burns, who is really no more a romantic than his English contemporary, Crabbe.

There is, indeed, much temptation to include Burns on grounds other than that of writing from the heart. He was certainly a radical: witness his toasts to Washington, and his prayer that the last king might be hanged in the guts of the last priest. Furthermore, many of his best poems and songs are post-revolutionary. Again, there is an element of primitivism in him. *The Cottar's Saturday Night* not only reflects the egalitarianism of 'A man's a man for a' that', but also provides a clear example of Hard Primitivism, in its picture of the unspoilt peasant. However, it is perhaps significant that this is one of the worst of his poems. The diction alone betrays it, lapsing incongruously into uncottarly, augustan abstraction:

> Is there, in human form, that bears a heart
>   A Wretch! a villain! lost to love and truth!
> That can, with studied, sly, ensnaring art,
>   Betray sweet Jenny's unsuspecting youth?
>   Curse on his perjur'd arts! dissembling smooth.
> Are Honour, Virtue, Conscience all exil'd.
>   Is there no pity, no relenting ruth,
> Points to the Parents fondling o'er their Child?
> Then paints the ruin'd Maid, and their distraction wild?

Perhaps one should not expect such a theme from the pen of a father of eleven illegitimate children to carry conviction. But the feeling that the whole thing is a facade is confirmed elsewhere – in the echoes of Gray, for instance. Thus stanza XIX concludes:

> The Cottage leaves the Palace far behind.
> What is a lordling's pomp! a cumbrous load
> Disguising oft the wretch of human kind,
> Studied in arts of Hell, in wickedness refin'd.

In contrast, Burns is better when less anglicised and less apparently romantic. The supernatural element in poems such as *Tam O'Shanter* and *Hallowe'en* gives them a superficially romantic appearance. But the supernatural is not taken with even pretended seriousness. *Tam O'Shanter* is racy and randy in tone, *Hallowe'en* is anthropological:

> The passion of prying into futurity makes a striking part of the history of Human Nature, in its rude state in all ages and nations; and it may be some entertainment to the philosophic mind, if any such should honour the author with a perusal, to see the remains of it among the more unenlightened of our own.   (*Proem*)

Hardly the voice of Enthusiasm.

Certainly these poems are not augustan, but neither are they akin to the poems of Coleridge or Keats. That they were ever considered so can have been due only to selective reading – a process furthered by the suppression of many poems Burns actually wrote and the sentimentalising rewriting he indulged in for the sake of respectable Edinburgh book-buyers.[1] Reverse this process, and Burns is at once seen to be at home only in an entirely different Scottish context. Not only is he far more akin to Dunbar and Henryson, and to his immediate predecessors Fergusson and Ramsay, but also many of his poems – particularly in the suppressed versions, circulated among his friends – are amplifications, or rewritings or fillings-in of old folk songs or fragmentary

---

[1] *The Merry Muses of Caledonia*, poems collected and written by Burns and published surreptitiously after his death, is difficult to come by. Some of these poems, however, are to be found in the Appendices to the limited edition of *The Common Muse*, (1957), ed. Pinto & Rodway. Cp., for instance, *Duncan Gray*, p. 429, with the 'authorised' version usually published.

ballads of the Scots countryside, poems whose earthy zest and unsentimental sentiment resemble the poetry of Burns at its most characteristic – a poetry by and for the whole man, not the man divided in conflict. Whereas the romantics found their inherited forms thwarting, and felt impelled to innovate in form, content or tone, Burns found to hand a surviving, irrepressible tradition in which he could express himself fully and easily. In this, if in little else, he resembles Crabbe.

Despite some romantic affiliations, Crabbe is more obviously not a romantic. He is neither a rebel nor a peasant, but an orthodox parson, aiming not at political or social reform or even – despite *The Village* – at literary reform, but at reform of the transgressor. Unlike the romantic, he is *outside* his theme, commenting tersely, pointedly, poignantly and above all realistically, but from the ground of Anglican orthodoxy. From that standpoint he attacks the individual transgressors rather than society – or at most he is neutral:

The Poor are almost of necessity introduced, for they must be considered, in every place, as a large and interesting portion of its inhabitants. I am aware of the great difficulty of acquiring just notions on the maintenance and management of this class of our fellow-subjects, and I forbear to express any opinion of the various modes which have been discussed or adopted.

(Preface to *The Borough*)

Imagine such forbearance in Byron or Shelley!

The Village, Crabbe's major work before the Revolution, is Johnsonian in tone, even echoing phrases from Johnson's *London*. It has the same monumental sobriety:

> And each in all the kindred vices trace
> Of a poor, blind, bewildered, erring race
> Who, a short time in varied fortune past,
> Die, and are equal in the dust at last.

And it has the same tendency to balance pity by censure:

> Nor are the nymphs that breathe the rural air
> So fair as Cynthia's, nor so chaste as fair.

It is worth noting, too, how the poetic diction in this couplet typically becomes an integral part of the poetry. Not only does it generalise and elevate the drab and narrow, but more important it gives a curious point to the poem's attack on the pastoral mode, for the elevation of language is deliberately incongruous with the unelevated content.

Crabbe does develop during his long poetic career, but not as a result of any change of attitude. Two apparent exceptions, *The World of Dreams* and *Sir Eustace Gray*, turn out to be sports—the results of opium not opinion. Neither of these fantasies of madness and nightmare is fused into a whole by some compelling belief, and both are poems of *admitted* fantasy from which an awakening is ardently desired (whereas the romantics gloried in their madness). They show some influence of their age, but it is significant that *Sir Eustace Gray* ends, like Crabbe's more characteristic tales, on a didactic note:

> Then let us keep our bosoms pure,
>   Our Fancy's favourite flights suppress
>   [*Hardly a romantic sentiment*]
> Prepare the body to endure,
>   And bend the mind to meet distress;
>   And then His guardian care implore
>   Whom demons dread and men adore

Huchon, Crabbe's biographer, is indeed so convinced his subject is not a romantic that he finds difficulty in admitting him as a poet at all, although he obviously likes his work. Crabbe rarely uses metaphor, and isn't elevated:

Poetry, which is emotion expressing itself in rhythmical language, demands a bold intellect, an enthusiastic and passionate mind. Too uniformly reasonable and calm, Crabbe becomes animated only on rare occasions and emits only transient gleams. Besides, he is hampered by the prosaic nature of his favourite subjects .... Where is the spirit of poetry to come from, which alone can breathe life into this refractory material?

(R. Huchon–trs. Clarke–*George Crabbe and his Times* (1907),
p. 479.)

Where, indeed, on romantic principles? But the passage implies an unconscious stipulative, and evaluative, definition of 'poetry'.

In any case it is arguable that Crabbe offers something different from M. Huchon's requirement but just as good. Whether you called it 'poetry' or not would hardly matter. However, what Crabbe's verse does in fact offer–apart from virtues in the content and construction of his tales–can properly be called 'animation', and it is as fully inherent in the use of language as anything the romantics offer. But this animation is not an emotive glow produced by the friction of verbal connotations, after the romantic manner; it is rather an aesthetic pleasure resulting from lively patterns of syntax. It may, then, turn out paradoxically that one distinguishing characteristic of augustan poetry is the possession of a more purely aesthetic element than is normally to be found in the succeeding work which intended to rely so much less on 'sense'. For it seems significant that Crabbe's verse, which yields little to modes of analysis suitable for romantic or symbolist work, can be illuminated by methods suitable for acknowledged augustan verse, which is typically more concerned with relationships than romantic states.

No such methods have, in fact, been demonstrated in detail, though Davie's *Articulate Energy* gives good general indications. However, since too much space has already been given to a poet who is *not* in 'romantic conflict', only two or three sample attempts at demonstration seem to be indicated. They should be sufficient, none the less, to show a *range* of differing critical approaches which is yet in its entirety appropriate for, say, Pope, and inappropriate for, say, Keats.

(*a*) In *Resentment*, from *Tales of the Hall*, Crabbe writes of a sick old man's predicament in the English weather:

> A dreadful winter came, each day severe,
> Misty when mild, and icy cold when clear.

To one whose literary sensibility has not been over-stimulated by romantic and post-romantic experiment, this couplet is likely to feel exquisitely pointed if a little formal. In its context of regular rhyme, metre and alliteration, the formality will seem proper enough, however. What is likely to escape *conscious* notice is that the pointedness results from an exceedingly complicated antithesis, whose beautifully interlocking implications are only just graspable as the attention passes over this little hillock in Crabbe's apparently flat narrative. Their existence can, however, be intellectually and visually demonstrated, briefly and clearly, by a sort of symbolic logic:

The key-words all have two aspects: of *value*, in so far as they are pointers of good or bad for the old man, and of *quality*, in so far as they are physical pointers. Each word is both an evaluator and a sensible. If we let x represent the bad, y the good; a mildness, and b clearness; then, with not-a ($-a$) and not-b ($-b$) for their opposites, cold and misty, we have a simple and adequate symbolism for analysing the antithetical patterns that give 'animation' to the line 'Misty when mild/ . . . cold when clear'. The synthesised perception, taken in by the sensitive reader as an aesthetic complex, is then as follows:

$$(x \text{ and } -b) \text{ and } (y \text{ and } a)/(x \text{ and } -a) \text{ and } (y \text{ and } b)$$

$$\text{Misty} \qquad \text{mild} \qquad \text{cold} \qquad \text{clear}$$

The interlocked antitheses are, of course, both separated alliteratively (by the m's and c's) and joined (by the w's): m w m/c w c. And the rhyme clips all this neatly to its main clause in the first line, as well as helping to make the formal pattern seem not unnatural.

(*b*) Alliteration also has a function, perhaps rather obviously, in this couplet from *The Village*:

> Who *f*ar from *c*ivil arts and *s*ocial *f*ly
> And *s*cowl at *s*trangers with *s*uspicious eye

But here the animation comes from syntactical variation which could more clearly be shown diagrammatically than algebraically. In the first line there is an eddy in the current of syntax. The strong impetus of the sentence to get as soon as possible to its verb is swirled by the impulse to set 'and social' before 'arts' where it comes from. In the couplet as a whole, too, there is a change of syntactical direction; the first verb comes at the end of its sentence, the second at the beginning.

In the first case, the variation from prose syntax seems to have a purely aesthetic effect, like a variation in a tune. In the second case, the change of structure from *subject–extension of verb–verb* **to** *subject–verb–extension of verb* elegantly illustrates Crabbe's turning from the villagers' negative, to their positive hostility.

(*c*) Another reasonably rewarding approach to Crabbe, which would show little profit on a romantic poet, is to consider the actual grammar in relation to the implications of metre or word-order. The following four lines reveal several of many possible effects. In general, we should note the energy obtained by the use of many active verbs and by leaving out–without loss of clarity–the weak auxiliaries 'was' and 'were' that ought to be in, strictly speaking.

1. Pinn'd, beaten, cold, pinch'd, threatened and abus'd–
2. His efforts punish'd and his food refus'd–
3. Awake tormented soon arous'd from sleep–
4. Struck if he wept, and yet compell'd to weep.

(Peter Grimes)

The most obvious effects seem to be as follows:

1. Two syllables that are metrically light get syntactically a heavy verbal stress. The effect of struggle and force is, of course, not just the result of extra stresses, but of extra stresses *against* a contrary tendency.

2. Alliteration and metre enforce the grammatical sense, further compacted by omission of 'were' and 'was'.

3. Off-beat parallelism and inversion. The word-order suggests a straightforward inversion with two parts in one half of the antithesis mirrored by two in the other (a.b/b.a). But 'Awake' is not quite equivalent to 'sleep' (but to 'asleep'). The one is an adjective and indicates a time ('When he was awake'); the other is a noun indicating a state. Nor is 'tormented' quite equivalent to 'arous'd', because it represents continuous action and is governed by a much stronger word than the weak adverbial 'soon'. Perhaps it is a rationalisation to say that this underlines the idea of alternating conditions which merge into each other, but it certainly has an effect comparable to 'off-beat' passages in otherwise regular music: it renews attention.

4. Straightforward antithetical structure emphasising the

dilemma given by the sense, but varied a little to avoid monotony (strong verb and weak verb; and 'wept' and 'weep'.)

To exclude Crabbe and Burns, then, while allowing for all the characteristics previously mentioned, it seems necessary now to deepen the conflict idea put forward in the Introduction by giving more emphasis to its inner aspect.

All the main writers of one recognisable type, whether radical or reactionary, have in common during this period the feeling of being outsiders. Adopt the hypothesis that romanticism is *the expression of the artist as outcast*, and not only is romantic conflict accounted for but all the loose ends can be brought together comprehensibly. For, with slight rephrasing to alter the emphasis, this hypothesis will allow the personal, psychological aspect of that conflict to be brought to the fore–a necessary procedure when one moves from general to more particular consideration of the poetry. Formulated as the 'Outcast Complex', the hypothesis will suggest a psychological approach which should be valuable if sparingly used–and on the poem rather than the poet; since the word 'complex', though analogical, tallies well with romantic poetry, if it is taken fairly strictly in its technical sense of a linked series of ideas and emotions subject to the accompaniments of total or partial repression: transformation, condensation, substitution and so forth, together with powerful feelings not rationally warranted by the ostensible cause. This indicates, it may be added, the *need* for firm anchoring to reality, and therefore the value of social commitment, for romantics. Otherwise delusion is apt to be the release from conflict, and the poetry fantastic instead of imaginative. The logical–or illogical–end of romanticism when the anchor is weighed is surrealism and its private worlds.

Such a definition accounts for the importance of Outcast figures in romantic poetry (the Wandering Jew, the Ancient Mariner, the Solitary), for the influence of Schiller's *The Robbers*–Karl being a typical romantic hero–and possibly for the attraction to *Macbeth*, *Hamlet* and the *Tempest*, in each of which the protagonist is a brooding outcast. Other romantic characteristics, too, fall into place. When a man's society and tradition, and therefore his own state of mind, become unsatisfactory there is a natural tendency to egotism, individualism, primitivism and melancholy, to looking before and after and pining for what is not.

In literature, dissatisfaction shows itself as a rebellion against older form or content, and a search for a preferable tradition, a haven of rest. Psychologically, as a desire to retreat to the shelter of the womb, or to find comfort in Nature as a substitute for the God of the old order. Sociologically, it may be revealed in political activity, if the dissatisfaction is strong enough, or in creative writing alone if it is not.

Such a hypothesis accounts for all the previously mentioned characteristics of romanticism, for all can be seen as the result of reactions against the inherited ideas, religion, or conditions of the age. It links up, too, with the outward variety of romanticism, since it accounts for the strong sense of self- and individualism, after all, is *necessarily* varied.

Individualism in turn tallies with the fact that the romantic peak comes in the era of *laissez-faire*, and that different psychological types (and not merely the introverted) are romantic. Typical of them all is the *Burning Heart*- to take a symbol from the magnificent last pages of Beckford's *Vathek* (1786): the mingled anguish and rebellion, the endless seeking of the outcast, his conflict and guilt. Hence spring the compensations of primitivism, mysticism, the ideal companion, or nature:

> No outcast he, bewildered and depressed;
> Along his infant veins are interfus'd
> The gravitation and the filial bond
> Of nature, that connect him with the world.
> (*Prelude*, II, 261/4 1805)

Hence, too, the admiration for those who are 'different' (the Superman, the Fatal Woman, the Rebel, the Seer, the Pilgrim, the Hermit) coupled, since man is a social animal, with a desire to be at one with the world (*v.* Blake's poignant cry 'O why was I born with a different face?', *The Poetry and Prose* (1948) ed. Keynes p. 873). Since the burning heart is fired by the surrounding civilisation, which is obviously a collective affair, it results in a concern for Freedom.

Here, the nature of English romanticism is seen most obviously to be related to its mutation, the increased intensity and density that comes in with the French Revolution and continues till the English Repression goes out. In that period, praise of Freedom becomes much more assured than it had been previously. The later romantic poets, definitely radicals, can project their desires into the impersonal channels of a political vision, so that egotism becomes altruistic. Hatred of oppression and of contemporary Britain gives two magnetic axes round which their dreams and eccentricities may be ordered. It gives a means of coherence-operative when they are at their rare best-to the poets' psychological contradictions; such as guilt with righteousness, or awed wonder at vastness with detailed particularising.

That this poetic mutation is not merely coincidental with the change in social pressures is evidenced by the fact that a similar increase of intensity is to be found in the development of criticism, of the picturesque, of a branch of architecture and of the horror novel. . . .

So far as concerns poetry, the incidence of forgery among the pre-romantics is significant. The poet lacks confidence; his rebellion against the age is half-hearted and escapist. In consequence, he is driven by shame to disguise his egotism, by wishful thinking, to present an ideal society as a real, historical one. Except when he is forging, his verse tends to reflect his outlook.

Of course, the great romantics make considerable use of earlier verse forms, in addition to creating new forms and diction. Technically speaking, it can be said that the Outcast Complex leads to a search for a soul-satisfying tradition and therefore to a preoccupation with supposedly kindred spirits of the past. Blake and Wordsworth look to Milton, Keats to Milton and Shakespeare, Shelley to Spenser and Shakespeare, Byron to Pope (his pseudo-augustanism being part of his rebellion-that part which attacked the insufficient romanticism of the turncoat Lake poets and the pre-romantics).

In both form and content, for earlier and later romantics, the search leads to the primitive, the natural, the gothic. The primitive is found, for instance, in the rhythmic prose of Ossian, which unfortunately provided a model for Blake's later free verse. It is found, too, in the psalm-like lines of Smart's *Jubilate Agno*. The natural appears in Cowper's modified poetic diction or Wordsworth's modified real language of men. The gothic, in Smart's *Song to David* or the stanza forms of much of Keats and Chatterton.

Yet when all is said, a general difference remains: where the pre-romantic seems to *borrow*, the romantic seems to *steal* his forms. That is to say, he makes them his own; they ring true. This matches the fact that where the pre-romantic forges, the romantic creates. Chatterton tries, as 'Rowley', to speak with the voice of the Middle Ages; Keats has sufficient confidence to let them speak with his voice.

In content, the same difference of emphasis is visible. Cowper carries a few Wordsworthian ideas gingerly like hot plates; Wordsworth is boldly convinced. Neither Smart nor Blake, perhaps, was quite sane. But Smart wrote best when he was least sane, and had contracted out of society, so to speak. The contrary is true of Blake.

Smart and Blake conveniently illustrate another cardinal difference. In the early period, the Church was corrupt but not oppressive, and its more rabid dogmas slept. Nor was this a period notable for cant or prudery. In the later period, the Church was flying at something higher than Game Laws. Allied with cant, a convenient bridge between commercial or political reality and Christian principles, it censured rebels and opposed the reform movement. Consequently, where Smart and Cowper could hold to old beliefs, Blake, Shelley, Keats and Byron abandon them altogether, and Wordsworth and Coleridge, in their creative period, radically alter them, with great benefit to their poetry.

The benefit in question is not merely the obvious one: that Christian imagery and vocabulary-like that of classical mythology-had got so hackneyed and blurred and controversial with centuries of use that it could hardly be made to convey fresh insights into human experience, even religious experience. The real benefit is rather that the abandonment of orthodox religion seems to be at the root of the amazing outburst of mythopoeic activity which did provide unhackneyed material—as it was then—for new insights.

Primitive myth, a systematic animation of the inanimate, seems to have arisen primarily from an effort to comprehend and control man's outer conflict with the forces of nature or other men. It was in fact ersatz science or history. But its magical, humanising mode naturally made it potentially expressive of inner problems. It is this aspect which is developed by the romantics (who are educated men, well informed in science and history). Their poetry, then, is mythopoeic but in no proper sense is it more primitive and regressive then that of the augustans. The romantics are not strong on analysis, so their work is rarely a good substitute for psycho-analysis, but the mythic power, organic growth and implicit symbolism of their best poems does organise, and exteriorise in graspable form, areas and complexities of being inaccessible to the augustans.

The same sort of difference of emphasis, between augustan and romantic, and earlier and later romantic, is evident in other fields. Just as Fancy becomes Imagination, and the mechanistic is replaced by the organic, so the attitude to Nature changes. The pre-romantic likes wilder scenery than the augustan and is less 'Newtonian' about it, but he still looks at nature in the Lockian way, as something apart from himself. The later romantic looks at in the Berkeleyan way, as something of which he is a part. Since Nature is usually not only scenery but a world spirit as well, this gives him the utmost opportunity of deification. He can become the seer, telling of the nature of reality, or the legislator for mankind, the defier of God, or even God himself. (Blake told Crabbe Robinson that Christ was the only God. 'But then', he added, 'and so am I, and so are you'.)

This attitude passes over into criticism. For the romantics, each true poem is an original manifestation of the universal Spirit, during a state of inspiration. It follows that it should be judged by the laws of its own situation, and this can be done only through sympathy, not by formula. But where they judge by exceptions, the augustans had judged by classical rules, rules equated with Good Sense which 'genius' was allowed, but not encouraged to break. On the whole, the poet tended to be generic and ethical, and he looked back to the sound model – a form of plagiary that perhaps encouraged pre-romantic forgery. In these procedures, he was aided by a classification of kinds of poem – ode, elegy, epic, pastoral and so forth – each having an appropriate form and style. Yet Pope, for instance, was quite ready to praise and help Thomson. Typically, the Rules were 'discover'd, not devis'd, Nature still, but Nature methodiz'd.' Consequently they could be modified as the idea of Nature changed. And, in fact, though pre-romantics gradually turned from social to personal poetry, though they emotionalised augustanism, they retained much that was augustan, including poetic diction. The real break comes only with Blake's violent rejection of augustan canons of taste. The poet then thinks of himself as revealing Nature's soul rather than painting its portrait, soignée or dishevelled. The romantic critic follows suit, ostentatiously concerning himself with the inner essence of the particular work. In contrast, the neo-augustan critics, headed by Gifford, Croker, Lockhart and the somewhat more tolerant Jeffrey, become much more rigid than their counterparts at the beginning of the century. Like literature and ideas of Nature, criticism reflects the social movement from compromise to extremism.

The same movement is seen in the development of the Picturesque, that pre-romantic application of the Fancy to nature. Again, Blake's tense art makes a late-romantic break, by turning from the atmospheric to the linear. Another sort of mutation, however, is typified by Turner, who leaves behind his Dutch period at the turn of the century to bring out whole-heartedly, even exaggeratedly, the impressionistic romanticism of atmosphere that was half-hearted in the Picturesque.

The term 'Picturesque' arrives with the publication of Gilpin's *Observations on the River Wye* (1782), but the practice goes back to the lifetime of Pope, when the landscape gardener, Kent, was planting dead trees in Kensington and Shenstone was planning the Leasowe's estate. It is implicit in Capability Brown's 'garden of ideas', laid out for 'associations' and therefore still linked with augustan psychology. Such gardens were, however, often combined with newly-built gothic ruins and paid hermits, and thus passed easily into the sort of garden more common after 1760, the 'garden of conflicting passions', where the emphasis was not on the associated but the unexpected. The visitor, advocated Chambers, the high priest of Chinoiserie, should sample the pleasing, the terrible and the beautiful, passing suddenly from the peace of goldfish and waterlilies to the Valley of the Shadow of Death, for instance. In the later romantic period, however, Price insisted on an organic approach. The emotional effect of the landscape as a whole was to be considered. The Fanciful, that is to say, is being replaced (to use Coleridge's words) by the Imagination which 'diffuses a tone and spirit of unity that blends, and (as it were) *fuses* each into each'. Thus landscape gardening comes to aim at an effect similar to that of Turner's painting or Shelley's poetry.

Architecture, too, changes from the mild mock-Gothic of Strawberry Hill (where Walpole appropriately printed the first Gothic novel) or the fanciful Chinoiserie of Kew Pagoda to the more excessive pseudo-Islamic flamboyancy of Brighton Pavilion.

In literature, the obvious connections are with the portrayal of the horrific, which though mostly Gothic was sometimes oriental or Arabian. The fake Strawberry Hill was paralleled by the 'forged' *Castle of Otranto* (allegedly transcribed from an old black-letter manuscript). The descriptive passages dwell lovingly, and irrelevantly, on the Gothic trappings; and the *enjoyable* melancholy of the conclusion confirms its pre-romantic status:

> But Theodore's grief was too fresh to admit the thought of another love; and it was not until after frequent discourses with Isabella of his dear Matilda, that he was persuaded he could know no happiness, but in the society of one with whom he could for ever indulge the melancholy that had taken possession of his soul.

(Comparable, this, to the play-element in contemporary works of sentiment. Thus Sterne's heart is touched–in *A Sentimental*

Journey-by the caged starling which cries 'I can't get out'. So he buys it-and gives it, cage and all, to Lord A so that *his* heart can be touched.)

In poetry, the 'terrible' of Chambers is constantly reflected.

> Their scenes of terror (he writes of his invented Chinese gardeners) are composed of gloomy deep valleys inaccessible to the sun, impending barren rocks, dark caverns and impetuous cataracts. The trees are ill-formed, forced out of their natural directions and seemingly torn to pieces by the violence of tempests .... the buildings are in ruins .... Bats, owls, vultures and every kind of prey flutter in the groves; wolves, tigers, jackals howl in the forest; gibbets, crosses, wheels, and the whole apparatus of torture are seen from the roads; and in the most dismal recesses of the woods, where the ways are rugged and overgrown with poisonous weeds, are temples dedicated to the King of Vengeance; deep caverns in the rocks and descents to gloomy subterranean habitations, are overgrown with brushwood and brambles.
>
> (Quoted Hussey, *The Picturesque* (1927), pp. 157/8)

This is obviously a product of the same state of mind that produced many of Chatterton's poems, or Beattie's *The Minstrel* with its twilit valleys where Young Edwin would 'dream of graves and corses pale' and harken to the clank of chains and 'the owl's terrific song'.

William Combe, the satirist of 'Tours' Gilpin, well caught the tone of this particular application of Fancy to nature and the supernatural:

The living, some wise man has said, Delight in reading of the Dead.
    What golden gains my book would boast
    If I could meet some chatty ghost,
Who would some news communicate Of its unknown and present
Some pallid figure in a shroud Or sitting on a murky cloud;   [state;
    Or kicking up a new-made grave,
    And screaming forth some horrid stave;
Or bursting from the hollow tomb, To tell of bloody deeds to come;
    Or adverse skeletons embattling,
    With ghastly grins and bones a-rattling;
Something to make the misses stare And force upright their curly hair;
    To cause their pretty forms to shake
    To make them doubt if they're awake:

And thus to tonish folks present The Picturesque of Sentiment!
(Canto 8. *The First Tour of Dr Syntax in Search of the Picturesque*
(1809))

He has caught the play-horror which contrasts strongly with the
nightmare-horror of the later romantics. Compare, for instance,
Shelley's turning death-horror into an attack on life, in *Adonais*:

> *We* decay
> Like corpses in a charnel; fear and grief
> Convulse us and consume us day by day;
> And cold hopes swarm like worms within the living clay

(Note how the worms are used as a psychological image now.)
Or, again, witness what Wordsworth makes of Mrs Radcliffe's
stagy scenery, or rather of scenery she makes stagy:

> Black drizzling crags that spoke by the wayside
> As if a voice were in them, the sick sight
> And giddy prospect of the raving stream
> The unfettered clouds and region of the Heavens,
> Tumult and peace, the darkness and the light.
>
> (*Prelude*, VI, 563/7. 1805)

Here is no attempt to stimulate the jaded reader, but a concrete
expression of the general *inner* romantic conflict between despairing recognition and idealistic aspiration, between actuality and
potentiality. The concretion, however, is largely effected by
implicit images of the *outer* conflict. Tumult and peace, and
darkness and light, obliquely reflect the struggles of armies and
ideas; while behind 'unfettered' is Wordsworth's concern with
prisons, and Liberty in general, at that period. 'Black drizzling
crags' seem to suggest the heights the poet has actually achieved-
from which he regards the giddy prospect of contemporary
fury-in contrast to the heights he longs for. The extra 'animation' this landscape gets is not from syntax, as with Crabbe, or
stage-effects, as with Mrs Radcliffe (to whom it may owe something), but from complex suggestion. Not that this need be taken
as a fully conscious achievement. The point is, that for Wordsworth, with good reason, such a scene had *a felt significance*. For
Mrs Radcliffe, it had not, so she had to invent one.

This contrast seems congruous with the sort of distinction which Coleridge had in mind (before turning metaphysician) when he associated Fancy with delirium, the mere disordering of ordinary reality, and Imagination with mania, the creation of a self-consistent private reality. In practice, both this distinction and the later metaphysical one too, boil down to pointing out a unity, urgency and purposiveness in one sort of creative art which is absent from another. It is, therefore, another instance of mutation in the evolution of romanticism in England. To this topic the whole subject of the horror novel is particularly relevant, for its influence on the poets is profound.

From *The Castle of Otranto* (1765), through *The Old English Baron* (1777) of Clara Reeve to Mrs Radcliffe's *Sicilian Romance* (1790) it remains fanciful and innocuous. Fleeing maidens are always chaste and never caught, the villains are invariably foiled. There is not enough blood and too little sex for the horror to have any chance of effectiveness. Moreover, sinister nature is merely put on for the benefit of the spectators. Adeline, of Mrs Radcliffe's *Romance of the Forest*, for example, rises 'at an early hour, eager to indulge the new and sublime emotion with which a view of the ocean inspired her'. Or again:

The gleams thrown across the fabric made desolation more solemn, while the obscurity of the greater part of the pile heightened its sublimity, and led fancy on to scenes of horror. Adeline now uttered an exclamation of mingled admiration and fear. A kind of pleasing dread thrilled her bosom, and filled all her soul.

(Pp. 332 and 23, Murray Rose's edn. 1904)

No such *pleasing* dread mars the horror of Monk Lewis. His sensational novel, *The Monk* (1796), is the first of a remarkable spate which characterised the revolutionary romantic period. In keeping with the changed attitude to nature (from pre-romantic portrayal to romantic possession) Lewis and his successors are interested in scenery as part of a state of mind rather than as a succession of backcloths. Moreover, the emphasis shifts from the struggle between heroine and villain to that within the villain's own dark and powerful soul. There is less description, more passion: blood, lust, rape, sadism and incest abound. Furthermore, Lewis is of his period in that he attacks the Church through his presentation of Ambrosio, while through the sufferings of Agnes he implicitly attacks current sexual respectability. Indeed, this point is made explicit by the concluding apostrophe to virtuous and severe women: 'to look with mercy on the conduct of others is a virtue no less than to look with severity on your own'.

The Monk is in fact humanitarian, like Lewis himself, yet its story traces with considerable zest the gradual debasement and growing hypocrisy of Ambrosio. A stern virtue, based on pride and bigotry, descends first to plain fornication, then to connivance at the torture of Agnes, and finally to incestuous rape and murder among the corpses of the vaults where Agnes is immured starving, her 'fingers ringed with the long worms which bred in the corrupted flesh of (her) dead infant', the 'bloated toad' dragging 'his loathsome length along her bosom.' Most of the better known perversions are exploited. From coprophilia the reader passes to the sadism of Elvira's suffocation and the lynching of the Prioress, or the combined necrophilia and sadism of the vault scenes 'where the gloom. . . and the resistance which he expected from her seemed to give a fresh edge to his fierce and unbridled desires'. Or, for variation, there is the voyeurism of the magic-mirror scene, and the latent homosexuality of Ambrosio's seduction by the supposed boy novice.

The source of this extremism is not so much earlier horror-novel literature as horror-novel life, in make-believe: pre-romantic ennui which expressed itself in the Hellfire and Sulphur clubs, imitated by Byron at Newstead Abbey during the period of his first and least original poetry. Of Medenham Abbey, the most famous– or infamous– we read:

> The cells were fitted up for all purposes of lasciviousness, for which proper objects were also provided (i.e. whores from the London brothels).
>
> (Johnstone, *Chrysal, or The Adventures of a Guinea* (1760–5),
> Bk. II, vol. iii, chap. xvii,)

Johnstone also reports, among other decorative effects, pictures of 'monks in attitudes and actions horrible to imagine', though, rather tantalisingly, without saying what they were.

From here it is obviously, only a short step to the anti-clericalism of *The Monk* and to Shelley's and Blake's identification of priests with tyrants and torturers, or to Byron's hero-villains, remorseful but unrepentant since their wickedness is caused by society which first thwarted them and then cast them out.

The horror novel, indeed, affects all the great romantics without exception, for horror is mainly an expression of unresolvable conflict and guilt, the nightmarish feeling of being cornered.[1] Tragedy represents the worst digested and turned into something acceptable; horror represents emotional nausea – often combined with the latent fascination of the fearsome. The ambivalence of *The Monk* is not accidental, for it is a reflection of the romantic conflict: the victims reject their age and yet are compelled to live in it, either compromising with standards (particularly sexual and religious ones) which they no longer believe in, or refusing to compromise and bringing suffering to themselves or others. Byron and Shelley, so to speak, *lived* the horror novel. Consequently, its influence on them is considerable, especially in their early and middle periods, before they were able sometimes to turn conflict into a complex unity unknown to their precursors.

Mary Shelley's *Frankenstein* (1818) enacts the romantic conflict, in both its inner and outer aspect, with greater control than most horror novels. The monster seems to be at once an image of popular violence and degradation, and of repressed, and therefore distorted psychological energies. Frankenstein, his creator, at once an image of tyrant-god or ruler and of the haunted neurotic. The external theme is clearly and consciously given in various places, particularly in chapter X where the monster appeals to his maker:

I will not be tempted to set myself in opposition to thee. I am thy creature, and I will be even mild and docile to my natural lord and king, if thou wilt also perform thy part, the which thou owest me. Oh,

[1] To a lesser extent it may be an expression of moral censorship. There are reasons for thinking that the high incidence of sadistic pulp fiction today is not entirely unconnected with the ban on straightforward bawdry or obscenity.

Frankenstein, be not equitable to every other, and trample on me alone, to whom thy justice, and even clemency and affection, is most due. Remember, I am thy creature. I ought to be thy Adam, but I am rather the fallen angel whom thou drivest from joy for no misdeed. Everywhere I see bliss, from which I alone am irrevocably excluded. I was benevolent and good. Misery made me a fiend. Make me happy and I shall again be virtuous. . . .

I will keep no terms with my enemies. I am miserable and they shall share my wretchedness. Yet it is in your power to recompense me, and deliver them from an evil which it only remains for you to make so great that not only you and your family, but thousands of others, shall be swallowed up in the whirlwinds of its rage.

Yet on the whole the reader's sympathy is urged for Frankenstein, not the unhappy monster, to the detriment of this external theme. The reason seems to be that the authoress was possessed by a theme of which she was not fully conscious, the inner aspect of the romantic conflict ('My imagination, unbidden, possessed and guided me, gifting the successive images that arose in my mind with a vividness far beyond the usual bounds of reverie', she writes in her Introduction). Indeed, only the presence of some such inner theme would seem to account for the book's long success, and for popular conflation of maker and monster. For though it is the first psychological novel, as well as the first *serious* horror novel, its psychology and style are both exceedingly crude.

The suggestion of psychological identity becomes convincing only in the chase to the north pole. Frankenstein is found to have no life apart from his obsessive and vengeful pursuit of his monster, and when he dies, unsuccessful, in the icy wastes, the monster commits suicide. An act as odd as his habit of leaving directions and caches of food for his pursuer–but right if both are parts of one personality.

Shelley's brilliant psychological image in *Epipsychidion* is worth recalling in connection with these polar deaths:

> What frost
> Crept o'er those waters, till from coast to coast
> The moving billows of my being fell
> Into a death of ice. . . .

Certainly Mary Shelley's novel, poor though it is, has more in common with what the romantic poets were trying to do than *The Monk* has, though Lewis's work had a much bigger influence on them. They were clearly trying to show horror in its moral, social and psychological connections, whereas his motives were more ambivalent. There is, therefore, no treachery in Byron's criticism:

These descriptions ought to have been written by Tiberius at Caprea—they are forced—the *philtered* ideas of a jaded voluptuary. It is to me inconceivable how they could have been composed by a man of only 20—his age when he wrote them. They have no nature—all the sour cream of cantharides.

(*Journal*. Dec. 6, 1813)

So, too, with his mockery in *English Bards and Scotch Reviewers*:

O wonder-working Lewis! monk or bard,
Who fain would make Parnassus a church yard!...
Or tracest chaste descriptions on thy page,
To please the females of our modest age.

It is one of the ironies of the age that the *Critical Review*, which said of *The Monk* that it was a romance 'which if a parent saw in the hands of a son or daughter he might reasonably turn pale', was but giving a mild foretaste of the criticism to be meted out to *Don Juan*. This, though, was not so odd as it seems, for Byron had something in common with Lewis, though at a higher level.

Typically enough, what most offended the age was not the descriptions, which apparently shocked Byron and are likely to bore the modern reader, but Lewis's moralistic suggestion that the Bible should be expurgated to protect the innocence of young girls. Similarly, what is attacked in the poets tends to be rather their irreligion and politics than the faults of style or the trashy shock tactics they derive from the horror novel.

Such derivative effects are seen most clearly in Shelley. Unlike the pre-romantics he does not give horror for horror's sake, to frighten himself out of ennui; nor, like Lewis, for secondary-largely sexual-sensation. But in his early period he comes close to doing both. The sole difference between *Zastrozzi* and *St*

Irvyne, Shelley's youthful novels, and *The Monk*, or Charlotte Dacre's *Zofloya*, which 'quite enraptured' him, is that his villains are really heroes made wicked by society which has cast them out.

Thus, 'In a short space of time, the high-souled and noble Wolfstein, though still high-souled and noble, became an experienced bandit' (*St Irvyne Complete Works*, 1926/30 ed. Ingpen and Peck, vol. v, p.113). Apart from this difference, the influence of *The Monk* is all-pervasive, and continues to taint his poetry to the end–particularly in its vague, excessive, neurasthenic expression. Not only is Verezzi, for instance, chained in a damp cell with twining worms for company, like poor Agnes; not only is Shelley's seductive villainess called, as in *The Monk*, Matilda, but above all there is a sedulous aping of style. Both Matildas, for example, speak in similar accents and with similar effect on the hero:

The fire of voluptuous, of maddening love, scorched his veins, as he caught the transported Matilda in his arms. . . . Wild with passion, she clasped Verezzi to her beating breast; and overcome by an ecstasy of delirious passion, her senses were whirled round in confusion and inexpressible delight. A new and fierce passion raged likewise in Verezzi's breast: he returned her embrace with ardour, and clasped her in fierce transports.

(*Zastrozzi, Complete Works* (1926/30) ed. Ingpen & Peck, vol. v,
p. 75.)

Cease to reproach me with having taught you what is bliss (cries Lewis's Matilda) and feel equal transports with the woman who adores you.

As she spoke, her eyes filled with delicious languour; her bosom panted: she twined her arms voluptuously round him, drew him towards her, and glued her lips to his. Ambrosio again raged with desire: the die was thrown: his vows were already broken: he had already committed the crime, and why should he refrain from enjoying its reward?

(p. 121. Bretano's reprint of 1st edn., 1924)

Add to this, a number of descriptive phrases from *The Monk* or *Zafloya*, which reappear almost verbatim in Shelley's novels (such as 'her hair was loose and flowed wildly upon her shoulders; her eyes sparkled with terrific expression') and it becomes evident that much of the overstrung unreality of passages in

Shelley's poetry purporting to be about physical love comes straight from the Horror Novel. Witness for instance these lines from Alastor:

> Sudden she rose,
> As if her heart impatiently endured
> Its bursting burthen: at the sound he turned,
> And saw by the warm light of their own life
> Her glowing limbs beneath the sinuous veil
> Of woven wind, her outspread arms now bare,
> Her dark locks floating in the breath of night,
> Her beamy bending eyes, her parted lips
> Outstretched, and pale, and quivering eagerly.
> His strong heart sunk and sickened with excess
> Of love. He reared his shuddering limbs and quelled
> His gasping breath, and spread his arms to meet
> Her panting bosom: he drew back awhile,
> Then, yielding to the irresistible joy,
> With frantic gesture and short breathless cry
> Folded his frame in her dissolving arms.

Obviously this is more efficient than *Zastrozzi* and *St Irvyne* but it has the same air of neurasthenic fantasy; it's a very disembodied bawdry.

A reading of *The Revolt of Islam* would strongly confirm the idea of such an influence. Quite apart from the horror of large-scale massacres, there is another union of lovers like that in *Alastor*-a union which begins in delirious passion and (too incredibly even for envy) does not end 'till, from the changing sky That night and still another day had fled'-even though the lovers' 'linked frames' are exposed to the bleak air of a mountain top (Canto 5, XXXIII/XXXVIII). But of course Shelley is not intending a versification of sexy horror-novel fantasy; he is intending a symbolic poetry which will elevate the soul and render it capable of transforming society.

That the effect is so different from the intention, seems to indicate a neurotic conflict in romanticism, springing from passions which cannot be converted into action. That this some-times leads to an energy and daring beyond the compass of the less deeply disturbed, should not lead us into mistaking the achievement of healing for healthiness itself. To be psychologically an outcast from one's society is to suffer mental strain, which is itself unwholesome, though it may bring into play reserves the victim did not know he had, and thereby produce great poetry. On the lower level, it will produce the Horror Novel and its poetic equivalents. Even at the highest level there are likely to be signs of the original dichotomy, showing like scar tissue. Blake's poem 'I saw a chapel all of gold' has transmuted his feelings about contemporary sexual morality, his view of commercialised, respectable marriage as priest-sanctioned rape, into an objective poetic myth, strong and controlled. To that extent it is wholesome, but it is not at ease. And in much of Shelley it is difficult not to feel that fascination looms as large as condemnation.

The point is seen more clearly in second-rate writers, in whom what is typical of their kind is more likely to be found. If, for example, John Cleland, the augustan counterpart of Monk Lewis, is compared with him, it is immediately apparent that he is catering for a less neurasthenic audience, an audience in fact at one with its age. Not that his work is less sexy. On the contrary, his *Memoirs of Fanny Hill* (1749) is hardly quotable, as the law stands, in a book like this. But the sensuality is of a healthier sort, as will appear from the companion book *Memoirs of a Coxcomb*, whose protagonist, being a man, can more appropriately stand comparison with Ambrosio anyway. He is a Morality (or Immorality) character and therefore, like Ambrosio, not fully human. But he is far more normal than Ambrosio, who is a mere force. The main difference, however, is one of tone, to be felt in the style. Thus the matter of male satiety is not dealt with by adjectival abandon in the manner of the horror novelists, but by a certain humour and realism:

> Women on these occasions have a quickness of sense and resentment that is neither to be lulled, nor imposed upon: and to say the truth there are certain test-acts, in the number and mark of which there is no trifling with their penetration.
>
> (1st ed., p. 93, B.M. 12611, e.13)

Similarly the psychology is not fantastic; it is credible, and indeed quite acute:

> But I became yet more unjust, even from a sense of my injustice, which having been riveted by her remonstrances, appeared so criminal and cruel even in my own eyes that I was half angry with Mrs Rivers for being the cause, however passive and innocent, of my making so bad a figure to myself. (p. 95)

The lush style for Ambrosio's raging desires may be compared with style of good sense used for the Coxcomb's, which has just wit enough to keep it sweet:

> . . . the whole, in short, of her person, spread out before me like a desert of dried fruit, exhibited such a picture of amorous fondness, as was even more ridiculous than distasteful and had nigh quelled my best of man. But as I was now in the pride of my spring, wellbottomed, and my blood fermented so strongly as to threaten the bursting its turgid and distended channels, so that love was rather a natural want in me than merely a debauch of imagination, the sympathy of organs established between the two sexes, sensibly exerted itself, and drove all delicacy and distinction of persons out of my head. I became then quite as naughty, to use her own term, as she could have wished, and piquing myself upon doing things conscientiously, I repeated a ceremony, which in some respects resembled that of the Doge of Venice, when he weds the gulph by way of asserting his dominion. (p. 206)

The comparative soundness is, surely, self-evident—and Cleland stands to the greater augustans as Lewis to the greater romantics. Nearer to the typical, each reveals latent strengths and weaknesses in the nature of augustanism and romanticism. Their difference is therefore significant; and it can be summed up in a sentence: the one book is a manual of seduction, the other a manual of rape. So the background of the age is again reflected in the literature, if only obliquely.

The tendency to algolagniac fantasy in the poetry of romanticism is simply one aspect of the period attraction to the horrific[1],

---

[1] For selected examples from available evidence *v.* note at the end of this chapter.

which intensifies after 1790 and culminates in the one great horror novel–unfortunately almost unattainable now–*Melmoth the Wanderer* (1820) by Charles Maturin. The horrific is the result of reaction against an age of prudery and repression—unnatural vice being a direct result of unnatural virtue. It also represents a crisis of opposition to the current order, felt to be inhuman and dehumanising. Horror, moreover, is a vehicle for conveying the guilt and conflict of the outcast. Hence, in the great romantics—by reaction from the Regency's combination of cynical license and cant–the mixture of *admiration* (for the honestly and beautifully evil), *exposure* (of the algolagnia latent in society, whether from moral-sexual or from political repression), *fascination* (of the tabooed subject, and the irreligious or anti-moral Superman), and *condemnation* (of sadistic tyrants and restrictive priesthood). This complex is part of the wider, nearly contradictory, romantic union of worship of Energy and Power with illimitable Pity for the downtrodden: a union symbolised in Blake's *Marriage of Heaven and Hell*. A remarkably unstable compound; but it is the great achievement of this period that occasionally incompatibles are miraculously combined, in accordance with Coleridge's precept for the Imagination. When that happens, an unexplored hinterland is put on the map—a map forever significant to those not at home in their society.

Each aspect of romanticism examined has further revealed its fundamental nature and shown the same sort of intensification in the revolutionary period. Final confirmation, as it happens, is provided by the development of the great poets of the war period, Wordsworth, Coleridge and Blake. To see them outlined against their background may, then, be an appropriate preliminary to a more specifically literary examination.

The effect of the French Revolution, we have suggested, was not only to arouse the enthusiasm of these poets but in its later phase to arouse conflict which caused them to explore first principles and thus made possible an imaginative audacity impossible earlier. This is confirmed by the fact that two people so utterly dissimilar as Wordsworth and Coleridge followed a similar course, and Blake radically changed his outlook on the outbreak of the revolution. All three, at its beginning, were at one with a very general outlook, for

> 'twas a time when Europe was rejoiced,
> France standing on the top of golden hours,
> And human nature seeming born again.
>
> *(Prelude,* VI, 352/4, 1805)

Consequently their poetry is less powerful than that written somewhat later, when their conflict was deeper.

Wordsworth's career has three phases, allowing for a little overlapping. Firstly, there is the period before he became a revolutionary in the France of 1792. This is the period of *An Evening Walk* and *Descriptive Sketches*, poems whose lack of passionate intensity of feeling for nature and large admixture of augustanism place them as pre-romantic in kind. Secondly there is the period of gradually decreasing radicalism, ending about 1804 when Napoleon accepted a crown. This is the period of Wordsworth's greatest poetry, and of his concern for 'the real language of men': a concern perhaps reflecting his feelings for the common people. It is also a period of unorthodox religion. He seems to have been a deist by 1790, when he abandoned his proposed career in the Church; in *Descriptive Sketches* he writes of pilgrims:

> My heart alive to transports long unknown,
> Half wishes your delusion were its own.

By the time of the first draft of the *Prelude* (1799–1800) this has become the poetic paganism of the 'Powers of Earth' which is converted into the pantheism of 'Presences of Nature' in the 1805 version, and then merges gradually into orthodoxy after that date.

Though the war with France and the onset of the Terror caused great strain, they did not alter Wordsworth's opinions. As late as 1794 he is proposing to start a propagandist magazine, and writes to his friend Mathews:

I solemnly affirm that in no writings of mine will I ever admit any sentiment which can have the least tendency to induce my readers to suppose that the doctrines which are now enforced by banishment, imprisonment etc, etc. are other than pregnant with every species of misery. You know perhaps already that I am of that odious class of men called democrats, and of that class I shall ever continue.

(*Early Letters* (1935), ed., de Selincourt p. 115)

The invasion of Switzerland, however, more strongly impelled him to the Right–though in 1804, after renouncing France, he still spoke, in Book X of *The Prelude*, of the Revolution as a 'Creed which ten shameful years have not annulled'. But that version was not published. In the 1850 publication the line is not to be found.

After a brief attempt to find faith in Godwin's *Political Justice*, Wordsworth retired to Somerset and then the Lakes, to seek it in Nature. This period, which produced most of his best poetry, is one of rationalisation (to fit a creed to his feelings), of adjustment of intellectual beliefs (in order to maintain emotional equilibrium), and of a radicalism now concerned with getting to the roots of human nature. But each fresh shock further disinclined him for this strenuous undertaking and shifted him towards orthodoxy. In 1802 he parted company with the Whigs on the issue of their attitude to the French war, and wrote the *Immortality Ode*, which gives the first hint of failing powers. By 1805 the process is complete. The *Ode to Duty* records Wordsworth's reformation. His conflicts are channelled off in the unthinking and insensitive orthodoxy of violent patriotism, antagonism to prison reform, and the defence of slavery, and of capital punishment for minor crimes. So the *Prelude* is his last truly *creative* work. Thereafter, comes much fine verse but it is an ever-colder repetition of previous original creation. The poet has become at one with his age.

The stages of Coleridge's slighter poetic career are essentially the same, though he differs personally from Wordsworth as much as any man well could. He reaches his peak in 1797 with *Kubla Khan*, *The Ancient Mariner*, and the first part of *Christabel*. In 1798, *France, An Ode* tells of disillusion and disgust brought about by the invasion of the free Swiss Republic (and is evidence that the changed tone of his poetry after this date cannot be entirely attributable to the failure of his marriage). In 1800 he is unable to finish the second part of *Christabel*. The *Ode to Dejection* in 1802 records the failure of inspiration (though largely on grounds of unhappy love). But as late as 1816 he is admitting, in the Preface to *Christabel* that his poetic powers have been in a state of suspended animation for sixteen years.

Like Wordsworth he turns from a deeply pantheistic, though nominally Unitarian, unorthodoxy to mysticism and then to orthodoxy in religion and politics, after about 1803; and this coincides with a cessation of creative originality.

Blake, at first sight, seems an exception, for the *Songs of Innocence* appear as part of a unified volume with the *Songs of Experience* in 1794, after the Revolution. Moreover, no poet is less *directly* concerned with the outside world. Taking Imagination to be 'the real and eternal world of which this Vegetable Universe is but a faint shadow', Blake concentrated on opening 'the immortal Eyes of Man *inwards* into Worlds of Thought, into Eternity'. But it is no part of this argument to maintain that the relationship between romantic poetry and the background is direct. On the contrary, the romantics' socially conscious work is often second-rate. What is valuable is the stimulus which stirs the poet to his depths.

Blake's main preoccupation is with this deep, inner conflict and the effort to resolve it. For this purpose, he constructs an elaborate rationalising metaphysic–despite his typically romantic rejection of 'Reason', as a force of restraint.

A Jungian psychologist, W. P. Witcutt (*Blake, a Psychological Study*, 1946) has argued that the effort to achieve Fourfold Vision and Eden is equivalent to a desire to regain the innocence of childhood, and is evidence of trauma, an obsession with early sin. This is probably much more profitable as a way of critical approach to Blake than any attempt to disentangle his confused metaphysic, but there is no conclusive biographical evidence for it. On the other hand, there is a good deal of evidence to show that the *poetic form* his conflicts took was conditioned by contemporary circumstances, particularly in *The French Revolution* (1791) and *America* (1792). An active radical, and a member of a revolutionary society, Blake was bold enough to wear the red cap of France during the early days of the repression, and was tried for treason in 1803 (which may partly account for increasing obscurity thereafter). It is in keeping with this activity that the real content of the Prophetic Books– where they reflect the experience of those who do not share, or follow, the metaphysic– is to be found in their dramatised conflict of imaginative freedom and repressive convention or law. However, the clearest indication of the effect of period on Blake comes when it is realised that the *Songs of Innocence* were written before the Revolution and published separately in 1789. So the *Songs of Experience*, completed in 1794, would seem to be not only a completion, but also a correction, recording a change of viewpoint.

Thus, in the pre-romantic period come *Poetical Sketches* (1769–1778), showing much less originality and genius than anything later. Just before the Revolution are *The Book of Thel* and the *Songs of Innocence*, original in style but orthodox in content. In *The Marriage of Heaven and Hell*, and the *Songs of Experience*, which are post-revolutionary, the change is startling. The emphasis on Passivity, Meekness, Charity, Love, and God as the good Father, is replaced by a cry for energy, justice, freedom; and God becomes a tyrant of imposture. Religion gives way to morality, acceptance to revolt. The Lamb of the *Songs of Innocence* has turned into a Tyger. After 1804, in *Milton* and *Jerusalem*, the process is somewhat reversed by the condemnation of selfhood, though not to the same extent as in the case of Wordsworth and Coleridge. And Blake's best work, like theirs, is that produced in the 1790s. But literary quality requires a more detailed and less sociological assessment. . . .

NOTE: The following may serve as sample instances of romantic fascination with the horrific:

1. *Blake* (*passim*) cosmic rape, lust and sadism, save in early work.

2. *Coleridge v.* the garish whore Life-in-Death of the *Ancient Mariner*, the following demon, slimy horrors, etc. The mariner's appearance at a wedding is probably derived from Lewis's ballad of *Alonzo the Brave* (which contained the memorable line

'The worms they crept in and the worms they crept out', plagiarised several times by Byron and Shelley). Or there is the Vampire, Geraldine, of Christabel—a relative of Matilda.

3. *Southey v.* epilogue to *Joan of Arc*, or the *Ode to Horror*.

4. *Wordsworth v. The Borderers*, concluding lines of *Yew Trees*, or the corpse and gibbet scenes in the *Prelude* (Bks. V & XII).

5. *Byron v.* the demonism of *Manfred*, prison scenes of *Prisoner of Chillon*, the Gothic of *Lara*, the incest theme of *Cain*, etc.

6. *Shelley v.* crucifixion and torment of Laon and Prometheus, sadism of *The Cenci* (and its incest) or the vast panorama of carnage, plague and terror in *The Revolt of Islam*.

7. *Keats:* influence of *Vathek* in Hyperion's palace, *Isabella* (*passim*), and the general influence of Mrs Radcliffe's descriptions. *The Eve of St Agnes* finely transforms passages from *The Mysteries of Udolpho*, which provides a girl, Maddelina, an old man whose spirit *fails* and whose eyes *ache*, faded tapestry, richly coloured casements and many other items found recombined and ensplendoured in Madeline's chamber.

(Further parallels are given by M. H. Shackford, "The Eve of St Agnes and the Mysteries of Udolpho" PMLA, (1921) vol 36)

Part Two

Part Two

PRE-ROMANTIC POETS

I

GENERAL

IF the romantic radicals are forced into reality by their social, as much as their personal situation, while the pre-romantics seem to be escaping from both by forgery, fantasy or pastoral, then it follows that the latter must be commanding their situation only by deliberately putting themselves into a simpler state of mind than they really possess, for they *know* theirs is not poetry of the whole truth. Though the later poets seem to hold Nature as a final arbitrary court of appeal, a sort of god, they are, in fact, genuinely unauthoritarian and unorthodox, so long as they remain nature-worshippers, for their 'natural' order is, in fact, found in the self. There is no church or dogma of 'Nature' and therefore no set rules or traditions by which all things are to be judged. This may encourage crankiness, but it also permits flexibility and subtlety to be shown when necessary. But the thoughts and feelings of the earlier poets usually put on a uniform – very ill-fitting sometimes – before they come out.

This unmutinous spirit probably accounts for stylistic peculiarities. Smart, Chatterton and Cowper all use different styles for different kinds of verse. That is to say, they have a style for a *type* of experience, not for *particular* experiences. Like the subject, the style tends to be either augustan, or romantic fancy-dress. Where the content is potentially new and exploratory, the form is therefore often inadequate for it. Consequently their poetry rarely shows that organic growth in unity which is characteristic of their successors' better work. Even within one poem, the style may so vary that it could be mistaken for the work of two different people; and their poetry as a whole can be divided into two broad and very different categories: the one inhibiting, the other permitting a disguised self-expression (a disguise to be dropped only in madness).

75

For these reasons, the opposing aspects of any conflict are rarely resolved in some richer unity–at least not at a level deeper than that of the convenient verbal formula. Instead, as each disturbance rises to consciousness it is usually fed into the appropriate channel (dogma, pastoral and so on) to be harmlessly led off. So, save for a few remarkable exceptions, one feels in these poems one part of a personality dealing superficially with each side rather than a whole, rich personality dealing with both. Thus the conflicts of the pre-romantic tend to be themes for mild speculation or uplift, until madness frees him from the inhibiting climate of his age. At that point only–and paying a heavy price for the privilege–he is able to immerse himself in the destructive elements of his experience. His style and form become both more expressive of the subject and more recognisably his. For a writer *not* immersed in his subject gives to it less than his whole being, so that his work paradoxically becomes both less objective and less personal.

But, even so, between the best in both periods there is still a difference–perhaps mostly a difference of power. Smart in his madness writes the best cat poem in the language; Blake, in his sanity, *The Tyger*.

II

SMART

In his little classic *The Psychology of Insanity* Bernard Hart concludes that

It is possible that the individual who is faced with an intolerable conflict between his primitive instincts on the one hand, and his environment and traditions on the other, and who has found a refuge by retiring into a world of phantasy and shutting out the world of reality, can only achieve this by dissociating herd instinct from the other primary forces of the mind and refusing to allow it any longer to play a part therein. . . . The only remedy would then lie in altering one or other of the antagonists so that incompatibility no longer existed. The primitive instincts cannot presumably be altered, and the attack would therefore have to be directed against the traditions and codes which obtain their force from the operation of herd instinct. . . . For it is at least conceivable that our present complacent assurance that every individual must live and act within the arbitrary limits assigned by conventional and purely artificial standards of conduct, or else be segregated from society, may be fallacious and inimical to the best development of the race.

(4th edn., (1946) pp. 170/1)

The relevance of these conclusions to the romantic mutation is apparent: the earlier romantics *retired* into a world of fantasy, the later *used* such worlds in an attempt to alter the arbitrary limits assigned by society. To suggest that the intricately logical ordering of Smart's *Song to David* indicates that he could not have been touched with his madness at the time of writing is quite beside the mark. For Hart's, and other studies in clinical psychology, prove conclusively that many maniacs have no lack of logic – it's their premises, their refusal to accept the material facts of experience, that are irrational. Indeed, the obsessive numerology of the *Song to David*, the grouping of stanzas in mystical threes and sevens, or their multiples, is an exaggerated example of a neurotic need for order which one senses in the form of many romantic poems – often no doubt as a compensation for frighteningly expansive feeling. Moreover, W. H. Bond's edition of *Jubilate Agno* (Hart-Davis, 1954) showed this poem – indisputably written in madness – to have had an equally 'logical' structure (an antiphonal one in which 'For' lines were matched by 'Let' lines).

Both of these long poems are characterised by a latent *folie de grandeur* and a Panglossian determination to find a providential purpose in everything, yet they remain his most impressive achievements (however lunatic *Jubilate Agno* may be). The reason can only be that madness, particularly when expressing itself in religious terminology, permitted the intermittent but memorable formulation of experience normally inhibited. At any rate, both the secular and religious poetry published after 1756, when Smart first lost his sanity, tend to be better than earlier work, but the religious poetry – in these two major poems – shows a far greater betterment. In both fields, too, romantic characteristics appear more frequently in the later work, but most strikingly in the religious poems.

This is, of course, what one might expect from the unconstrained self-expression of a personality compounded of fantasy, sensuousness, and persecution mania, and gifted with naively literal and acute observation. Augustanism is adult, and these are childhood qualities. Religion gave both refuge and compensation–sometimes over-compensation–to such a personality: the personality, moreover, of a man sensitive about his physical littleness and his moral failings, and conscious of being out of tune with the age. But, on the whole, if religion and romanticism stand out in his later work, secular and augustan poetry is best exemplified in the earlier.

Reading, as it were, between the lines of his poetry we see that Smart's *personal* conflicts must have been manifold, and note that these extremes of temperament–bravado and gentleness, erudition and simplicity, grandiosity and microscopy–seem to have been resolved in a richer unity only in the *Song to David*. But confining ourselves to the *poetic* themes, we see that these personal conflicts can be conveniently reduced to a literary opposition of Reason and Imagination in his secular poetry, and an opposition of Senses and Spirit in his religious poetry.

Apart from occasional lines or brief passages, Smart's secular poetry is almost entirely augustan before 1756 or thereabouts. The pleasant immorality of the tale of Susan and the lost poker, is as typically augustan, for instance, as the pleasant morality-poem *Care and Generosity*, which ends:

> (Ruined Generosity) wept, she rav'd, she tore her hair,
> When lo! to comfort her came Care–
> And cried 'my dear, if you will join
> Your hand in nuptial bands with mine;
> All will be well–you shall have store,
> And I be plagued with Wealth no more.
> The Bridal came–great was the feast
> And good the pudding and the priest.
> The bride in nine moons brought him forth

A little maid of matchless worth:
Her face was mix'd of care and glee,
They christened her Oeconomy:
And styled her fair Discretion's queen,
The mistress of the golden mean.
Now Generosity confin'd
Is perfect easy in her mind;
Still loves to give, yet knows to spare,
Nor wishes to be free from Care.[1]

The whole poem is a seamless unity, whose conclusion charmingly dispels any suggestion of priggishness by its bland play-wit. Yet it obviously leaves out a good deal in order to achieve its limited perfection; there is glaring disparity between its creator and the vain, lying, drinking, extravagant Smart of whom Gray correctly prophesied that he 'must come to gaol or bedlam, and that without any help, almost without pity'. So it is scarcely surprising that the poem reflects the manifest man of great talent, who won the Seatonian Prize at Cambridge five times in six years, rather than the latent man of genius.

However, even the early poems show signs of things to come—often in the shape of lines too rich for their context, and thus, on a purist view, flaws in the poem. Even a trifling poem like *The Duellists*, for instance, though it derives from Dryden's Zimri contains a few splendid lines of a romantic sort:

A thousand trifles not worth naming
In whoring, jockeying and gaming,
Shall cause a challenge's inditing,
And set two loggerheads a-fighting.
Meanwhile the father of despair,
The Prince of vanity and air....

Quite unaugustan in its imprecise play of emotive overtone and suggestion ('air' as invisibility, ubiquity, vastness and mere emptiness, 'vanity' as vainglory and futility, Milton's magnifico swooping through the void), it looks forward to the *Song to David*.

---

[1] All quotations, save those from *Jubilate Agno*, are from N. Callan's edn. (1949). For *Jubilate Agno*, W. H. Bond's re-edited edition (1954) has been preferred.

Later on, this romantic element in his work grows larger, even in oetry which is secular and entirely sane. In *Munificence and Modesty*, for example, there is an anticipation of the Blakian characteristics of his *Song to David*:

> Consider for the poor infirm,
> The harmless sheep, th'obnoxious worm,
> The stooping yoke that turn the soil,
> And all the children of thy toil.

The systematic humanisation of the animal (and in other poems the animation of the inanimate) which is so marked in his two major works is clearly beginning. Again, if the quotation from *Care and Generosity* is compared with one from the later *Reason and Imagination*, it is clear that the poetry of Beauty has come to engage more of Smart's talent than the poetry of Prudence:

> Imagination in the flight
> Of young desire and gay delight,
> Began to think upon a mate;
> As weary of a single state;
> For sick of change, as left at will,
> And cloy'd with entertainment still,
> She thought it better to take up and save.
> She therefore to her chamber sped,
> And thus at first attir'd her head.
> Upon her hair with brilliants grac'd,
> Her tower of beamy gold she plac'd;
> Her ears with pendant jewels glow'd
> Of various water, curious mode,
> As nature sports the wintry ice
> In many a whimsical device.
> Her eyebrows arch'd upon the stream
> Of rays beyond the piercing beam;
> Her cheeks in matchless colour high,
> She veil'd to catch the gazer's eye;
> Her paps as white as Fancy draws,
> She covered with a crimson gauze;
> And on her wings she threw perfume
> From buds of everlasting bloom.

The allegorical figure is now more lifelike, the tone more

sensuous and the diction somewhat less orthodox. Yet the fact that Smart's conflict is rendered in the title of the poem symbolises a lack of depth and density in it. One may infer from it more than it says, but that is also more than Smart intends. In other words, though it earnestly records a rake's desire to reform, it makes the white-papped pin-up, Imagination, a good deal more attractive than the grave, saving, sober augustan Reason. This would seem to tally with Smart's real inner experience, if the slackened tension and pedestrian movement of the rejection verses which follow is good evidence. Certainly the reader feels surprised to find Reason rejecting the proffered marriage:

> I cannot take thee for a mate;
> I'm lost if e'er I change my state.
> But whensoe'er your raptures rise
> I'll try to come with my supplies.

This guarded attitude seems to indicate a fear of Imagination just about commensurate with the attraction to it. But Smart is not sufficiently aware of this complexity in his experience to make much of it. Moreover, the style he has inherited is suitable only for the simple pre-Coleridgian psychology he actually uses (reason being rushed up whenever rapture seems likely to get out of hand), and the guilty associations of Imagination with shameful behaviour prevent his probing too deeply into his experience – or at any rate prevent his expressing it fully – until the revelation of madness, when he lived in a shameless world whose every characteristic was deified: the world of the later romantics mirrored in a twisted glass. In *Reason and Imagination*, however, he ended with a weak compromise, Reason promising

> To act conjointly in the war
> On dullness whom we both abhor.

Thus, half-heartedly echoing Pope, the poem remains an in-adequate embodiment of his real, or at least his potential experience.

His religious poems, perhaps rather surprisingly, follow the same course, in so far as they do not engage his whole personality until the period of, and immediately after, his confinement. One might have expected religion, in any period, to offer the poet a way into the subconscious, or a new and interesting slant on life. In fact, the earlier poems are mere exercises in orthodoxy. To compare the frigid competence of Smart's sub-Miltonic verses *On the Eternity of the Supreme Being* (1750) with the rather uncontrolled power of, say, Blake's apocalyptic vision in *Vala* is to see at once that comparisons are going to be much more odious to Smart. To the theologian, no doubt, these poems are the more approvable; but the literary critic, *as* critic, is concerned with doctrinal expressions only in so far as they reflect, or reflect on, human experience. A religious poem, like a mythological or fabulist poem, is for him saying something which ought in principle to be equally comprehensible to well-informed readers of any creed or none, and it is to be assessed according to the quality of its expression of life, not according to the 'correctness' of its dogma. In principle, it could reflect the same reality (or perhaps fantasy) in other terms–such as the 'Nature' of the later romantics, or the 'Art' of the symbolists.

What the religion of his mad period gave to Smart was a release from conflict and inhibition. This had its drawbacks, in the shape of childishness of one sort or another, but it also had the great advantage of permitting the poet to indulge his childlike attributes in full confidence: to look with a child's unspoilt eye, to speak what he felt, unabashed, and to use imaginative fantasy to express things his augustan 'reason' would have repressed– and all without faltering, that sign of known falsity which tends (however unnecessarily) to occur in pastoral or primitivistic creations, which are products of 'fancy' not 'faith'.

His *Hymn to the Supreme Being*, conceived during 'a dangerous fit of illness' in 1756, occasionally modulates into the mood of the *Song to David*:

> Chief of metallic forms is regal gold;
>   Of elements the limpid fount that flows.
> Give me 'mongst gems the brilliant to behold;
>   O'er Flora's flock imperial is the rose;
> Above all birds the sov'reign eagle soars;
> And monarch of the field the lordly lion roars.

The augustan Principle of Plenitude enables Smart to console himself with this firm vision of a fusion in nature of the spiritual and the material. For after all, 'What are these to man, who bears the sway, For all was made for him. . . ?' Later it will allow him an almost romantic pantheism: a way of imprinting his inner world on the outer one, and so seeing it as a meaningful object. But in this hymn Smart cannot sustain any pressure. When he is forced to turn from what he believes to be God's plenitude to what he knows to be his own, he lapses into constrained super-ficiality:

> My little prattlers lifting up their hands,
> Beckon me back to them, to life and light;
> I come ye spotless sweets! I come again,
> Nor have your tears been shed, nor have ye knelt in vain.

Only with the composition of *Jubilate Agno* (1759–63) does he become consistently unconstrained. Freed from the literary, moral and rational restraints of his period he patchily succeeds in the typically romantic task of embodying the spiritual and rational-ising the intuitive.

Three factors help to bring about that success–where success there is. Firstly, Smart is able to believe quite literally in a divine unity in the world, a unity not only of all things, but of things and emotions. Believing, that is to say, that the physical is a plenitudinous expression of the spiritual, he can be as naively literal and sensuous as a child in humanising the inanimate: he can explore the world of his suppressed self without knowing it to be so, and therefore without self-consciousness. At the same time, his learning gives him suitably impersonal moulds, biblical, masonic or medieval. The second factor follows from the first, for in this state no period training or inhibition prevents his utilising to the full his talent 'to give an impression upon words by punching, that when the reader casts his eye upon 'em, he takes up the image from the mould I have made'. Thirdly he can be insanely scientific and logical about intangible worlds. On the whole, of course, the results of this last factor are now of psychiatric, rather than strictly literary interest, since the science is pseudo or outdated and the logic ascends from crazy premises, but occasionally the childlike honesty and the talent for 'punching' combine with this pseudo-science to give unforgettable expression to some acute perception of sensation or feeling or judgement:

For Frost is damp and unwholesome air candied to fall to the best advantage. (B2.326)
For an Ague is the terror of the body, when the blessing of God is withheld for a season. (B2.474)
For stuff'd guts make no musick; strain them strong and you shall
. have sweet melody. (B2.307)

All three factors immensely assist in the foremost of the romantic poet's tasks, the creation from the psyche's amorphous chaos of an acceptable, consistent, experiential world. What operates against Smart in this work, rendering his successes accidental and intermittent, is his mania.

His chief technique is to obliterate the distinction between analogy and identity, leaving the assertive grammatical structure to telescope idea and object, sense and spirit, or reason and fantasy. In Fragment A the obliteration is rarely complete. Though the syntax states a double identity, an implied analogy is apparent ('Let Soloman praise with the Ant, and give the glory to the Fountain of all Wisdom' (A.43) seems to equate man and insect, but only through an implied common attribute, wisdom). Such lines are clear, but not always so common-sensical. Indeed the cumulative effect is neither that of a series of propositions nor of a hymn or praise. Rather, the ecstatic tone and the determination to laud, indeed to become one with, all creation, finally records a pantheistic *feeling*, not a coherent *creed*. Everything, from the weasel to the tarantula is blessed (the latter on the odd ground that its lurking makes 'the pilgrim take heed to his way'). Sometimes the result is downright contradictory (as in A.70 where the canker-worm is blessed and condemned at the same time). At other times, however, a real complexity rather than a confusion is punched home, and something more than a rapt feeling is conveyed. Thus in the line:

Let Susanna bless with the Butterfly—beauty hath wings, but chastity is the Cherub. (A.93) a complex statement is 'candied to fall to the best advantage', so to speak. The main idea presumably is that Susanna's chaste spirit is of greater worth (a higher link in the Chain of Being) than her bodily beauty. But the full statement conveyed by the form in which this idea is rendered goes further than the mere contrast of beauty and chastity. Susanna and the Butterfly are identified as things of beauty, which is a blessed gift; and chastity, despite the 'but', is made to seem a more highly evolved butter-fly-beauty with a plus-quality about it. So the spiritual and the physical in Susanna become terms of each other. Chastity, by spiritualising beauty, renders it more beautiful; and beauty, by making chastity voluntary, not a mere lack of wings, renders it praiseworthy.

At times, Smart is exceedingly sane and penetrating in his madness. Two aspects of the pre-romantic predicament are perfectly put :

For where Accusation takes the place of encouragement a man of
  Genius is driven to act the vices of a fool. (B2.365)

For I bless God in the rising generation, which is on my side. (B1.10)

Smart shares too the tenderness for animals which is so notable an extension of human sympathy in the later romantics:

For the merciful man is merciful to his beast, and to the trees that give
  them shelter. (B1.13)

In the wonderfully lithe and vital lines on Cat Jeoffrey (B2. 697/ 770), however, this characteristic catches up others like a magnet, so that the cat becomes a centre of intense life, which the reader shares. From the cat, currents of feeling constantly flow from animal to human, beauty to goodness, physical to spiritual, Smart to the world, the literal to the imaginative–and they flow without a break for Smart's punching, assertive lines do, in fact, convince anyone who knows cats that what he sees–once it has been pointed out–is in fact potentially there, at least by sug-gestion, metaphor or analogy:

For he rolls upon prank to work it in. . . .
For he counteracts the powers of darkness by his electrical skin and
  glaring eyes. . . .

For the dexterity of his defence is an instance of the love of God to him
  exceedingly....
For having considered God and himself, he will consider his neighbour.
For if he meets another cat he will kiss her in kindness....
For he is hated by the hypocrite and miser....
For he is a mixture of gravity and waggery....
For there is nothing sweeter than his peace when at rest.
For there is nothing brisker than his life when in motion....
For he can spraggle upon waggle at the word of command.

To see, and *sense*, so much in and through one animal almost
makes one envious of insanity.

Such a feeling, however, is likely to be modified by other
parts of the poem. The childlike, startling vision often degenerates
into childish vanity and boasting:

For Newton nevertheless is more of error than of the truth, but I am
  of the WORD of GOD (B1.195)

Let Fig, house of Fig rejoice with Fleawort. The Lord magnify the
idea of Smart singing hymns on this day in the eyes of the whole
University of Cambridge. Novr 5th 1762. N.S. (D.149)

Feelings are rationalised, without any compensating insight or
cattish wit, merely to fit phenomena into a personal notion:

For the phenomenon of the horizontal moon is the truth—she appears
  bigger in the horizon because she actually is so (B2.426)

Or again:

For the devil hath most power in winter, because darkness prevails
  (B2.296)

Here the effect depends entirely on the ambiguity of 'darkness',
and it disappears as soon as one analyses the word into (1) absence
of light, and (2) sin. One might give meaning to the line by
arguing that winter implied old age or depression, but nothing
in Smart encourages such inferences, which must therefore be
rejected as invented, not inherent meanings. Smart is being
literal in intention but hasn't noticed the two-facedness of his
substantive. Surely, though, many of Wordsworth's statements in

the Immortality Ode are literally and logically as meaningless[1] (in so far as they are subject to no possible verification or are self-contradictory)? True, but Wordsworth, whether he believes them literally or no, does not *rely* on their literal truth. His poem states a psychological truth (verifiable, at least hypothetically, by reference to common experience) which does not depend on the unverifiable propositions about insubstantial realms where Child-seers and 'our life's star' originate. That poem's more controlled complexity not only permits, but enforces analogies with the reality of youth and age which we all share, if only in some lesser degree than the poet. But Smart's is an uncontrolled complexity, so that the same technique–of taking the figurative as literal–which elsewhere candies tenuous perceptions here achieves only a mirage.

The rest of *Jubilate Agno* shows the same erratic variations of quality. In his lines on the alphabet, there is sometimes a remarkable synæsthesia of sound with sight or movement ('For C is a sense quick and penetrating', B2.515) or a brilliant, surrealistically witty, relating of physical and mental:

For H is not a letter but a spirit. (B2.520)

H is made by a breath and breath is the spirit of God breathed into Adam. There is, too, a subdued pun on aspirate and aspiration. On the other hand, much is pedestrian ('For F is faith') or pointless punning ('For B pronounced in the animal is bey importing authority').

Similarly, on the colours, Smart's delicate sensuous apprehension of

For Red is of sundry sorts till it deepens to BLACK. For Black blooms and it is PURPLE. (B2.659/60)

degenerates into silly lines like this:

For the next is PALE. God be gracious to W. Whitehead (B2.662)

The *Song to David*, however, seems to be free from erratic variation, and the Reverend Christopher Hunter has been much

---

[1] 'Our birth is but a sleep and a forgetting', for example, logically implies that the assertion itself has been made in a dream when the facts were forgotten. Further, since 'sleep' gets meaning by contrast with 'waking'–both states of life–the statement that *all* life is a sleep is literally meaningless.

censured for omitting it from the 1791 edition of Smart's work, as showing proofs of his 'recent estrangement of mind'. The omission was certainly a mistake, but not so inexcusable a mistake as later (post-romantic) critics have made out. As a clergyman, Hunter must have found it exceedingly unorthodox and inconsistent, and as an augustan exceedingly lacking in Good Sense. Indeed, one could say paradoxically that while it is *greater* than any of Smart's augustan poems it is not so *good* as many–and being only a little malicious one might suggest that for some critics 'great' has signified the capacity for giving a sense of generalised uplift without committing the reader to any particular sort of behaviour. A satisfying feeling to have, of course, but one indicating in the poem only the virtue of being 'opium for the people'. Considered in augustan terms, in fact, the *Song to David* is little more. It is an example of the Sublime–badly flawed because it so nearly touches the ridiculous at times; and it lacks such virtues as attention to things as they really are, consistency of argument, discrimination in terms of a standard, a developing theme, and so on. Moreover, while far less erratic than *Jubilate Agno*, it is not so thoroughly controlled in its sense and tone as the arithmetical strictness of its form leads one to think. It ignores the true facts of what Hart calls 'the world of reality', and its varying moods are all contained within a general tone of manic elation. To be sure, it is not a mad poem as *Jubilate Agno* is (and therefore its best passages are the less striking), but the Reverend Christopher Hunter was right in thinking it showed *signs* of his 'recent estrangement'. Where he was wrong was in assuming full sanity to be essential for good poetry. For romantic work it is not (though it is desirable for the best results), since much of its function is to explore and map–or, as second-best, just reveal–jungle territory uninhabited by augustans.

A Song to David is more profitably approached as a poem of shared experience, an experience powerful though limited, but within its limits richly variegated: so variegated indeed that it can include all Smart's conflicts within the one general euphoric experience, and *needs* the ingenious rigidity of its plan and stanza-form to retain unity. It develops like a plant watched by

time-lapse photography, in changing sameness, till the sun-
flowering of the last, 'Glorious' stanzas.

As a technical feat it is outstanding[1]; and in relation to content
the form of the poem is as the One to the Many. That is to say,
it matches the theme of a world whose plenitude is united in
God–in psychological terms a world in which disturbing conflicts, the differences of good and evil, of material and spiritual
are contained in a general euphoria, saved from dullness by the
colouring of different moods: admiration, pastoral peace, awe,
adoration, sweetness, strength (not to mention a little moral
superiority, patronage and indirect self-satisfaction). Thus, like
Blake, he has not only a sensuous delight in animal life but a
tenderness for it:

> Be good to him that pulls thy plough
> Due food and care, due rest allow
> For her that yields thy milk.   (XLII)

But this homeliness is only one viewpoint, the microscopic.
With a change of mood–measured for the reader by a newly
majestic movement within this grid of strict stanza-form–life is
seen telescopically:

> He sung of God–the mighty source
> Of all things–the stupendous force
> On which all strength depends;
> From whose right arm, beneath whose eyes,
> All period, power and enterprise
> Commences, reigns and ends. (XVIII)

> The world–the clust'ring spheres he made,
> The glorious light, the soothing shade,
> Dale, champaign, grove and hill;
> The multitudinous abyss,
> Where secrecy remains in bliss,
> And wisdom hides her skill. (XXI)

The two stanzas in between, though, are among those in which
the sublime leans precariously towards the ridiculous. With their

---

[1] Details are to be found in *Havens Review of English Studies*, (April 1938)
(vol. 14, pp. 178–82) or more handily in the notes in Donald Davie's collection,
The Late Augustans, 1958.

'Angels. . . Which to and fro with blessings speed' and 'the Saint elect For infinite applause' it is difficult not to associate Smart with Logan Pearsall Smith's gently satirised parsons (in *All Trivia*):

All the same I like Parsons; they think nobly of the Universe, and believe in Souls and Eternal Happiness. And some of them, I am told, believe in Angels–that there are Angels who guide our footsteps, and flit to and fro unseen on errands in the air about us.

Again, there are many confusions in the poem (apart from the undiscriminating approval of *everything*) such as that pointed out by Davie, in stanza XLIV, where it is impossible to reconcile the injunctions to 'Use all thy passions!' and to curb concupiscence with fear, and psychologically difficult to dissociate the 'rapture to transport' from the 'concupiscence' that must be curbed since they come in successive lines.

But as a whole–and unlike *Jubilate Agno* it is a whole–the poem conveys an impression of great psychic release and sincerity, of a spiritualised joy in the senses. It becomes, in effect, a sensuous and emotive revelling in the beauty of animal and inanimate nature, a romantic appreciation of different qualities in it: of strength, sweetness, delicacy or glory.

How does all this differentiate it from a poem of 'mere uplift?' Well, it removes the 'mere'. Yet it is true that Smart's religion allows him to ignore harshness and evil and cruelty. So neither unity nor madness compensates adequately for the lack of that external stimulus granted to the post-revolutionary romantics. In so far as *A Song to David* expresses the synthesis Smart was capable of, it does so once for all. His was not an inspiration which could develop, for it assimilated too much. Such inclusive feeling for the goodness of the world is one thing and demands only one satisfying expression. Not surprisingly, therefore, his later Parables and Hymns, though admirably competent, add nothing to his achievement. The 'Nature' of the later romantics, however, though in some ways a substitute for 'God', tends to force them nearer to the complexities of good and evil in reality, so that they have far greater possibilities of development.

III

CHATTERTON

Like Smart, Chatterton had two main types of poetry and two main styles. Although he died by his own hand at the early age of seventeen, he had through one of these manners more influence on the later Romantics than any poet of his period. His achievement, however, fell short of his influence, for his incomparable promise was thwarted not only by the brevity of his creative life, but also by his need to work, first in an attorney's office and then at the incessant labour of hack journalism for the 'patriotic' (Whig reformist) side, when the market was contracting and the hacks were exploited.

In these political poems, and in his bawdry or his orthodox amatory and adulatory odes and addresses–the poems he wrote, so to speak, 'as himself'–Chatterton was almost invariably augustan. But, again like Smart, he was more personally expressive when he was 'not himself', for he then had his subject in mind, not his audience, and was therefore able to project his genius more whole-heartedly, in the egocentric romantic manner. As Chatterton, he wore a mask; as Rowley he was freely himself– at any rate so far as the necessity of faking permitted. His supposed medieval poet expressed a very eighteenth-century Middle Ages: witness for example the minstrels' fondness for Nature in *Aella*, the latent doctrine of 'universal benevolence'in the *Balade of Charitie*, or the general primitivism. And the heroes of these pseudo-medieval poems–transcribed with infinite pains on to stolen candle-smoked parchment–turn out to be dramatised aspects of his own character.

When he presented feeling for Nature in his contemporary manner (not a religious feeling, as in Smart's case, but a feeling for the picturesque) there was inevitably a clash between style and subject. A third, minor manner appears, inferior to either of the main ones. The reader comes to dread the inevitability of the all-too-appropriate adjective, and the sandy absorption of individual perceptions by the orthodox diction. On the other hand, style and subject seem well matched in political satires like

The Prophecy. These poems resemble the Augustan work of Smart in being very competent if not inspired. Like him, Chatterton appears to have needed a different style to produce his best poetry; for such verse is not a suitable medium for embodying either aspect of the romantic conflict.

Consequently, he produces not poetry of depth and intensity when he writes in his own person on subjects which would allow him to embody the frustrating contraries that most pre-occupied him – rather he produces poetry of uncertain mien and incongruous imagery. In generalised form, these contraries yield the poetic themes of the conflict of Joy and Melancholy, of Senses and Spirit (themes which figure largely too in the poetry of Keats, a great admirer of Chatterton). Obviously, an *Elegy on the Death of Mr Phillips* – Chatterton's school usher and good friend – invited the use of such themes. The result, though, was not as might have been expected, the *growth* of a poem getting down to the roots of sorrow and comprehending their ramifications, but rather an *addition* of disunited sentiments in different stock styles. Thus, the first of these stanzas is clearly augustan ('inspired' by Gray's *Elegy*), the second a mixture of augustanism and pre-romanticism, and the third is purely pre-romantic:

> No more I hail the morning's golden gleam,
> No more the wonders of the view I sing;
> Friendship requires a melancholy theme,
> At her command the awful lyre I string!

> Now as I wander through this leafless grove
> Where tempests howl and blasts eternal rise,
> How shall I touch the chorded shell to move,
> Or stay the gushing torrent from my eyes? ...

> When golden Autumn, wreathed in ripened corn,
> From purple clusters prest the foamy wine,
> Thy genius did his sallow brows adorn
> And made the beauties of the season thine.

In the last, most romantic stanza, one senses the poet's own spirit struggling feebly beneath the smothering influence of Milton and the conventionally adjectival diction. In a later stanza, too, there is a flash of personal vision and felicitous usage:

> Peace decked in all the softness of the dove
> Over thy passions spread her silver plume;
> The rosy veil of harmony and love
> Hung on thy soul in one eternal bloom.

That last line might well have been early Keats. But the poem degenerates immediately into Peace's 'silver pinions wet with dewy tears.' The same uncertainty of attitude and variation of style is seen even more clearly in *The Complaint*, a poem which seems to have influenced two of Keats's odes and his description of the snake in *Lamia*.

Similarly, the self-dramatisation of the threatened suicide in the last stanza of Chatterton's poem ('No; if I still must meet your scorn/I'll seek the realms of night') is crude in movement, expression and mood in comparison with Keats's '*half* in love with easeful death'. Possibly Chatterton was sincere – since he did kill himself later – but his poem isn't, for its language won't let it be; and the experience presented by the poem, not that perhaps initially presented to it by the poet, is what the reader is concerned with.

Chatterton is again like Keats in his wish for, and disbelief in, immortality. But here again he is unable to relate the two, and simply contradicts himself. The *Last Will* is satirically sceptical:

> My powers of utterance I give to the Reverend Mr Broughton, hoping he will employ them to better purpose than reading lectures on the immortality of the soul. I leave the Reverend Mr Catcott some little of my freethinking that he may put on spectacles of Reason, and see how vilely he is duped in believing the Scriptures literally.

His *Verses to a Lady in Bristol* express the creed of romantic naturalism in literature, morality and theology:

> The bard alone by nature taught
> Is to that nature just. . . .
>
> But ask your orthodox divine. . . .
> Will all his sermons, preaching, prayers,
> His hell, his heaven, his solemn airs,
> Quench nature's rising fires?

In natural religion free
I to no other bow the knee
Nature's the God I own.

On the Immortality of the Soul, however, cannot bear the thought that experiences of the senses and the spirit alike are doomed to 'non-futurity,' and it ends in Christian orthodoxy. Chatterton, in fact, always had religion to fall back on in time of stress, so that his worship of nature does not go so deep as that of his successors. It does not even go so deep as that of Smart, who was able at the end to identify all the feelings and aspirations he personified by 'God' with natural things and creatures. Hence Chatterton's unstable wavering not only between augustanism and romanticism, but also between religion and naturalism, rebellion and acceptance. The conflicts are never worked out personally, because the conventions, religion or diction of his period can be made shift with.

Of the Rowley poems, however, this charge is less fully justified. True, there is inevitably an element of masquerade in them, but they give him a world on to which he can project his romanticism without fear of exposing himself to ridicule. Pre-romanticism was a matter of Fancy more often than Imagination. An escape from, rather than an attack on the present, it preferred a bright bubble to a dull world. Not surprisingly, therefore, Chatterton is at his best in the Rowley poems when he is being most fantastic, for he then taps springs normally denied outlet. When trying to express directly some moral or material truth he is at his worst, lapsing into priggery or didacticism, or into rather crude sadism and action (as in the battle scenes of *The Battle of Hastings*).

When he abandons himself to the atmosphere of his private world he creates something as remotely meaningful as stained-glass windows (whose light is so lucid while their content is usually so obscure). Though the language is phony, translation leads to loss, not gain:

The blaunchie mone or estells to gev lyghte
(*Eclogue the Second*)

Apart from the illegitimate and temporary attraction of quaint-
ness, there are here enriching suggestions of 'blanch', 'blank',
and 'fearful', of 'spangles', 'sparks', and 'constellations' which
disappear if the line is rendered:

> The silver moon or stars to give (us) light.

And how would one translate 'the lordynge toad'? To say that
Chatterton, with this *invented* word, meant merely 'standing on
his hind legs' is to lose the suggestion–which contemporary
poetic theory and diction would have denied him–of a fat,
loathed eighteenth-century milord.

When this sort of rebelliousness comes out into the open it is
much less effective, for Chatterton shared in an extreme degree
the romantic dilemma of wealth. He admired both the natural
simplicity of the primitive life and the glamour of immense
riches. *Eclogue the Third* is vitiated by this uncertainty. Chatterton
cannot decide whether to approve or condemn the peasant who
would 'be moe great'.

In view of such uncertainty, it is remarkable how rarely in the
Rowley poems he lapses into the failings of his other work.
Often this technical improvement is put at the service of extravagant period horror (as in *The Tournament* or the matter of the
heroine's necrophilia in *Elinour and Juga*), but there is usually
some compensating merit. *The Tournament*, for instance, contains
at least one example of vivid seeing. 'Wythe *passent* steppe the
lyon mov'th alonge'–that is, walking leisurely, not melo-
dramatically ramping.

But on the whole, it has to be admitted, these poems are
not only forgeries; they are fakes. They offer a facade instead of
an experiential whole–as one sees clearly on the rare occasions
that something first-rate does crop up. The most notable
example perhaps is in *The Dethe of Syr Charles Bawdwin*, whose
subject, the tyrant's martyrdom of a rebel, was congenial enough
to engage Chatterton's full participation and remote enough for
him to view it unrhetorically, to let the romance of the scene
speak for itself. Joy of the senses (the splendour, the sun on the
axe, and so on) is fused with the melancholy of the event, and

these are respectively associated with the tyrant's triumph and the rebel's death:

> And nowe the horses gently drewe
> Syr Charles uppe the hyghe hille
> The axe dydd glyster ynne the sunne
> Hys pretious bloude to spylle

In its context, how sinister, distancing and remorseless that 'gently' becomes! And how well the stresses and alliteration of 'Chárles uppe the hýghe hílle' convey a sense of purposeful effort.

Something of the same grasp of actuality is evident, too, in *Aella*. The description of autumn, for example, is excellent descriptive writing, evocative of a medieval-primitive ideal; and the acceptance of the inseparability of joy and melancholy in these lines:

> Hys goulde hond guylteynge the falling lefe
> Bryngynge oppe Wynter to folfylle the yere

gives depth to the spiritual-sensuous implications of the conclusion:

> Thenne, bee the even foule or even fayre,
> Meethynckes mie hartys joie ys steynced with somme care.

But though this is basically similar to Keats's *Ode to Autumn*, it falls far short of it in complexity. In the same way, *An Excellent Balade of Charitie* is indeed excellent of its kind, in its period, but by comparison with Keats's poem of the same kind, *The Eve of St Agnes*, it is a minor work. The difference between the opening description of the cold in the later poem and the description of the storm in the earlier is characteristic. Keats's description is an integral part of the whole poem. So, it might be said, is Chatterton's; but if so it is part of a different sort of whole–it is part of the story. The pilgrim must get drenched in order to be spurned by the abbot and helped by the poor monk. Not the *feeling*, but only the *fact* of the storm is an essential part of this whole. The archaic language is not animating but decorative here. Whereas Keats evokes a feeling of intense cold.

In short, even in the Rowley poems, the presented experience often becomes a linguistic legerdemain: apparent complexity, originality or starkness of vision being in fact due to the novelty of a diction which has become a reflection of a fantasy. The body of real meaning easily slips out of this sort of work, leaving the verse behind, standing in virtue of its decoration, like a dress of stiff brocade.

Had circumstances been other than they were, Chatterton might have been the greatest of romantic poets, but he lived too early and died too young to fulfil his brilliant promise. By the mid-May of 1770, the year in which Chatterton went to London to live by his pen, the printer of the *Middlesex Journal* had been tried by the House of Lords and committed to Newgate, and Fell of the *Freeholders Magazine* was in the King's Bench, both victims of the Government's drive against political satire. In August, penniless, starving, and probably ill, the 'wonderful boy' killed himself, leaving behind his most bitter satirical verses:

> Farewell Bristolia's dingy piles of brick,
> Lovers of Mammon, worshippers of Trick!
> You spurned the boy who gave you antique lays,
> And paid for learning with your empty praise.
> Farewell, ye guzzling aldermanic fools,
> By nature fitted for Corruption's tools!
> I go to where celestial anthems swell.
> But you, when you depart, will sink to hell.
> Farewell, my mother! cease my anguished soul,
> Nor let Distraction's billows o'er me roll!
> Have mercy Heaven! when here I cease to live,
> And this last act of wretchedness forgive.

Ironic, that at the end the poet admired by Blake, Wordsworth and Coleridge, by Keats and Shelley, should have spoken in so unRowleian a manner.

COWPER

Cowper has a greater poetic range than Smart and Chatterton, but he shares many of their characteristics. His innate timidity turns into religious mania, though of a morbid methodistical sort, without Smart's exultation. Like Chatterton, he takes the Whig side in politics. In a letter to his bad angel, the Reverend John Newton (March 29, 1784) he states his opposition to the Crown:

> I thought myself, however, happy in being able to affirm truly that I had not that influence for which he sued; and for which, had I been possessed of it, with my present views of the dispute between the Crown and the Commons, I must have refused him, for he is on the side of the former.
>
> *(Letters* (1912), ed. Frazer, vol. 1, p. 286)

Like these poets he attacks various abuses – corruption, the slave trade, the depression of the agricultural worker, the extreme accumulation of wealth – and he does so in a manner predominantly augustan. In the romantic fashion, he also displays signs of a literary reaction: opposing his own translation of Homer, for instance, to that of Pope, which he thought too artificial, and censuring Pope's followers (in *Table Talk*). He is to be aligned, too, rather with Smart and Chatterton than (say) Byron and Shelley in so far as both reactions are fairly tame, and in so far as his most romantic poetry, the product of instability, is by far his best.

This last, and most important point, however, has been blurred by a persistent critical fallacy, whose latest victim, astonishingly in so good a critic, is Donald Davie:

> Without help from the biographer (he writes) his poems lose much of their point and poignancy. This is true not only of short lyrical pieces like *The Castaway*, but also of longer poems like *The Task* or *Friendship* or *Table Talk*. . . . (They) take on much extra significance when the reader knows they were written under the shadow of psychosis. . . . And when we know of Cowper's private infirmity, we admire him the more for having so resolutely turned his eyes away from his private world.
>
> *(The Late Augustans* (1958), pp. 26/27)

Certainly, such biographical knowledge may make us admire *him*, but if it leads us to revise upwards our assessment of his *poetry* solely on such sympathetic grounds it is leading us into sentimental criticism, since the 'extra significance' is extra-literary. Of course, biographical information, like information about social background or obscure references, may well be useful in inclining us to notice virtues in the poem that we might otherwise have overlooked, but it cannot create virtues from a poetic void. In the case of *The Castaway*, for instance, some knowledge of Cowper's condition may ensure that the less practised reader does in fact take the poem metaphorically, as he must for an adequate response; but in the case of *Friendship* or *Table Talk* such knowledge can only act as an *excuse*. For the fact is that while we may admire him for writing so in the circumstances, the poetry we should admire, on literary grounds, is that in which, far from 'resolutely turning away', he entered his psychotic world. *The Castaway* is a unique, first-rate, pre-romantic poem, whereas *Friendship* and *Table Talk* are common-place, third-rate, degenerate augustan works.

It is difficult, indeed, to find much to praise in Cowper's most public poems, his moral satires *Table Talk*, *Progress of Error*, *Truth*, *Expostulation*, *Hope*, *Charity*, *Conversation*, *Retirement*. Cowper himself obviously staked his claim mainly on their improvement-value:

> A. Hail Sternhold, then, and Hopkins hail!
> B. Amen
> If flattery, folly, lust employ the pen . . .
> Though Butler's wit, Pope's numbers, Prior's ease,
> With all that Fancy can invent to please,
> Adorn the polished periods as they fall,
> One madrigal of theirs is worth them all
>
> (*Table Talk*, 760/7)

He was sufficiently perceptive to allow A. to comment:

> Such lofty strains embellish what you teach:
> Mean you to prophesy, or but to preach? (478/9)

All these poems are inordinately long and lacking in structure or sense of climax. They seem to make the same points (in no particular order), and in the same style–a style ridden with clichés, devoid of the syntactical animation appropriate to heroic couplets (and of course lacking the romantic sort of animation): it is 'natural' only to be flat. Having indignation without wit, and making no tonal discrimination between grave and trivial faults, they succeed in being utterly unmemorable, and leave behind only an impression of peevish railing.

This monotonous rhetoric cannot be said, either, to compensate by romantic content for the conspicuous failings of its feeble augustan form. Certainly, the reader gathers that Cowper is thoroughly dissatisfied with his age, but his remedy is neither 'nature' nor republican reform; it is the pulpit:

> The pulpit, therefore (and I name it fill'd
> With solemn awe, that bids me well beware
> With what intent I touch that holy thing)–
> The pulpit (when the satirist has at last,
> Strutting and vapouring in an empty school
> Spent all his force and made no proselyte)–
> I say the pulpit (in the sober use
> Of its legitimate, peculiar powers)
> Must stand acknowledged, while the world shall stand,
> The most important and effectual guard,
> Support, and ornament of Virtue's cause.
>
> (*The Task*, Bk. II, 326/37)

Nature is a comfort sometimes, but never engages much of the poet's deeper experience because it is always secondary to God, at best 'Borrowing a beauty from the works of grace' (*Retirement*); and at worst–'the more we learn/Of nature overlooks her author more' (*The Task*, Bk. III).

Considering the fierce and arbitrary character of Cowper's God, operating above the moral law, the remedy must seem of dubious efficiency. Indeed, it adds to an impression slowly gathered from the rest of Cowper's public, pulpiteering work: that these poems have inconsistencies rather than conflicts. He will not admit to friendship the man who should tread upon an insect, but is cruelly rigorous (in Bk. III of *The Task*) to the adultress. Here his religion intervenes between his subject and his naturally sensitive nature, so that moral subtlety disappears and he comes to share with various eminent coarse-grained moralists some simple stereotype of the homebreaker, ignoring the range of situations 'adultery' can cover. Shelley is far more flexible. The same passage requires payment in blood for anyone proving slack when his country requires 'His every nerve in action and at stretch'. Hardly consistent with Cowper's own armchair existence. Again, his attachment to the idea of a Great Chain of Being is incompatible with his complaints about various classes of people and various fields of public affairs (but like most augustans he makes no attempt to relate the two views in a more comprehensive one):

> Great Offices will have
> Great talents; and God gives to every man
> The virtue, temper, understanding, taste,
> That lifts him into life, and lets him fall
> Just in the niche he was ordained to fill....
>
> To monarchs dignity; to judges sense;
> To artists ingenuity and skill;
> To me an unambitious mind....
>
> (*The Task*, Bk. IV, 788/98)

Compare the attack on the bloated folly and drivel of kings and the vices of eminent men, in Book V.

To inconsistency, we may add impercipience and naive patriotism. Only seven years before the outbreak of the French Revolution, Cowper is to be found boasting (in *Table Talk*) of the healthy, noble, freedom-loving British peasant (a picture very different from that given in Bk. IV of *The Task*) and comparing him with the frivolous slaves over the Channel:

> Not form'd like us, with such Herculean powers,
> The Frenchman, easy, debonair, and brisk,
> Give him his lass, his fiddle, and his frisk,
> Is always happy, reign whoever may,
> And laughs the sense of misery far away....
> Fill'd with as much true merriment and glee
> As if he heard the king say–'Slave, be free'. (235/45)

Most of Cowper's *un*orthodox satire, in fact, turns out to be directed *from* England rather than *at* it in the romantic manner. If his orthodoxy seems to be a crutch for a crippled personality-the stricken deer's attempt to feel part of the herd-the half-hearted unorthodoxy seems to be a substitute for the expression of his real minority feelings (of guilt, timidity and *personal* despair). He is a romantic less in his slight social rebellion-usually dressed in a reachmedown augustan garment, anyway-than in his personal sense of guilt.

With the feebleness of the poems quoted above, compare the power of these sapphics written during his first serious attack of madness in 1763. This inner world is what *really* matters to Cowper, not the public or churchly world that he thinks really matters to him:

> Man disavows and Deity disowns me,
> Hell might afford my miseries a shelter;
> Therefore Hell keeps her ever-hungry mouths all
> > Bolted against me.
>
> Hard lot! encompassed with a thousand dangers;
> Weary, faint, trembling with a thousand terrors
> I'm called, if vanquished, to receive a sentence
> > Worse than Abiram's.
>
> Him the vindictive rod of angry Justice
> Sent quick and howling to the centre headlong;
> I, fed with Judgement, in a fleshy tomb, am
> > Buried above ground.
> > (*Lines Written under the Influence of Delirium*)

Directness of impact and linguistic concentration are combined with a masterly command of movement and alliteration quite absent from his less personal poems.

This case holds even for poems with whose content everyone must be sympathetic, and whose form does not suffer by provoking comparison with Pope. The good intentions of *The Negro's Complaint*, for instance, are evident, but merely quoting a few stanzas will make equally evident the poor effects:

Why did all-creating Nature
    Make the plant for which we toil?
Sighs must fan it, tears must water,
    Sweat of ours must dress the soil.
Think, ye masters iron-hearted,
    Lolling at your jovial boards;
Think how many backs have smarted
    For the sweets your cane affords.

Is there, as ye sometimes tell us,
    Is there one, who reigns on high?
Has he bid you buy and sell us,
    Speaking from his throne, the sky?
Ask him, if your knotted scourges,
    Matches, blood-extorting screws,
Are the means that duty urges
    Agents of his will to use?

Hark! he answers wild tornadoes,
    Strewing yonder sea with wrecks;
Wasting towns, plantations, meadows,
    Are the voice with which he speaks.
He, foreseeing what vexations
    Afric's sons should undergo,
Fix'd their tyrants' habitations
    Where his whirlwinds answer–no.

There are obviously striking discrepancies between purport and form, form and subject, and subject and content: the jaunty rhythm is more suitable to a comic poem, the pseudo-dramatic rhetorical mode hardly matches the pitiful situation, and the providential argument– apart from being a blatant rationalisation– is so extraordinary as to undermine the ostensible theme. In addition to being tortured the negroes, one gathers, are to be drowned while *en route* for the plantations or flattened when they arrive, by a cross but unthinking deity.

Such negative evidence, of course, is not conclusive. It has to be conceded that Cowper does write occasional short poems in his public satirical mode which are effective (usually though, in a humorous way), there are one or two good epigrammatic couplets in the moral satires, a few short humorous pieces in an urbane augustan manner, such as the case of the Nose and the Spectacles, and above all there is *John Gilpin*–the single complete success achieved by 'turning resolutely away' from his morbid guilt-feelings. But it surely owes its effectiveness to the fact that the poet chose to write up the story, given him by Lady Austen, in the street-ballad manner: a manner encouraging broad fun, objectivity, and concentration on story rather than morality.

On the other hand, there is much positive evidence that guilt was central and essential in Cowper's life. *The Memoirs of William Cowper Esq, Written by Himself* reads like a casebook history of neurotic guilt and terror. *The Task* and various other poems reveal a predilection for retreat—into greenhouses, groves, alcoves or Russian ice-palace—combined with a sense of its impermanence and futility. In 1795, moreover, he wrote an almost Kafkan letter to Lady Hesketh:

What a lot is mine! Why was existence given to a creature that might possibly, and would probably, become wretched in the degree that I have been so? and whom misery such as mine, was almost sure to overwhelm in a moment? But the question is vain. I existed by a decree from which there was no appeal, and on terms the most tremendous, because unknown to, and even unsuspected by me; difficult to be complied with, had they been foreknown, and unforeknown, impracticable. (*Letters* (1912), ed. Frazer, vol. II, p. 412)

This guilt accounts for the main characteristics of Cowper's poetic output—he is at his worst in public utterances in the mode of augustan satire; he is better in poems of a meditative, personal sort or in passages of this nature in the longer satirical poems (whose rambling method at least has the virtue of letting in such valuable irrelevances); and he is at his best in confessional poems of deep despair. The first mode allows him to evade grappling with his real conflicts, by offering substitute ones with an old-established solution supplied. The second mode leads to his most important technical discovery, the discovery of intimacy–a way of writing poems *not* suitable for reading aloud in the coffee-house. And the discovery of intimacy prepares the way for full confessional expression.

If we take *Gilpin* as the best example of the first, outward-turning mode, then, by virtue of the ballad form they have in common, *the Epitaph on a Hare* will make a transition to the second, semi-inward category:

> Old Tiney, surliest of his kind,
>   Who, nursed with tender care,
> And to domestic bounds confined,
>   Was still a wild Jack-hare.
>
> Though duly from my hand he took
>   His pittance every night,
> He did it with a jealous look,
>   And, when he could, would bite.
>
> His diet was of wheaten bread,
>   And milk, and oats, and straw;
> Thistles, or lettuces instead,
>   With sand to scour his maw.
>
> On twigs of hawthorn he regaled,
>   On pippins' russet peel,
> And, when his juicy salads fail'd,
>   Slic'd carrot pleased him well.
>
> A Turkey carpet was his lawn,
>   Whereon he loved to bound,
> To skip and gambol like a fawn,
>   And swing his rump around.

This shares the tenderness for animals which is so evident in Smart, but it is less generalised and hortatory. It takes the reader into the poet's drawing-room and then into a close particularised relationship with this one particular object of his affection—a natural unforced affection, not blinking surliness and snappiness, yet in strong contrast to the rigour of the poet's *acquired* morality. Similarly, *The Task*—which contains far more personal passages than the earlier satires—lets the reader first share the poet's fireside and then, for a while, his unmoralised, his self-revealing meditations:

Me oft has Fancy ludicrous and wild
Sooth'd with a waking dream of houses, towers,
Trees, churches, and strange visages, express'd
In the red cinders, while with poring eye
I gazed, myself creating what I saw.
Nor less amused have I quiescent watch'd
The sooty films that play upon the bars
Pendulous, and foreboding in the view
Of superstition, prophesying still,
Though still deceived, some stranger's near approach.

                                        (Bk. IV, 286/95)

These lines read like the speech of a recluse talking to himself – a quality shared by certain passages of compensatory nature-poetry.

Cowper is the first poet to write of nature without didactic or picturesque overtones, and without being entirely flat. Certain latent conflicts – particularly that between delight-in-nature and terror-of-death – give the poetry overtones of its own. Even so, Cowper's nature poetry is often insipid by comparison with that of the later romantics, because his outlook prevents him from associating nature dynamically with his 'progressive' views or his psychological needs; whereas, for the later poets, a complex interrelated background of ideas gave to descriptions of nature much submerged metaphor. Imagery of man and his society and ideas – as well as his emotions – came to be implicit in the subject-matter. Therefore, a 'unified' imaginative effect could take the place of the allegorical effect produced by Cowper's habit of using an extended natural simile to make some moral or religious point, separately expressed. Even of the wonderful description of the frost at the millrace, hanging 'the embroidered banks/With forms so various, that no power of art... may trace the scene' (Bk. V), one is forced to admit that it is minor art, since it is decorative rather than significant – icing without the cake – for no theme or conflict is embodied; nothing is implied of man.

It is significant that in the one early case in which Cowper tries to neutralise the terror of death by delight in nature (in *Retirement*), he creates his best poetry of the period – by being honest enough to confess failure. Theoretically, nature is

a scale, by which the soul ascends
From mighty means to more important ends,
Securely, though by steps but rarely trod,
Mounts from inferior beings up to God,
And sees, by no fallacious light or dim,
Earth made for man, and man himself for Him. (111/16)

This comforting picture is soon overwhelmed by a fiercer one:

The waves o'ertake them in their serious play,
And every hour sweeps multitudes away;
They shriek and sink, survivors start and weep,
Pursue their sport and follow to the deep. (157/160)

To be sure, an attempt is made to reconcile these disparate pictures by the rationalisation that the godly will not be swept into the sea but 'snatcht away/From scenes of sorrow into glorious day'. But almost at once Cowper lurches into confessional honesty:

'Tis not, as heads that never ache suppose,
Forgery of Fancy, and a dream of woes;
Man is a harp whose chords elude the sight
Each yielding harmony disposed aright:
The screws reversed (a task which if he please
God in a moment executes with ease),
Ten thousand thousand strings at once go loose,
Lost, till he tune them, all their power and use.
Then neither heathy wilds, nor scenes as fair
As ever recompensed the peasant's care,
Nor soft declivities with tufted hills,
Nor view of waters turning busy mills,
Parks in which Art preceptress Nature weds,
Nor gardens interspersed with flowery beds,
Nor gales that catch the scent of blooming groves,
And waft it to the mourner as he roves
Can call up life into his faded eye
That passes all he sees unheeded by. (323/40)

Since this is one of the very rare examples of the conflict of delight-in-nature and terror-of-death being woven into a single web which seems genuinely to express a complex experience, without falsification, it is significant that it is an example of the third, confessional mode.

The Shrubbery, Yardley Oak, The Castaway and *On the Receipt of my Mother's Picture*, four other magnificent poems mainly in the same mode, are built on Cowper's deeply felt contrast between society and the outcast. Like the first conflict, this seems to be a literary form of the unresolved contradiction in Cowper's life between his *theory* of the goodness of the senses and the happiness to be derived from them, and his *practice* of retirement, shyness, melancholy and despair. Naturally, then, he fails when he tries to be orthodox in form and content, because he was not at one with his society, but a lonely, tormented 'different' soul–a hunted hare.

In *Yardley Oak*, for once, he finds a perfect objective correlative in nature for his own state of soul, and a verse-form which matches it. This is the last poem in which his deep sense of guilt and despair are not conquerors but conquered:

> Embowelled now, and of thy ancient self
> Possessing nought but the scooped rind–that seems
> A huge throat calling to the clouds for drink,
> Which it would give in rivulets to the root. . . .
> Yet is thy root sincere, sound as the rock,
> A quarry of stout spars and knotted fangs,
> Which crook'd into a thousand whimsies, clasp
> The stubborn soil and hold thee still erect.

The Shrubbery has not quite so fine a fusion of form, tone and content. But this poem on Cowper's personal suffering is far better than (say) *The Negro's Complaint*, a poem on the sufferings of others. Perhaps it is morally better to write such poems, and in Cowper's own day it must have been socially valuable. But such willed work reads now as the propaganda it is; and today it is the self-centred work which survives, for its memorable personal revelation:

> This glassy stream, that spreading pine,
> Those alders quivering to the breeze,
> Might soothe a soul less hurt than mine
> And please, if anything could please.

> But fix'd unalterable care
>   Foregoes not what she feels within,
> Shows the same sadness everywhere
>   And slights the season and the scene....
>
> The saint or moralist should tread
>   This mossgrown alley, musing, slow;
> They seek like me the secret shade,
>   But not, like me, to nourish woe!
>
> Me fruitful scenes and prospects waste
>   Alike admonish not to roam:
> These tell me of enjoyments past,
>   And those of sorrows yet to come.

Here is not only clear-sighted self-knowledge but also perfectly controlled expression. The management of vowel and consonant, of alliteration and assonance and, surprisingly, of half-rhyme, gives resonance to the sense. (Witness the dying fall of the last line of the second stanza quoted, whose assonance– 'season ... scene'–ironically echoes that of 'please ... please' in the corresponding line of the preceding stanza.) Moreover, the comma after 'please' forces one to read according to speech rhythm rather than metre; after the pause the voice must quicken a little, and therefore no artificial stress need fall on '-thing'. Or, again, the spondee (and the long vowels) of 'Foregoes' appropriately slows the movement and gives slightly more emphasis to 'not'. Similarly the trochee in the next line, 'Shows the' throws a light stress on to 'same'. This syllable would otherwise have been unstressed–but in terms of sense the sameness is as important as the sadness, and it is therefore fitting that 'same sad' should become a spondee.

My Mother's Picture starts as a meditative, personal poem of the past, though one senses in the background Cowper's present feeling of 'difference' and isolation in society. As usual, the couplet is handled a little uneasily, making statement often stiffly simple instead of naturally so. Yet the general effect is tender and moving; and one element of the stiffness is indeed

positively beneficial. The touches of artificial diction save sentiment from turning sugary. Witness the effect, for instance, of
'pastoral' and 'confectionary' below:

> Where once we dwelt our name is heard no more,
> Children not thine have trod my nursery floor;
> And where the gardener Robin, day by day,
> Drew me to school along the public way,
> Delighted with my bauble coach, and wrapp'd
> In scarlet mantle warm, and velvet capp'd,
> 'Tis now become a history little known,
> That once we call'd the pastoral house our own. . . .
>
> Thy nightly visits to my chamber made,
> That thou mightst know me safe and warmly laid;
> Thy morning bounties ere I left my home,
> The biscuit, or confectionary plum. . . .

Yet for all its distinction the body of the poem is less powerful
and less outstanding, than the conclusion which reflects the
torment at the heart of the outcast much more directly. As so
often in Cowper it does so through the image of a castaway:

> So thou, with sails how swift! hast reached the shore,
> Where tempests never beat nor billows roar . . .
> But me, scarce hoping to attain that rest,
> Always from port withheld, always distress'd –
> Me howling blasts drive, tempest-tost,
> Sails ripp'd, seams opening wide, and compass lost,
> And day by day some current's thwarting force
> Sets me more distant from a prosperous course.

It is less impressive than *The Castaway* itself only because it is a
little more crude. In the latter poem Cowper talks about himself
obliquely, in his imaginative reconstruction of the feelings of a
man literally 'washed headlong from on board', and he is able
to convey poignancy as well as terror by contrasting him with
the 'society' of his fellows left on board, who can give only help
that will prolong his agony but not save him. The attempt to
give metaphorical implication, moreover, leads to one or two

subtle psychological touches not found elsewhere in Cowper, such as the frighteningly convincing paradox on the swimmer, waging

> With death a lasting strife,
> *Supported by despair of life.*

Yet even in this, Cowper's most personal and least conventional poem, a hampering effect of his age is to be detected. As Dr Leavis has pointed out[1], there is a hint of discrepancy between the sober hymnic form and the personal agony of the content–a significantly pre-romantic characteristic.

[1]*Revaluation* (1956), p. 121.

RADICAL ROMANTIC POETS

I
GENERAL

THE pre-romantic is not only divided against himself, but also in rebellion against his own revolt, for he has some sympathy with the orthodoxy of his age. The later romantic, generally speaking, is emotionally more radical and, moreover, has a theory which enables him to be unashamedly 'different'.

It is one of the more piquant historical ironies that the ordering effort of State and Church brings to greatness – by directing their attention outwards – poets passionately individualistic and anti-establishment. Poets, too, less likely than their predecessors to be driven out of a precarious sanity by their isolation. Where Cowper speaks of himself regretfully as a deer which has 'left the herd', Shelley thinks of himself in *Adonais* as a 'herd-abandoned deer', and attacks the herd. It's the rest of the regiment which is out of step and being 'unnatural'.

Such an attitude, of course, has disadvantages as well as advantages. It leads to certain psychological dilemmas. Napoleon, for instance, is felt to be condemnable as a tyrant, but on the other hand he is felt – particularly by Byron – to be admirable as an example of the poor man rising by *natural* greatness to overthrow the *artificial* greatness of proud kings and prelates. Similarly, 'cold philosophy' has to be condemned for its associations, but on the other hand poetry must claim philosophical insights – claim to be more than merely subjective – because the poet wants to be thought *right*. Furthermore, although these poets are supported by their fervour and their convictions, they are bitterly aware of being in a small minority, hated and despised by their own countrymen. How should they know it was their period, the Romantic Period?

Such feelings aggravate the conflicts and compensations mentioned in *Part I*. In terms of theory, too, they lead to maintaining in the religious manner a Two-Truths hypothesis, the unconscious being the repository of a special unscientific 'truth'; it then follows that metaphor is the most poetic device and lyric the best poetic form[1]. In terms of practice, it often leads to using imagery to intensify emotion or to insinuate value-judgements,[2] instead of using it in the less rhetorical way to draw attention to illuminating analogies. However, it is one of the great virtues of the later romantics that, though often self-*centred* they are rarely limited to the personal. Even of Wordsworth, the poet of the 'egotistical sublime' we have already seen this to be true. It is important, then, to regard the compensations and conflicts of the romantic attitude more as literary than personal determinants. Purely personal factors, such as early parental or later marital relationships, are no doubt immensely influential but they are dangerous critical tools: not only because they are not as irrefutably available as the text but because the work of these poets usually takes a general or public colouring. Blake, Wordsworth, Coleridge, Shelley, Byron and Keats all have highly intelligent independent minds and a wide range of interests. Furthermore, they are capable of some self-analysis and become aware, in varying degrees at different times, that they are subject to conflict. This they tend to attribute to the shortcomings of the age, and thus are able to see personal incompatibilities as reflections of larger disharmonies. It is in this way that they can be unashamedly anti-social. For by attacking current morality–regarded as the cant of dullness and oppression–they act as bards pointing the way to a natural morality.

Self-awareness is, however, limited. They are rarely conscious how much of their rejection of current morality and orthodox religion is founded not on the abundant rational arguments available in the work of various sceptics but on emotion–and what's more, often not on emotion resulting from intuitions of truth, but on seeming intuitions of truth resulting from emotion.

Of no poet is this more true than of Blake. But Shelley, Byron

[1]M. H. Abrams deals fully with these points in *The Mirror and the Lamp* (N.Y., 1953).

[2]R. A. Foakes amplifies these points in *The Romantic Assertion* (1958).

and Keats–and Wordsworth and Coleridge sometimes and to a lesser extent–also reject or revise Christianity less on the rational grounds of improbability and supernaturalism than because of their feelings about liberty. All, at their nearest to Christianity–at any rate if we limit Wordsworth and Coleridge to their creative period–are not the children but the father of their God, their religion being a form of self-expansion in the face of thwarting social institutions. The authority on this subject is Fairchild,[1] and while one may well disagree with many of his valuations and implications it is hard to avoid the conclusion of his detailed study of romantic self-deification: that in the romantics' religion 'Man, in short, is God' (p. 362).

However, their religion is usually not very near to Christianity at all. Blake turns it inside-out, regarding godliness as satanic and praising Christ as a breaker of all ten commandments, and Byron, Shelley and Keats are sceptics[2] (though they often take over the vocabulary of Christianity for propagandist purposes). Hence, feelings that in another age would have gone into some form of dogmatic religion go into Nature. But admittedly Nature is hardly separable from human nature, and the tendency to self-deification leads the poet to feel at one with the Spirit of Nature (or the Good, the Beautiful, the One).

The same destination–on the whole beneficial, though not

---

[1] Fairchild, *Religious Trends in English Poetry* (1942/9), vol. III (Columbia Univ. Press, 1949). Cp. also Basil Willey on 'that divinization of Nature' (including human nature) whose tentative beginnings are found in Shaftesbury: *The Eighteenth Century Background* (1940), p. 64.

[2] As late as 1822 (11 April. Letter to Horatio Smith), Shelley is condemning Christianity and 'the monstrous superstitions of popular worship', in the same letter stating that 'the delusions of Christianity lie', for Byron, 'in ambush *in the hours of sickness and distress*'. This tallies with the scepticism of many of Byron's letters in hours of health (e.g. to Hodgson 3.9.1811, 'I am no Platonist, I am nothing at all' or *Detached Thoughts* 15.10.1821 – 18.5.1822, No. 96, 'It is useless to tell me *not* to *reason* but to believe. . . .'). Of Keats, G. F. Mathew writes that 'he was of the sceptical and republican school. . . . A faultfinder with everything established' (Quoted by Colvin *John Keats* (1920), p. 25. Note also the sonnet *Written in Disgust of Vulgar Superstition*, and the letter congratulating Hunt for having 'levelled a battering-ram against Christianity' in *The Examiner* for May 4, 1817 (*Letters*, ed. Forman, 1935, p. 23).

metaphysically as the poets would have wished, but psychologically–is reached by another route which also starts in conflict
rather than cold consideration. Lacking the support of convention,
the outcast is thrown back upon his own resources. His will and
creative power are the sole substitutes for the protection the
conventions afford. This throwing away of crutches can undoubtedly develop the self. But it is vitally necessary to the
romantic that he should *have* an essential self. Since, however, he
would never have thrown away the crutches of convention if
he had not been in conflict he is in a predicament. He knows he is,
and is right, but he does not know *what* he is. Hence he needs to
see himself reflected in something solid (Nature as scenery) or to
lose himself in something more harmonious but not essentially
different (Nature as spirit). Thus 'Nature' furthers poetic unification–or sometimes, of course, confusion–by allowing the
metaphorical expression, at one and the same time of the poet's
disparate experience of material facts and spiritual aspirations.

II

BLAKE

Though Blake is the most obviously 'romantic' of all romantics,
it is far from obvious at first sight that his work probably confirms
more strongly than that of any other poet the critical usefulness
of approaching romantic poetry through the idea of related
social and psychological conflicts. To be sure, his general development was found, in *Part I*, to approximate to that of Wordsworth
and Coleridge, the other great poets of the wartime group. But
in his case: the stages of development are less clear-cut; from
stage to stage theme and content repeat themselves to a greater
degree (so that change is more a matter of emphasis); within
each stage inner and outer aspects of the romantic conflict are
less distinguishable; and the whole is conditioned by a metaphysical refusal to distinguish subjective from objective reality.
Besides these differences–all of which militate against any

obviousness—there are special difficulties, not applying to Wordsworth and Coleridge.

In a study of this sort, where so much material has to be
manhandled into a limited space, it is impossible to deal fully
with these matters; but perhaps something may be done to dispel
certain bugbears and rationally account for others. If, in addition,
a new way into the poems can be opened up, the usefulness of
the present method will indeed have been confirmed, for the
vast jungle of Blake criticism—like Blake's work—is frighteningly
dark and tangled. . . .

Firstly, then, to place the difficulties in perspective—a somewhat
more inward perspective than that of *Part I*—and relate them to a
general difficulty common to all the poets to be considered later.

Secondly, to consider the special difficulties in Blake.

Thirdly, to give reasons for preferring to attack them psychologically, by-passing the metaphysical approach seemingly
insisted on by Blake himself. (That the psychological expands
from time to time into the social is very important, since what is
only personal in Blake strongly inclines to be *private*.)

And finally, to attempt a brief chronological critique of
representative poems in the light of the foregoing.

Blake's joining *Songs of Experience* to *Songs of Innocence* seems
to introduce early the theme of the need to resolve conflicts in a
more inclusive harmony than that represented by the simplici-
ties of innocence. The title of *The Marriage of Heaven and Hell*
would seem to indicate that such a harmony was to be one not
based on the suppression of any part of man's humanity. And
even in this early period it is clear, both from what the poetry
says and what it sometimes enacts, that the exercise of a Coleridgian 'creative Imagination' was to be the means, and unity
of being—later styled 'Eden' or 'Jerusalem' or 'Fourfold Vision'—
the end. Moreover, it is evident even in his latest period, when
Blake was as orthodox and withdrawn as he was ever to get,
that unity of being was to include not only self-completion but
full involvement of the self and the environment. So causes of
division and repression (inner and outer causes never being clearly
separated) are castigated to the end. Witness this expression of

anger at the restrictive codes and conventions of the age, in his last poem:

> I saw the limbs form'd for exercise contemn'd, & the beauty of
> Eternity look'd upon as deformity, & loveliness as a dry tree.
> I saw disease forming a Body of Death around the Lamb
> Of God to destroy Jerusalem & to devour the body of Albion,
> By war & stratagem to win the labour of the husbandman.
> Awkwardness arm'd in steel, folly in a helmet of gold,
> Weakness with horns & talons, ignorance with a rav'ning beak,
> Every Emanative joy forbidden as a crime
> And the Emanations buried alive in the earth with pomp of
> > religion,
> Inspiration deny'd, Genius forbidden by laws of punishment.
> > (*Jerusalem*, Bk. 1, p. 441)[1]

It might seem, then, that Blake's work could be adequately surveyed solely in terms of changing form: from knotty rhymed songs at the beginning to expansive free-verse epics at the end, from enacted conflict to enacted harmony. Certainly, Blake sometimes speaks in the later poems as if he had achieved harmony and were zealously revealing it:

> ... I rest not from my great task!
> To open the Eternal Worlds, to open the immortal Eyes
> Of Man inwards into the Worlds of Thought, into Eternity
> Ever expanding in the Bosom of God, the Human Imagination.
> > (*Jerusalem*, Bk. 1, p. 436)

However, it is not so simple. Not only is there no such steady evolution of form, but it is clear that what he wrote in a letter to Wm Hayley on the 4th December 1804 (p. 900) was reflected in all his work, early or late:

> I have indeed fought thro' a Hell of terrors & horrors (which none could know but myself) in a divided existence.

In fact, it is apparent that what Blake found when he turned his eyes inwards into the world of thought and imagination, to

---

[1]All quotations are taken from *The Poetry and Prose of William Blake* (1948), ed. Geoffrey Keynes, and page-references are to that volume.

write the late poems, was an analogue of the world of war and stratagem outside, and not an exemplary fourfold harmony or Eden. No matter what is asserted or implied, *Jerusalem* is, in effect, no more an *exemplum* than the early *London*. Both are psycho-social *myths*.

Even if Blake had been temperamentally capable of contemplating 'a divided existence' from a position of achieved unity, his metaphysical refusal to distinguish object and subject would have pushed him towards myth: work existing somewhere between concept and representation. In any case, though he always has integrity, he never has unity; and his major achievement is not what the metaphysic desiderates and the poetry aims at (and occasionally accomplishes), a larger harmony, but the pungent revelations of life as it actually was, and is, in a time of 'terrors and horrors'.

However, the special difficulties in Blake spring less from any contradiction between intention and attainment than from the fact that he took his myth-making to have metaphysical validity, to be *true*. This certainly checks a tendency to over-conceptualise, to write parables; but since the metaphysic is generally obscure, often incoherent and sometimes self-contradictory (though also sometimes brilliant and profound) it has the bad effect of distorting representation.

But before examining these difficulties in more detail, it is perhaps helpful to discuss briefly a general source of unclarity in the poets of this period. All romantic 'philosophies' seem to be sophistications of a basically primitive and childlike tendency: the tendency to interpret the world anthropomorphically because you are fixated on your own feelings and actions and cannot fully separate self from surroundings, and, further, to imagine you can influence the world magically by analogous performance or creation

Then I asked: 'Does a firm persuasion that a thing is so, make it so?'
He replied: 'All poets believe that it does, and in ages of imagination this firm persuasion removed mountains. . . .'
I heard this with some wonder, and must confess my own conviction.
(*Marriage of Heaven and Hell*, p. 186)

Perhaps the most sophisticated form of such primitivism is that of Plato whose notion of Ideal Forms, insubstantial but more 'real' than their earthly equivalents, seems to reflect the anthropomorphic projection of a mind-body relationship on to the world—as in the cases of 'Giant Albion' and 'Nature'—but his reflection is less direct than that of the romantics. Its proximate cause would seem to be Plato's interest in geometry, in which the hypothetical figure with nondimensional lines and points *is* better than its drawn imitation.

Since all the romantic theories are tinged with platonism (usually thickened by an element of pantheism), it is necessary to insist that philosopical weakness in poems may be more than compensated by psychological strength, or simply the framework usefulness of their theory. Even of the most obvious nature poetry, it is true to say that where it has merit that merit lies not in what is said of nature but in what is revealed of man.

In Blake's case this is particularly evident. He was a Londoner and therefore not such a devotee of the country as the other poets. At any rate, he was clearer than they about the distinction between Nature as scenery and Nature as Spirit. Moreover, he did not need to use Nature against God and the Church—he used Christianity (of his own brand) against them:

> Natural Objects always did & now do weaken, deaden & obliterate Imagination in Me.
> (*Annotations to Wordsworth*, p. 821)

> The Vision of Christ that thou dost see
> Is my Vision's Greatest Enemy....
> Both read the Bible day and night,
> But thou read'st black where I read white. (2a, p. 133)

> He had only to say that God was the devil
> And the devil was God, like a Christian Civil. (2d., p. 137)
> (*The Everlasting Gospel*)

With these points in mind, we can begin listing the special difficulties of Blake. He criticises Wordsworth on the grounds that in him the Natural Man rises up against the Spiritual (p. 821).

This is as much as to say that Wordsworth does not trust himself entirely to intuition unchecked by the senses. In a word, he is not mystical enough for Blake. In view of Blake's laudation of sex and his assertion of the union of body and soul, this seems queer. But it was a mystical sort of sex and a mystical sort of unity:

... the whole creation will be consumed and appear infinite and holy, whereas it now appears finite and corrupt.

This will come to pass by an improvement of sensual enjoyment.

But first the notion that man has a body distinct from his soul is to be expunged.   (*Marriage of Heaven and Hell*, p. 187)

All Bibles or sacred codes have been the causes of the following Errors:

1. That Man has two real existing principles: Viz: a Body & a Soul.

2. That Energy, call'd Evil, is alone from the Body; & that Reason, call'd Good, is alone from the Soul.

3. That God will torment Man in Eternity for following his Energies.

But the following Contraries to these are true:

1. Man has no Body distinct from his Soul; for that call'd Body is a portion of Soul discern'd by the five Senses, the chief inlets of Soul in this age.

2. Energy is the only life, and is from the Body; and Reason is the bound or outward circumference of Energy.

3. Energy is Eternal Delight.

(*Marriage of Heaven and Hell*, p. 182)

It is apparent from these and other passages that Blake envisaged the senses—and particularly sex—as a way to mystical illumination, and that the unity of body and spirit was a one-way matter: there could be no body without spirit, but there could be a pre-existing spirit without body. Blake is not altogether consistent on this point, but such seems to be his general opinion—as indeed it has to be if he is to maintain, as he does, that reality is mental and 'Man is all Imagination'. One of many potential confusions in this viewpoint is to be seen in the conjunction of the ideas that energy is from the body and that energy is eternal delight. One must either define 'eternal' so that it is not inconsistent with bodily mortality or envisage a disembodied 'energy' delighting a non-body.

Secondly, there is a difficulty inhering in the idea of Blake as a myth-maker, for the implications of the statement that his work exists between concept and representation have not yet been fully teased out. We have seen from the comment on Wordsworth that Blake was opposed to sensation; we may add that he was opposed to reason; his myths therefore are neither sensory nor rational. They speak in images, and are therefore vivid, but are conceptually unclear wherever the theme is really abstract and involved. Since the images are not of sensory reality, but of inner vision, they are vivid but representationally indirect: the light of empirical reality is refracted through the prism of a visionary system. All this points to the 'somewhere' in which his work exists between concept and representation.

Thirdly, Blake seems in fact to represent *symbolically* in this way the forces of man and nature. But there is evidence that at least some of the time he *believed in* these forces (or 'Eternals') not merely as personifications but as personages: figures of some spiritual 'reality' constricted in matter, though rather less constricted than men. To be sure, there is evidence on the other side: often, perhaps usually, he regards them as useful embodiments of psychological or physical characteristics or drives. But even then they are universals (drives of mankind or earth, not of this man or this place) and therefore rather diagrammatic. Thus, Blake writes frequently in terms of subjective myth:

And now fierce Orc had quite consumed himself in Mental flames.
(*Vala*, Night 9th, p. 357)

Daughters of Beulah! Muses who inspire the Poet's Song,
Record the journey of immortal Milton thro' your Realms
Of terror and mild moony lustre in soft sexual delusions
Of varied beauty, to delight the wanderer and repose
His burning thirst & freezing hunger! Come into my hand,
By your wild power descending down the Nerves of my
right arm
From out the portals of my Brain, where by your ministry
The Eternal Great Humanity Divine planted his Paradise.
(*Milton*, Book the First, p. 376)

This tallies perfectly well with the psychologism of much earlier work:

> Without Contraries is no progression. Attraction and Repulsion, Reason and Energy, Lone and Hate are necessary to Human existence.
>
> From these contraries spring what the religious call Good & Evil. Good is the passive that obeys Reason. Evil is the active springing from Energy.
>
> Good is Heaven. Evil is Hell. (p. 181)
>
> The ancient Poets animated all sensible objects with Gods or Geniuses, calling them by the names and adorning them with the properties of woods, rivers, mountains, lakes, cities, nations, and whatever their enlarged and numerous senses could perceive.
>
> And particularly they studied the genius of each city and country, placing it under its mental deity;
>
> Till a system was formed which some took advantage of, and enslav'd the vulgar by attempting to realize or abstract the mental deities from their objects: thus began Priesthood;
>
> Choosing forms of worship from poetic tales.
>
> And at length they pronounc'd that the Gods had ordered such things.
>
> Thus men forgot that All deities reside in the human breast. (p. 185)

These passages from *The Marriage of Heaven and Hell* might well have been written today–or even tomorrow. But is *this* a deity existing only in the human breast?

> Thinking as I do that the Creator of this World is a very Cruel Being, and being a worshipper of Christ, I cannot help saying: 'the Son, O how unlike the Father!' First God Almighty comes with a Thump on the Head. Then Jesus Christ comes with a balm to heal it.
>
> (*Addition to a Descriptive Catalogue*, p. 651)

Perhaps, of course, he is speaking loosely, jocularly, taking over current modes of speech for the occasion. But, if so, the habit is sufficiently frequent to cause confusion. Anyway, it is difficult not to take Blake seriously in such a passage as the following:

> Man Passes on, but States remain for Ever; he passes thro' them like a traveller who may as well suppose that the places he has passed thro' exist no more, as a Man may suppose that the States he has passed thro' Exist no more. Everything is Eternal. (*loc. cit.*, p. 640)

This tallies with various other passages which suggest that various states of mind (or being) – Imagination, God, Eternity, Jesus, Jerusalem, Los and so forth – nevertheless exist when there is nobody to experience them. There sometimes appears to be Imagination without an imaginer, for instance. This seems to be a simple category – mistake, due to a subconscious assumption that nouns must always be *names*, and encouraged by a tendency to platonism (obviously present in Blake despite denials and denunciations of it).

These points lead into the fourth cause of difficulty: the fact that in his bloated later works the personages multiply, their names have no traditional associations (or if they have, as in the cases of God, Jesus, Jerusalem, Satan, they are utterly flouted), and the metaphysic is excessively complex and (on principle) unexplained. True, a good many interpreters have stepped in and explained it, but many have been cranks, those who were not have differed from each other, and the explanations have themselves often required explaining (in so far as they merely translated Blake's crankinesses into other, usually occult, crankinesses). So the difficulty remains.

Basically, Blake's position seems simple enough. He reacted against Locke's divided world of subject and object, and followed Berkeley in believing that reality is mental. The dilemma that such a view leads to is neatly summed up in the well-known anti-Berkeleyan limerick:

> There once was a man who said 'God
> Must think it exceedingly odd
>   If he finds that this tree
>   Continues to be
> When there's no-one about in the Quad'

The reply leaves a yawning gap between God and man: between two meanings of 'reality':

> 'Dear Sir, Your astonishment's odd.
> I am always about in the Quad,
>   And that's why this tree
>   Will continue to be
> Since observed by Yours faithfully, God'

Blake bridges this gap by maintaining not only that reality is mental and varies according to the quality of perception ('The fool sees not the same tree the wise man sees') but also that man is God (or Satan, Angel, Spirit, Demon, Spectre, according to the quality of his imagination).

This might be well enough, but none of these words is used straightforwardly-not even *parodoxically* straightforwardly. In *The Marriage of Heaven and Hell*, a comparatively simple work-and probably Blake's greatest achievement, although it largely forsakes the aid of verse-it seems at first as if one could simply invert customary meanings. For, though the title advocates a *marriage* of human faculties, the tenor of the work is strongly favourable to Hell or Energy. 'God' then equals passivity, reason, chastity, restraint, tyranny and is really *evil*. 'Satan' equals energy, vitality, sensuality, imagination and is really *good*. But soon we find these words being used in a more orthodox sense. And this is not only because Blake forgets his own system or doesn't care about consistency (though the evidence of other works indicates that such may be part of the cause); it is also because you cannot fly in the face of common usage if you want to affect the common reader. In the 'Proverbs of Hell' section Blake wishes to enforce acceptance of the *goodness* of several of the 'deadly sins': pride, lust, wrath. It is consistent that the proverbs should emanate from Hell (which is good). But had Blake said that these qualities were from Satan, as he should have, his reader would have sagely agreed and taken the proverbs as confirmation of wickedness. Consequently, we have the oddity of the devil attributing satanic qualities to God (who for the moment must have *good* associations):

> The pride of the peacock is the glory of God.
> The lust of the goat is the bounty of God.
> The wrath of the lion is the wisdom of God.
> The nakedness of woman is the work of God. . . . (p.183)

> As the caterpiller chooses the fairest leaves to lay her
> eggs on, so the priest lays his curse on the fairest joys. (p. 184)

In the later, long didactic symbolic works this tendency to

inconsistent usage is much increased. One always has to look closely at the surrounding context before deciding what a name stands for. This increased tendency is in turn complicated by Blake's development of a system, in which there are four main mythical personages, Luvah, Urizen, Tharmos and Urthona, each of whom may divide into a male Spectre and a female Emanation (with different names) or may change into any of the others if he passes into a different one of the four states of vision, Ulro, Generation, Beulah and Eden: that is, single vision symbolised by rock, sand, ice and metal, the visionary world of Locke, Newton and Urizen (who is usually, but not always, God–and bad); double vision, that of the average man in the world of subject and object, and often symbolised by plants and sadistic sensualists; threefold vision, the world of sexual innocence, where sensuality becomes love, a world of moon-gardens and lovers; and fourfold vision, the world of full Imagination in which all man's contraries are harmonised, some of its symbols being the city, sun, a hermaphrodite, or the four Zoas round the throne of God.

In a recent article (*Essays in Criticism*, July 1959) W. H. Stevenson has spoken of the 'confusion, illogicality and inconsequence' of *Jerusalem*, and these words are by no means too strong for *Vala* and *Milton* as well. He has added with equal justice that

Too often this sort of thing [a turgid and tedious round of incidents without any real purpose] indicates that Blake is not using his imagination. Images have become formalised and abstracted into ideas without material significance. . . . Many of his images are not images at all, but ideas expressed, through force of habit, in figures of speech. (p. 260)

When, finally, one adds to all this a deliberate choice of obscurity when clarity became dangerous, it must be evident that the difficulties are both real and damaging.[1]

[1] *The French Revolution* was set up in type in 1793 but not printed. While etching *America* Blake cancelled a plate referring to George III by name, and next year hid the names of Paine, Washington and Franklin under Los and Orc–Urizen's antagonists. Wise precautions, these, since the members of the *London Corresponding Society* were on trial at the time, and Blake was a member of a much more treasonable secret society, which met in the house of his publisher Johnson. After his trial for treason in 1803, of course he had further cause for caution.

To sum up, then, Blake is inherently difficult and obscure owing to:

distrust of the evidence of the senses (the Natural Man) combined with an elevation of sensory ecstasy;

distrust of reason combined with commitment–particularly in his later period–to a complicated system (which is therefore often bafflingly unsystematic);

uncertainty of attitude between empirical hypothesis and metaphysical belief;

inconsistent use of terminology, incoherent narrative, and distrust of explanation;

and chosen obscurity, together with the crankiness of an artist without an audience.

It is clear that any interpretative approach is likely to be unprofitable; the difficulties are in the grain.

If, however, we ask *Why* is there no separation of body and soul, hell-qualities and heaven-qualities, subject and object in Blake's desiderated state of Eden? it seems likely that there is a psychological answer. We need not follow Witcutt[1] to the bitter end and postulate a trauma due to Blake's childhood relation with his father. But we can say that the later *poetry* is traumatic: it makes better sense as an analogue of psychological conflict written in the light of a yearning for a childlike innocence and unity of being than it does as a metaphysical interpretation of man and nature. The metaphysic, in fact, becomes comprehensible as a rationalisation of such a psychological state–whether real or imagined for poetic purposes. Furthermore, the mythic method, together with much of Blake's beliefs, is accounted for by assuming him to be–or to have imagined himself into the world of–a rare psychological type, the intuitive introvert *to whom the inner world of imagination is more vivid and actual than the outer world.* That inner world, consequently, seems to need no explanation, but only presentation. It is the truth for such a type and once seen must be believed. This at any rate tallies with the nature of Blake's mythological figures, with his view of corporeal nature as a veil, and with his refusal to distinguish between

[1] *Blake: A Psychological Study* (1946).

objective and subjective realities. Several other things, too, fit this diagnosis. There is the identification of Imagination and Reality, and of Reality and Eternity. (Imaginative states are freed from the usual temporal limitations of living.) And in a letter to Dr Trusler in 1799 (p. 835) Blake interestingly refers to imagination as 'Spiritual Sensation', which certainly suggests that he found inner images as vivid as outer sense-data. Next there is the sado-masochism and incest in Blake's writings, and the stress on energy and sex-indications of writing that taps the libido. Then there is the characteristic thinking in images, and the endless conflict of the personages in a psychosociological cycle of repression and revolt. Finally, there is the close correspondence with the Jungian scheme of psychological types–which seems, together with the idea of introversion and extraversion, to be an acceptable formulation, whatever else of Jung is to be rejected. Indeed, Blake's own diagram of intersecting circles (*Milton*, Bk. the Second, p. 421) matches exactly the Jungian cross one would make from the longer works on the basis of our hypothesis. Significantly, too, Blake marks Adam north of the centre (towards his preferred pole, the intuitive or Urthona end) and Satan–not favoured here–south of the centre (towards the reasoning or Urizen pole). The Jungian cross would look like this:

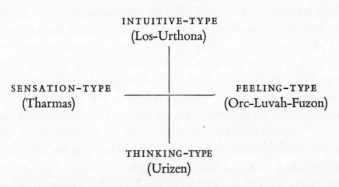

INTUITIVE-TYPE
(Los-Urthona)

SENSATION-TYPE   FEELING-TYPE
(Tharmas)   (Orc-Luvah-Fuzon)

THINKING-TYPE
(Urizen)

If Blake's imaginative vision of an inner and outer world of conflict were indeed the specialised one of an intuitive introvert one would expect Los to be often allied with Tharmas and Orc but always opposed to Urizen, save on very rare occasions of integration. This is, in fact, what we do find.

Much in Blake supports such a view:

> Four mighty Ones are in every Man; a Perfect Unity
> Cannot exist but from the Universal Brotherhood of Eden,
> The Universal Man. . . .
> > Sing
> His fall into Division and his Resurrection to Unity.
>
> > (*Vala*, Night the First, p. 252)

Or:

> They saw the Wheels rising up poisonous against Albion:
> Urizen cold and scientific, Luvah pitying and weeping,
> Tharmas indolent and sullen, Urthona doubting & despairing,
> Victims to one another & dreadfully plotting against each other.
>
> > (*Jerusalem*, Bk. II, p. 487)

It may be objected that such an approach merely allows one to see the late, long works as vast deserts of delirium instead of deserts of confused and cranky metaphysic. Certainly, no approach will turn a bad poem into a good one, and these poems undoubtedly suffer from the failure of imagination diagnosed by Stevenson, from the baleful influence on their style of Ossianic prose, from padding, from narrative that is repetitious instead of progressive, from turgidity, tediousness, nonsense, and verbal inconsistency. Yet to be given the experience of delirium – even if little is made out of it poetically (as opposed to metaphysically) – is to be given something: an insight into a type of human nature in a given certain situation. Whereas to be given the experience of a confused metaphysic is to be given nothing – it is like being offered a wrongly-worked mathematical problem; the experience of confusion is not what such working is for and has no value. Furthermore, to approach the works psychologically at least has the negative virtue of preventing overvaluation of their literary merit *because* they have a metaphysic delightful to the interpretative critic. Most importantly, perhaps, this approach (combined with an awareness of the social background) helps to prevent the reader's attention from being distracted by irrelevant difficulties and thus allows him to receive what vision of reality the work really has to offer.

This is probably better illustrated by an obscure but good poem: that very fine work, in terse rhymed verse, *The Mental Traveller* (p. 110). It could be explained in metaphysical terms: the woman would be Nature, on whom the infant or undeveloped man is dependent. He is passive and suffers by her. As he grows up he becomes as powerful as she and gets even with her, in both senses of the phrase. (In effect she becomes younger–turns from mother to wife. This would be the state of Generation.) He then looks on her as something separate and thereby relapses into Ulro, Urizen's dead world, becoming a terror. And the cycle begins again. The poem, however, could equally well be interpreted as a myth of the seasonal cycle, the progress of life and love, or the cycle of civilisations. All these interpretations would be in part permissible, for a poem in unexplained images is limited only to the fan of meanings given by all possible and consistent suggestions of the image-sequence. But in order to experience the poem–and not merely to understand it–it is much more helpful (as indeed the title suggests) to approach it as a formalisation of the conflicts of the unconscious–the archetypes which can be reflected in so many things precisely because our minds are predisposed to see so. The power of the poem, and the mixture of tenderness and sadism then come through, and certain wonderful lines (such as 'The wild game of her roving Eye'), ceasing to be isolated felicities, take their place as parts of a grasped, controlled and exteriorised whole.

The longer poems, too, contain their felicities, but these remain isolated oases in the deserts, and usually occur when Blake's social concerns remain sufficiently strong to give the reader a lifeline to a public reality. The sexual and religious concern, for instance, is powerfully expressed in *Visions of the Daughters of Albion* (p. 198):

> With what sense does the parson claim the labour of the farmer?
> What are his nets & gins & traps; & how does he surround him
> With cold floods of abstraction, and with forests of solitude,
> To build him castles and high spires, where kings and priests
>   may dwell;
> Till she who burns with youth, & knows no fixed lot is bound

In spells of law to one she loathes? and must she drag the chain
Of life in weary lust? must chilling murderous thoughts obscure
The clear heaven of her eternal spring; to bear the wintry rage
Of a harsh terror, driv'n to madness, bound to hold a rod
Over her shrinking shoulders all the day, & all the night
To turn the wheel of false desire, & longings that wake her womb
To the abhorred birth of cherubs in the human form,
That live a pestilence & die a meteor, & are no more.

The military and industrial concern is equally well expressed in
Vala, Night 7th (b), (p. 327), and is repeated in *Jerusalem*, Bk. III
(p. 517):

And all the Arts of Life they changed into the Arts of Death.
The hour glass contemn'd because its simple workmanship
Was as the workmanship of the plowman, & the water wheel
That raises water into cisterns, broken & burn'd in fire
Because its workmanship was like the workmanship of the
    Shepherd,
And in their stead intricate wheels invented, wheel without wheel,
To perplex youth in their outgoings & to bind to labours in
    Albion
Of day and night the myriads of eternity, that they might file
And polish brass & iron hour after hour, laborious task,
Kept ignorant of its use: that they might spend the days of wisdom
In sorrowful drudgery to obtain a scanty pittance of bread,
In ignorance to view a small portion & think that All,
And call it Demonstration, blind to all the simple rules of life.

Similarly, in *The Book of Los* (p. 242) there is a development of
pastoral idealism, in a vision of what might be, in man and
society, which is superior to anything in the *Songs of Innocence*:

O Times remote!
When Love & Joy were adoration,
And none impure were deem'd:
Not Eyeless Covet,
Nor Thin-lip'd Envy,
Nor Bristled Wrath,
Nor Curled Wantonness;

But Covet was poured full,
Envy fed with fat of lambs,
Wrath with lion's gore,
Wantonness lull'd to sleep
With the virgin's lute
Or sated with her love;

Till Covet broke his locks & bars
And slept with open doors;
Envy sung at the rich man's feast;
Wrath was follow'd up and down
By a little ewe lamb,
And Wantonness on his own true love
Begot a giant race.

And as late as *Vala* (1795-1804) there is a symbolic picture of the facts as they actually are which is nearly as pungent as the better *Songs of Experience* and gives point to his comment that 'the Creator of this World is a very Cruel Being'—whether he meant by 'Creator' an independent entity (in which case the animals of the poem are to be taken literally) or an aspect of man (in which case they are to be taken analogically):

Why does the Raven cry aloud and no eye pities her?
Why fall the Sparrow & the Robin in the foodless winter?
Faint, shivering, they sit on leafless bush or frozen stone
Wearied with seeking food across the snowy waste, the little
Heart cold, and the little tongue consum'd that once in thoughtless
   joy
Gave songs of gratitude to waving cornfields round their nest.

Why howl the Lion & the Wolf? why do they roam abroad?
Deluded by summer's heat, they sport in enormous love
And cast their young out to the hungry wilds and sandy desarts.
Why is the Sheep given to the knife? the Lamb plays in the Sun:
He starts! he hears the foot of Man! he says: Take thou my wool,
But spare my life: *but* he knows not that winter cometh fast.

The Spider sits in his labour'd Web, eager watching for the Fly.
Presently comes a famish'd Bird & takes away the Spider.
His Web is left all desolate that his little anxious heart
So careful wove & spread it out with sighs and weariness. (p. 264)

In general, however, the best of Blake is not to be found in these long-lined literary dinosaurs, but in the rhymed verse of *Songs of Experience* and Miscellaneous Poems, and the prose of *The Marriage of Heaven and Hell*. These middle-period works, from 1790 to 1804 or thereabouts, contain passages of a pungency, profundity, psychological insight and originality unequalled in English–qualities just as much due to the disturbance of the times as is the long-winded crankiness which mars so much of his other work. However, though one needs to bear in mind what was to come, the works of Blake's greatness are better approached from what came before. . . .

The *Poetical Sketches*, mostly written in the 1770s, show few typically Blakian characteristics. On the whole they are excellent but imitative: prentice work. Occasional references to the Almighty give no hint of any conception other than the normal one of a benevolent despot existing as an independent entity, and the attitude to law is orthodox to the point of naivety–witness the conclusion of *Blind Man's Buff*:

> When men were first a nation grown,
> Lawless they lived–till wantonness
> And liberty began t'increase,
> And one man lay in another's way:
> Then laws were made to keep fair play.

This seems perfectly comparable with the *Songs of Innocence* (which were written, engraved and separately published before the Revolution–the *Songs of Experience* being added five years later, in 1794). *The Chimney Sweeper*, for instance, ends piously:

> And the Angel told Tom, if he'd be a good boy,
> He'd have God for his father, & never want joy.
> And so Tom awoke; and we rose in the dark,
> And got with our bags and our brushes to work.
> Tho' the morning was cold, Tom was happy & warm;
> So if all do their duty they need not fear harm.

Similarly, *Holy Thursday* concludes with the poor children in St Paul's raising 'to heaven the voice of song' while

> Beneath them sit the aged men, wise guardians of the poor;
> Then cherish pity, lest you drive an angel from your door. (p. 59)

Neither in content and style nor in the simple hymnic rhythm of these and other poems is there any indication of irony. Nor is there any suggestion that Blake intended them to represent an innocent naivety needing the complement of Experience. (Would he have published them separately in that case?) The implication is that Blake was orthodox before the Revolution-at any rate, an orthodox nonconformist-and meant the songs to be what many still seem, Sunday-school propaganda:

> To Mercy, Pity, Peace and Love
> All pray in their distress;
> And to these virtues of delight
> Return their thankfulness.

> For Mercy, Pity, Peace and Love
> Is God our father dear....
> (*The Divine Image*, p. 58)

There is no indication in the original *Songs of Innocence* that in a few years time the writer would be matching this simple lilt with the biting irony and sardonic speech-rhythm of *The Human Abstract*:

> Pity would be no more
> If we did not make somebody Poor;
> And Mercy no more could be
> If all were as happy as we....

> Soon spreads the dismal shade
> Of Mystery over his head;
> And the Caterpiller and Fly
> Feed on the Mystery. (p. 75)

Nor is there any indication that he knew he would soon be regarding *Holy Thursday* so:

> Is this a holy thing to see
> In a rich and fruitful land,
> Babes reduc'd to misery,
> Fed with cold and usurous hand? (p. 66)

Or *The Chimney Sweeper* in these terms:

> And because I am happy & dance & sing,
> They think they have done me no injury,
> And are gone to praise God & his Priest & King,
> Who make up a heaven of our misery. (p. 70)

The change tallies with that between the pre-Revolutionary *Thel*, which is meek and mild in style and content, and the post-Revolutionary *Marriage of Heaven and Hell* which has even more aphoristic pungency than the *Songs of Experience* and is profoundly original in style and content.

Why then did Blake not repudiate the *Songs of Innocence* instead of incorporating them in a joint volume 'Shewing the two contrary States of the human Soul'? The answer would seem to be that the idea of a rich integration of personality, desiderated in the title *The Marriage of Heaven and Hell* (a work coming between the Songs of Innocence and those of Experience) was already preoccupying him when he was writing the Experience poems. By juxtaposing some of them he could give to the earlier poems a reflected symbolic quality. They would come to suggest a too-simple ideal, a world of wishfulfilment – yet still worth bearing in mind as a corrective contrast to the corrective cynicism of the state of experience. Together, when read in the light of the intervening *Marriage of Heaven and Hell*, the *Songs of Innocence and Experience* point to the need for a more inclusive state of being, in which the possibilities of innocence will be realised without the repression of instinct. This will come about by a diminution of sexual guilt, restraint and possessiveness, a humanising of abstract moral codes, and the abandonment of coercion.

In short Jealousy and Authority are seen as the great stumbling-blocks in the way of human fulfilment. That Freud says the same thing is by no means irrelevant, for it seems probable that Blake will survive not through his later theoretical works (for the reasons given) or his early songs (fine though one or two of them are), but through the astonishing examples of intellectual penetration and the amazing variety and vigour of style in the *Marriage of Heaven and Hell* and, above all, for his gift of expressing original and profound psychological insights with the utmost pungency in that work, and with the utmost concretion–so that they are proved on the pulses–in his shorter poems. The whole race of psychologists is anticipated by the line 'Sooner murder an infant in its cradle than nurse unacted desires'–and they have perhaps not yet arrived at the insights implicit in 'Damn braces. Bless relaxes' or the cutting comment 'As the plow follows words, so God rewards prayers'. And what of this psychological relativity, pointedly phrased in religious terms as a reminder of a major source of repression:

> It indeed appear'd to Reason as if Desire was cast out; but the Devil's account is, that the Messiah fell, and form'd a heaven of what he stole from the Abyss.
>
> (*Marriage of Heaven and Hell*, pp. 185, 184, 182)

Similarly, the corrective cynicism of the Pebble in *The Clod and the Pebble*, with its bitter recognition of the actual, reproves the whole race of sentimentalists–including Blake's earlier self. However, the merits of Blake's middle period poetry may best be seen by a brief analysis of one or two short poems.

In *The Tyger* Blake's desired inclusiveness is actually achieved, not discussed, in the texture of the verse. But this has been so well analysed by D. W. Harding in the *Pelican Guide to English Literature* (5) as to make any addition, in a work of this scope, unnecessary. But some of the Miscellaneous poems (p. 87) are almost as interesting. One mentioned earlier seems to deal with the sort of arranged marriage implicitly condemned in the passage already quoted from *Vala* (that containing the phrase 'all the night To turn the wheel of false desire'). A comparison of that passage–fine though it is–with this poem would serve to indicate the general superiority of the short rhymed poems over the free-verse epics.

In *Part I*, the work in question, 'I saw a chapel all of gold' was said to be an embodiment of Blake's view of marriage as a priest-sanctioned rape. We are now in a position to expand this statement briefly:

> I saw a chapel all of gold
> That none did dare to enter in

So far we have an implicit vaginal image combined with a hint of that 'sensual enjoyment' which could make everything appear 'infinite and holy'–a hint qualified by the second line which picks up a secondary, but equally 'holy', suggestion of 'chapel': the symbol of an anti-sexual religion. (Cp. the chapel in *The Garden of Love*, p. 74, with 'Thou shalt not' writ over the door, 'And Priests in black gowns. . . walking their rounds, And binding with briars my joys & desires'.) The last two lines of the stanza amplify this suggestion, and the last word 'worshipping' adds a note of contempt to the tone, hitherto neutral:

> And many weeping stood without,
> Weeping, mourning, worshipping.

The next two and a half stanzas lack this inherent fusion of social and psychological reference. They are pure dream-images of rape, whose sacramental imagery gives intensely the idea of defilement and perversion, and whose rhythms (particularly of the third line of each stanza) act as sensory reminders:

> I saw a serpent rise between
> The white pillars of the door,
> And he forc'd & forc'd & forc'd,
> Down the golden hinges tore.
>
> And along the pavement sweet,
> Set with pearls and rubies bright,
> All his slimy length he drew,
> Till upon the altar white
>
> Vomiting his poison out
> On the bread & on the wine.

Yet the wider social reference of the first stanza has set in motion a generalising tendency, so that one can hardly help feeling subconsciously that the dream-images of rape are also symbols of what current Christian morality is doing to human joys and desires. So the final lines of biting contempt for society–which would seem extravagant if taken as simply referring to limited instances of literal marital rape–seem inevitable and fitting:

> So I turn'd into a sty
> And laid me down among the swine.

Soft Snow (p. 96) grows even more compactly from this psycho-social background, but is a brief myth of young love, not of marriage:

> I walked abroad in a snowy day:
> I asked the soft snow with me to play:
> She play'd & she melted in all her prime,
> And the winter call'd it a dreadful crime.

Of this poem it is probably only necessary to remark its associative compression, and the assimilation of sexual loving to the innocent joys of childhood, the loss of chastity to a natural–and thawing–process. With the background material in mind, it is evident that 'winter' is not only an aspect of nature but of society–and thereby of man perverted into an 'unnatural' state in which experience cannot be assimilated to a more inclusive innocence because of the shaming condemnation of a wintry code. Nothing could be more lucidly complex; and in this the stanza is typical of its period.

To see what became of Blake's gift, it is not necessary to examine further the longer poems. The briefest possible commentary on a late poem in rhymed verse, which *seemingly* exemplifies that gift will sufficiently signpost the change. The poem in question is that most popular and most misunderstood of all Blake's works, the miscalled *Jerusalem* which is prefixed to *Milton* (1804–8).

Those who sing these verses in churches and Women's Institutes think of them as constituting orthodox uplift, as a hymn in fact. F. W. Bateson, however, has pointed out with only a very little exaggeration in his *Critical Introduction to English Poetry* (pp. 7/9) that it was intended by Blake to be an anti-clerical poem in favour of free love. Certainly, Blake had not reverted to his pre-Revolutionary views or become an orthodox reactionary like Wordsworth. By 'Satan' he means what the modern hymnist would call 'God', and the 'dark Satanic Mills' were the altars of churches, where humanity is ground down. Witness the following lines further on (Bk. the First, p. 386):

> And the Mills of Satan were separated into a moony Space
> Among the rocks of Albion's Temples, and Satan's Druid sons

Offer the Human Victims throughout all the Earth, & Albion's
Dread Tomb, immortal on his Rock, overshadow'd the whole
    Earth,
Where Satan, making to himself Laws from his own identity,
Compell'd others to serve him in moral gratitude & submission,
Being call'd God, setting himself above all that is call'd God;
And all the Spectres of the Dead, calling themselves Sons of God,
In his Synagogues worship Satan under the Unutterable Name.

The 'Arrows *of desire*' were to be taken literally as well as symbolically, and the 'Bow of burning gold' and 'Chariot of fire'
evidently carried sexual implications. Witness, *inter alia*, the
following phrases on p. 565 (*Jerusalem*, IV):

> The Bow is a Male and Female. . . . the Arrows of Love. . . .
> and each Chariot was Sexual Threefold. . . .

Furthermore Jerusalem was not a place but a state of mind
('Imagination is surrounded by the daughters of Inspiration, who
in the aggregate are call'd Jerusalem', p. 638) and the 'holy Lamb
of God' was not an historical figure but a personification of
mankind in fully imaginative, fourfold state.

Yet are the hymnists wholly to be blamed? The tone of the
poem has a simple hymnal elevation; its complexity is an
artificial, verbal matter. One has, as it were, to row hard against
the current of connotation in order to *make* the poem mean
what it was consciously intended to. It is not writing which
draws in a general way on a background; it is writing in a *code*.
Subconsciously, it would seem, Blake had come to terms to a
greater extent than he knew–though to a much lesser extent
than Wordsworth and Coleridge did. Hence the diffuse rhetorical
quality of the later works, and their comparative lack of impact
and clarity.

However, one point remains to be added: Blake's constant
devotion to line and particular image.

To generalise is to be an Idiot. To Particularise is the Alone Distinction of Merit.   (*Marginalia to Reynolds's Discourses*, p. 777)

The great & golden rule of art, as well as of life, is this: That the
more distinct, sharp and wiry the bounding line, the more perfect the
work of art.   (*Descriptive Catalogue*, p. 617)

If, then, we bear in mind the habit of tense energetic definition carried over from painting to poetry and the method of symbolism, as well as the idea of approaching Blake's metaphysic through psychology, we seem to be impelled to some such summing-up as the following:

Blake's political and social comments are valuable for their provocative power rather than their balance; they are not really separable from his comments on character, for social shock released psychic energies that found their most fruitful field, in one of Blake's make-up, in sharply drawn psychological myth with social and ethical overtones. And finally, even his most delirious reflections of conflict are not merely psychological documents; they combine implicit comment and generalisation with their revelations, by reason of the myth-form, the symbolism and the intrusive background.

III

WORDSWORTH

> Two voices are there: one is of the deep;
> It learns the storm-cloud's thunderous melody....
>
> And one is of an old half-witted sheep
> Which bleats articulate monotony....
>
> And Wordsworth, both are thine.
>
> (*A Sonnet*, J. K. Stephen)

Few critics would disagree with Stephen. There *are* two voices (at least), and one is decidely inferior to the other. There is general agreement, too, that the inferior voice droned down the other with increasing frequency as the poet got older. F. W. Bateson is not out of step when he notes that

> Wordsworth wrote very good poems and less good poems in both his early and later manners, but I am not aware of the existence of one poem of his written after he had reached poetic maturity in 1797 and before the gradual degeneration set in about 1805 that can be called a really bad poem.   (*Wordsworth, a Re-interpretation* (1954), p. 10)

Shelley also noted the fact, in one of the two most brilliant pieces of Wordsworth-criticism ever written (the other being that of Coleridge in *Biographia Literaria*), and he related it, as we have done, to the retreat into orthodoxy:

> For he now raved enormous folly,
>   Of baptisms; Sunday-schools, and graves.
> 'Twould make George Colman melancholy
> To have heard him, like a male Molly,
>   Chanting those stupid staves.
>
> Yet the Reviews, who heaped abuse
>   On Peter while he wrote for freedom,
> So soon as in his song they spy
> The folly which soothes tyranny,
>   Praise him, for those who feed 'em.
>
> He was a man too great to scan;
>   A planet lost in truth's keen rays;
> His virtue, awful and prodigious;
> He was the most sublime, religious,
>   Pure-minded poet of these days.
>   (*Peter Bell the Third*, Pt. VI, XXXII–XXXIV)

The effect? 'A disease soon struck into/The very life and soul of Peter'; the world and the people in it 'All grew dull as Peter's self'.

Even of the great Wordsworth, Shelley had his reservations—the right ones:

> He had a mind which was somehow
>   At once circumference and centre
> Of all that he might feel or know;
> Nothing went ever out, although
>   Something did ever enter.
>
> He had as much imagination
>   As a pint-pot;–he never could
> Fancy another situation,
> From which to dart his contemplation,
>   Than that wherein he stood.
>   (Pt. IV, VII–VIII)

But on the other hand Shelley is wonderfully sensitive to the particularly Wordsworthian strength:

> Yet his was individual mind,
>   And new-created all he saw
> In a new manner, and refined
> Those new creations, and combined
>   Them by a master-spirit's law.
>
> Thus – although unimaginative –
>   An apprehension clear, intense,
> Of his mind's work, had made alive
> The things it wrought on; I believe
>   Wakening a sort of thought in sense. (IX–X)

The precise *sort* of sort is unforgettably evoked in Part V.

> But Peter's verse was clear, and came
>   Announcing, from the frozen hearth
> Of a cold age, that none might tame
> The soul of that diviner flame
>   It augured to the earth:–
>
> Like gentle rain on the dry plains,
>   Making that green which late was grey,
> Or like the sudden moon that stains
> Some gloomy chamber's window-panes
>   With a broad light like day.
>
> For language was in Peter's hand
>   Like clay while he was yet a potter:
> And he made songs for all the land
> Sweet both to feel and understand,
>   As pipkins late to mountain cotter. (XIII–XV)

How well such lines capture that capacity to embody the intangible in concrete particulars which Wordsworth shares with Blake at his best. One is tempted to believe them psychologically akin. Certainly, Wordsworth's note on the 'Intimations of Immortality' ode would not sound out of place in Blake:

I was often unable to think of external things as having external existence, and I communed with all that I saw as something not apart from, but inherent in, my own immaterial existence.

The note goes on, however, to introduce an overtone of prudence, caution, even perhaps of fear, which is foreign to Blake:

Many times while going to school have I grasped at a wall or tree to recall myself from this abyss of idealism to the reality.

Unlike Blake and Coleridge, Wordsworth never wholly accepts the primacy of mind, of intuition as the main road to reality. He clings to the idea of an equal partnership of mind and matter, idealism and sense-experience.

Of this overtone, too, Shelley was not unaware. He detected beneath the greatness that lack of full commitment which so often shows itself as an absence of energy and sensuality:

> But from the first 'twas Peter's drift
> To be a kind of moral eunuch:
> He touched the hem of Nature's shift, –
> Felt faint, – and never dared uplift
> The closest all-concealing tunic. (Pt. IV, xi)

Does this, one wonders, provide a clue to the explanation of the current apathy of the younger generation towards Wordsworth? The idea of Two Voices, allocated according to period, hardly does so; nor does a division by manner: augustan and romantic, or pedestrian and rhetorical; for today there is little enthusiasm among students for either period or any manner. Even for poems in his best period and combining the best in all manners, admiration is generally inert.

No doubt we should not overlook the possibility of biographical explanation. Much is repellent in Wordsworth's life and personality: the insensitive egotism, the assumption of moral superiority, the ratting on his principles, the nastiness to Coleridge about Sara Hutchinson, and to De Quincey because his wife bore his child some months before marriage – barely excusable in one concealing his own shabby behaviour to Annette Vallon. Then there is the niggardliness: giving visitors a cup of tea, but telling them they must pay if they wanted anything to eat; the grudging attitude to other poets – witness the cold comment to Keats on *Endymion*, 'A pretty piece of paganism'. There are the 'unromantic' vignettes: the great poet expatiating about his rheumatic knees, or, toothless, conversing vainly to Harriet Martineau's ear-trumpet. Moreover, there is the constant tendency of the teacher to overcome the poet, to make Nature your Sunday-school teacher. Yet other poets have had unsympathetic personalities without destroying enthusiasm for their best poetry. Surely, then, there must also be some literary reason in Wordsworth's case–and that reason is implicit in the last sentence of the Note quoted. He is a man fighting against the void: a conflict remote from general experience.

In consequence, he is impelled to manufacture a protective outside skeleton, like a crustacean–or rather, perhaps, to borrow empty shells like the hermit crab. In rough chronological order these are earlier poetic forms and manners, Godwinism, Nature, and religious and political orthodoxy. Only in the case of 'Nature', (for the reasons given in *Part I*) does this bring about a balance of enrichment and stability, rather than security by impoverishment–and even then, as we have seen, it is often at the cost of a certain severity and coldness. His 'joy' or 'glee' is typically ruminative and trancelike, not energetic and dramatic, and it is usually the product of solitariness, even of bleakness. Still, in this period his work, so to speak, has an articulated inner skeleton which renders it both strong and flexible. In the other cases, the void gets form (and the poet identity) only at the price of constriction and rigidity; 'Avaunt all specious pliancy of mind', and the approval of man as slaughterer for the Lord of Hosts, of Carnage as the daughter of God (*Ode*, 1815), nicely symbolise the fact.

At first, this fault is due largely to imitativeness; later, to his retirement into a shell of theory so that didacticism and exhortation come to supplant the attempt to render and fix his full real experience. Both cases can be clearly illustrated by comparison.

The early *Vale of Esthwaite* falsifies the poet's real experience by forcing it into the form of a pre-romantic horror ballad (the same influence being apparent also in *Three Graves*, *Fragment of a Gothic Tale*, *The Convict* and other early works):

> I lov'd to haunt the giddy steep
> That hung loose trembling o'er the deep,

> While ghosts of Murtherers mounted fast
> And grimly glared upon the blast

Compare *The Prelude* (1805), Bk. I, 34:

> Oh! when I have hung
> Above the raven's nest, by knots of grass
> And half-inch fissures in the slippery rock
> But ill sustain'd, and almost, as it seem'd,
> Suspended by the blast which blew amain,
> Shouldering the naked crag; Oh! at that time,
> While on the perilous ridge I hung alone,
> With what strange utterance did the loud dry wind
> Blow through my ears! the sky seem'd not a sky
> Of earth, and with what motion mov'd the clouds!

(It seems *apropos* to mention that the next line referring to 'The mind of Man' is trancendentalised to 'the immortal spirit' in the 1850 version.)

As great a change for the worse is seen when we move from middle-period to late works. *The Convict* is by no means one of the best poems of *Lyrical Ballads*. But the sense of freedom and beauty in the expanse of nature makes a quietly effective contrast with the dungeon. There is emotional honesty in the poet's reluctance to turn from beauty to suffering, and there is pity for the suffering. In the language, the muted drama rarely approaches theatricality. In the verses below, for instance, 'Glory' and 'glimmering' underline the difference of condition, 'outcast of pity' is finely ambiguous (implying both 'piteous outcast' and 'cast out from (society's) pity'), and 'Rang' is a daring sense-image for a psychological state – a very different state from that implied by 'Resound':

> The glory of evening was spread through the west;
> – On the slope of the mountain I stood,
> While the joy that precedes the calm season of rest
> Rang loud through the meadow and wood.
>
> 'And must we then part from a dwelling so fair?'
> In the pain of my spirit I said,
> And with a deep sadness I turned, to repair
> To the cell where the convict is laid.

> The thick-ribbed walls that o'ershadow the gate
> Resound; and the dungeons unfold:
> I pause; and at length, through the glimmering grate
> That outcast of pity behold.

How well these first three stanzas compare[1] with the unctuous complacency, the dead rhetoric, and the lying picture of this later view of the convict in the *Sonnets Upon the Punishment of Death* (XII):

> See the Condemned alone within his cell
> And prostrate at some moment when remorse
> Stings to the quick, and, with resistless force,
> Assaults the pride she strove in vain to quell.
> Then mark him, him who could so long rebel,
> The crime confessed, a kneeling Penitent
> Before the Altar, where the Sacrament
> Softens his heart, till from his eyes outwell
> Tears of salvation. Welcome death! while Heaven
> Does in this change exceedingly rejoice;
> While yet the solemn heed the State hath given
> Helps him to meet the last Tribunal's voice
> In faith, which fresh offences, were he cast
> On old temptations, might for ever blast.

Is this the same man who had himself dreamed of 'implements of death, and long orations which in dreams' he 'pleaded Before unjust Tribunals, with a voice Labouring, a brain confounded'? The rebel who had dragged 'all passions, notions, shapes of faith, Like culprits to the bar'? The answer is Yes, indeed, the same man, but when he had ceased to 'grasp at a tree or wall' to recall himself to reality.

In *Part I*, it was noted how the verbal form of conflict in Wordsworth's poetry often took on a social or political cast. It is perhaps now time to emphasise that in his case–as in that of other romantics–social pressures often merely gave a means of

---

[1] Cp., too, the sentiment of the last lines quoted with those of the sonnet:
> At thy name though compassion her nature resign,
> Though in virtue's proud mouth thy report be a stain,
> My case, if the arm of the mighty were mine,
> Would plant thee where yet thou might'st blossom again.

expression, and a valuable way of generalisation, to what were primarily personal conflicts. Bateson attributes the obvious guilt-feelings behind much of Wordsworth's most powerful poetry to a suppressed incestuous love for Dorothy, pointing out (with the support of Coleridge's authority) that 'Lucy was almost certainly Dorothy Wordsworth' and going on correctly to add 'Sooner or later apparently Wordsworth *had* to kill the thing he loved, even though it was only in poetry' (p. 67, *op. cit.*). The list includes Lucy, Mary of Esthwaite, Annette–and himself. The original Ms of *There was a boy* shows that initially the grave the poet brooded over was his own. This was written in 1798. So if it is true, as Bateson suggests, that Wordsworth killed a part of himself when he married in 1802, it is evident that he was only doing what he had already been tempted to do. Significantly this date coincides with the period of growing rejection of his earlier unorthodox ideas (Southey's and Coleridge's 'conversions' took place at about the same time). What is likely, then, is that political, sexual and religious guilt-feelings are branches of a deeprooted insecurity resulting from his inability to commit himself trustingly either to the external world or the 'abyss of idealism'. From this major, underlying conflict seems to come his strength in the period of probity and probing, when the external world is firmly, even desperately grasped, and made to record echo-soundings of his own depths. From this also his weakness in the period of substitute systems.

It is remarkable how often nature takes on a punitive aspect quite out of proportion to the *ostensible* cause of guilt recorded. The small boy takes a bird from a snare and lo!

> I heard among the solitary hills
> Low breathings coming after me, and sounds
> Of undistinguishable motion, steps
> Almost as silent as the turf they trod.
>
> (*Prelude*, Bk. 1, 329/32)

He borrows someone else's rowing boat, and

> a huge Cliff,
> As if with voluntary power instinct,
> Uprear'd its head. I struck, and struck again,

> And, growing still in stature, the huge Cliff
> Rose up between me and the stars, and still,
> With measured motion, like a living thing,
> Strode after me. . . .
>   And after I had seen
> That spectacle, for many days, my brain
> Work'd with a dim and undetermin'd sense
> Of unknown modes of being; in my thoughts
> There was a darkness, call it solitude,
> Or blank desertion, no familiar shapes
> Of hourly objects, images of trees,
> Of sea or sky, no colours of green fields;
> But huge and mighty Forms that do not live
> Like living men mov'd slowly through the mind
> By day and were the trouble of my dreams. (Bk.1, 406/427)

The fact that these passages are preceded by 'Fair seed-time had my soul' and succeeded by 'Wisdom and Spirit of the Universe...' gives an effect of rationalisation and willed optimism rather than unflinching interpretation; for these are surely passages which externalise the feelings of a betrayer, one who must betray either the world or the Ideal. The *record* is a fine result of conflict, the *comment* a harmful result.

Had he been a different sort of poet, it might not have mattered which side was betrayed. But Wordsworth was exceedingly uncritical both as a poet and a philosopher. Consequently, it paid him to betray the ideal: to be primarily a poetic recorder, not a poetic exhorter. At worst, the recorder might be tedious (not merely grasping a tree to reassure himself of the existence of reality, but measuring a pond and giving the dimensions without comment, as if others craved equally for reassurance). At best, he could embody psychological experiences beyond the grasp of even his own consciousness (as in the passages quoted above), or wonderfully evoke the life of sensation – as in the brilliant skating scene which immediately follows the 'Wisdom and Spirit' passage. This latter passage, however, amply illustrates what could happen when poetry of rhetoric took over from poetry of experience. The significant difference is excellently analysed by Winkler in the *Pelican Guide to English Literature*, (5):

... Some of it we are likely to find obscure: what is 'the Eternity of Thought' and what is the 'discipline' referred to, for example? We may guess or be told, but we ought not to have to ask. We are prompted to ask by the controversial presentation ('the mean and vulgar works of Man'), and by the provocative pulpit tone ('soul', 'everlasting', 'purifying', 'sanctifying' etc), but there is no argument or demonstration here that will convince us if we are not already convinced.

He contrasts this with the marvellous matching of matter and manner in the lines that follow on, which prove their point on the pulses, and rightly concludes:

The difference, in terms of effectiveness of communication and richness of experience, between this part of the poem and that of the rhetorical prolegomena need hardly be emphasised. It achieves by *creation* something of what the prolegomena merely asserts. In itself, however, it hardly goes all the way to validating the large cheque drawn by the prolegomena. It is not easy to see, for example, how 'pain' and 'fear' are 'sanctified' as a consequence of experiences such as these. (pp. 155, 159)

But at least it can be said that Wordsworth hardly ever cheats. He doesn't write one sort of thing and pretend it is another. Even if his integrity were in question, his lack of critical ability would prevent him from doing so. So where there is waste it shows up. Auden advises poets to

> Be subtle, various, ornamental, clever,
> And do not listen to those critics ever
> Whose crude provincial gullets crave in books
> Plain cooking made still plainer by plain cooks.
> (*The Truest Poetry is the Most Feigning*)

Wordsworth's is the plainest of cooking, especially when he is writing according to his critical theory. And this has at least the virtue of letting you see clearly when the answer *is* cooked. . . .

About the early poems not much need be added to what has already been said. They say little that is original either about the world or the writer, because there is little originality of thought, form or language. Any problems or conflicts are absorbed by the language or substituted by stock literary responses. Even the best poems of this period, *An Evening Walk* and *Descriptive Sketches* (1793), are derivative: augustan in form, pre-romantic in content. It is significant that the latter was begun (in 1790) under the title *Picturesque Sketches*. It has the aesthetic, visual approach, as well as something of the language, of pre-romantic Picturesque poetry. Somewhere in its ancestry is the Claude-glass carried by picturesque tourists like Gray so that they might look at a small image of the landscape instead of the landscape itself, the better to judge the relationship of masses and perspectives.

In the *Lyrical Ballads* Wordsworth speaks with his own voice: crude and provincial perhaps, but genuine. Further, his interests are more social and human than they were. Where these poems are faulty they are so not through falsity but through dullness. They lack the qualities Auden recommends.

At first sight, Wordsworth's contributions to this volume seem to contradict a point made in *Part I*, that romantic poetry gets a great deal of its effect from connotation–from using the harmonics of language, so to speak. But in fact the poems succeed only when Wordsworth does this; then, they may well acquire the heightened effect commonly attendant on results obtained by unexpectedly simple means. In other cases, there is an effect of stubborn adherence to theory–a mistaken theory–with all the attendant ills Coleridge pointed out: the feeling of *accidentality* and irrelevant matter-of-factness, of garrulity, of incongruity (between this sort of language and the rhymed metrical form), and of ventriloquism. It is no accident that *Tintern Abbey*, the most widely acknowledged success, should be the poem least consonant with Wordsworth's critical theory but most relevant to his basic need to reconcile matter and mystery. Gently gathering up a mild landscape, the poem moves effortlessly into:

> that blessed mood,
> In which the burthen of the mystery,
> In which the heavy and the weary weight
> Of all this unintelligible world
> Is lighten'd:– that serene and blessed mood,
> In which the affections gently lead us on,

> Until, the breath of this corporeal frame,
> And even the motion of our human blood
> Almost suspended, we are laid asleep
> In body, and become a living soul:

The tone, of elevated meditation, is matched by the solemn muted rhythm, itself matching the utterly unrustic language. The validity of this intangible 'mood' is sustained, for the reader, by that implicit in the landscape it rises from, where 'steep and lofty cliffs' 'connect the landscape with the sky'. Moreover, it is guaranteed by an honesty which admits this may 'Be but a vain belief'. Whatever its status as a 'belief', it stands secure as a shared experience from an identity not based on the betrayal of either aspect of humanity. Immaterial and material worlds are similarly fused in the rich evocation that follows, of 'What then I was' when 'The sounding cataract/Haunted me like a passion'. It is when the poet begins to theorise that doubts begin. Just as one feels in Yeats's *Sailing to Byzantium* a discrepancy between the *tone* of attraction to a life of the senses, in the first stanza, and the contrary *assertion* of the theme thereafter, so here it is difficult to believe that Wordsworth found in *meta*physical pantheism the 'Abundant recompense' he alleges for the loss of the vitality of his youthful response to nature (even if one suspects that was a little over-intense as a compensation for a repressed inclination to the void). The poet himself says he '*would* believe' it so, and his precariousness protects itself by language no less elevated but rather less precise than that on the 'blessed mood' which is now being explained:

> And I have felt
> A presence that disturbs me with the joy
> Of elevated thoughts; a sense sublime
> Of something far more deeply interfused,
> Whose dwelling is the light of setting suns,
> And the round ocean, and the living air,
> And the blue sky, and in the mind of man,
> A motion and a spirit, that impels
> All thinking things, all objects of all thought,
> And rolls through all things.

It is difficult to know what precisely could be meant by the statement that something (undefined) has a 'dwelling in the *light* of setting suns'. How could one possibly know this? And does this differ from the light of rising suns? Perhaps the idea of setting is intended to give a melancholy touch? If so, it contradicts 'joy'. Further, with *what* is the something 'interfused'? And 'more deeply' than *what*? If the interfusion is that of a spirit with material nature, then it contradicts the idea of its intangible dwelling-place in sunset light (though it allows for its being in the minds of 'thinking things'). Perhaps it is 'the sense sublime' which is more deeply interfused with the poet's animal feelings than it used to be in youth. If so, it is a very badly expressed psychological statement which would hardly warrant the empirical assumption of a spirit dwelling in media as disparate as light, sea, objects and minds. It is hard to resist the impression that what we have here is metaphysical rhetoric masquerading as shared experience—though not to such an extent that it spoils the balance of conflicts, the rich tension, characteristic of the poem as a whole.

Others among the *Lyrical Ballads* draw their strength rather from the facts given than from merits of style—when the facts are significant, and not mere barriers against solipsism. On themes of poverty and oppression, and particularly of seduced and abandoned women, like Annette, the bareness of the language acts as a guarantee against evasion by rhetoric. It is necessary to point out, however, that the bareness is relative. No Female Vagrant, for instance, ever spoke like this, though the vocabulary is ordinary enough:

> Peaceful as some immeasurable plain
> By the first beams of dawning light impress'd,
> In the calm sunshine slept the glittering main.

A fine objective correlative, in which each key-word gives off reverberations, while 'glittering' picks up ironically a reference to the sword in the previous stanza. The point is made rather unnecessarily explicit in the following lines, but then the stanza ends with one of those striking insights which, so often in Wordsworth, compensate for all the tedium he inflicts on his audience. And what perspectives the preposition 'along' conjures up!

> The very ocean has its hour of rest,
> That comes not to the human mourner's breast.
> Remote from man, and storms of mortal care,
> A heavenly silence did the waves invest;
> I looked and looked along the silent air,
> Until it seemed to bring a joy to my despair.

Where there is undeniable prosiness and yet none of the banality or sense of incongruity with verse-form usually attending it, we shall invariably find that a *selection* of detail has a similar effect to that interplay of connotation–the sign of inclusive tension (or of confusion) resulting from conflict–which is characteristic of romantic poetry. Thus:

> It is the first mild day of March:
> Each minute sweeter than before,
> The red-breast sings from the tall larch
> That stands beside our door.
>
> There is a blessing in the air,
> Which seems a sense of joy to yield
> To the bare trees, and mountains bare,
> And grass in the green field.

Keeping strictly to questions of implication, it is easy enough to see how the first two lines imply a sunny day growing in warmth, the third reminds us of winter. (The redbreast is not only a winter bird, but is still used to being near the door.) This conjunction of facts implies pleasurable surprise at such early mildness, a feeling developed in the first two lines of the next stanza; while the last two imply the idea of an advance guard from summer, in the green grass which contrasts with the still bare trees and mountains.

During the years which began with the *Lyrical Ballads* and ended with the completion of the first version of the *Prelude* in 1805 (a version he no longer dared to publish) the proportion of poor work in Wordsworth's output is very small. Even when he is monotonous, it is with– as John Jones puts it in *The Egotistical Sublime* (1954)–'an inspired monotony'; and when he is not monotonous he is magnificent. *The Reverie of Poor Susan*, for instance, images the poet's views without a trace of didacticism, his feelings without a trace of self-pity. Seen in perspective, the situation generates sadness without sentimentality. The thrush that sings in its cage, is like Susan in the city; the city is like a cage set in the countryside; the poet sings like the thrush, shares Susan's sense of alienation (or, more precisely, is able to evoke what she feels because he shares analogous feelings), and has known the fading of a visionary, yet sustaining, 'Nature'. It is this latent structure which gives overtones to, say, 'enchantment' and 'vision', 'bright' and 'vapour', 'vale' and 'Cheapside' in the simple but moving second stanza:

> 'Tis a note of enchantment; what ails her? She sees
> A mountain ascending, a vision of trees;
> Bright volumes of vapour through Lothbury glide,
> And a river flows on through the vale of Cheapside.

And, of course, there is the honesty, the refusal to cheat by rhetoric or a compensatory metaphysical moral:

> The stream will not flow, and the hill will not rise,
> And the colours have all passed away from her eyes!

The first four stanzas of the *Intimations of Immortality* ode, written some years later (1802) share something of this quality, though not in quite so high a degree. The difference between the stanzas lamenting the loss of 'the visionary gleam' and the remainder, written a year or two later to proclaim, not Nature, but 'the faith that looks through death', 'the philosophic mind', and to offer thanks and praise 'for those obstinate questionings/Of sense and outward things'–that difference is the first clear sign of the poet's decline from a self-questioning observer to a preacher with a cut-and-dried creed. Coleridge's detailed and devastating analysis[1] of stanza VIII so brilliantly proves the inferiority and confusion of this part of the poem that any addition seems superfluous.

But more subtle signs of the future are to be found elsewhere. *She was a Phantom of Delight* (1804) is a fine poem; but is it not a little *too* detached, a little less humanly sensitive than *Poor Susan*?

> And now I see with eye serene
> The very pulse of the machine;
> A Being breathing thoughtful breath,
> A Traveller between life and death.

Possibly, too, one might be tempted to detect a little lack of critical strength, a hint of the coming escape from probing into some shell, some compensatory creed, in the lack of a fourth stanza. The poem progresses from 'Phantom of delight' to 'A Spirit, yet a Woman too!' and on to 'A perfect Woman, nobly planned', but stops well within the temperate zone of acquaintance. Again, there is not only a difference of emphasis between the two versions of the *Prelude* but also a difference *within* the first version. Book I speaks of 'the love, the life In common things' and of hopes 'that with a frame of outward life, I might endue, might fix in a visible home Some portion of those phantoms of conceit That had been floating loose about so long' (117/131). But by the conclusion of the last Book this aspiration for a psychological union of inner and outer has turned to a desire to sanctify and

> Instruct them how the mind of man becomes
> A thousand times more beautiful than the earth
> On which he dwells, above this Frame of things
> (Which, mid all revolution in the hopes
> And fears of men, doth still remain unchanged)
> In beauty exalted, as it is itself
> Of substance and of fabric more divine.

Such instances as these prepare one for the extraordinary disparity of quality within the *Excursion* between the first Book (c.1797) and the remaining eight (1806–14). That first Book

[1]*Biographia Literaria*, chap. XXII.

contains in the story of Margaret (originally published as *The Ruined Cottage*) what is probably the finest piece of any length that Wordsworth ever wrote. The gradual decay of the cottage and its garden unobtrusively becomes an objective correlative to the breakdown of its inhabitant, and her situation is shown as typical and symbolic (though she remains a rounded individual character):

> A second infant now
> Was added to the troubles of a time
> Laden, for them and all of their degree,
> With care and sorrow: shoals of artisans
> From ill-requited labour turned adrift
> Sought daily bread from public charity,
> They, and their wives and children – happier far
> Could they have lived as do the little birds
> That peck along the hedge-rows, or kite
> That makes her dwelling on the mountain rocks.
>
> (556/565)

Here the generalising comment is made in language properly plain and unrhetorical but not wilfully simplified as if the poet were playing at being a peasant. Elsewhere, the language is evocative – but with wonderful tact, so that its significance seems to spring from the chance occurrence of details, that turn out to be *clues:*

> Daisy flowers and thrift
> Had broken their trim border-lines, and straggled
> O'er paths they used to deck: carnations, once
> Prized for surpassing beauty, and no less
> For the peculiar pains they had required,
> Declined their languid heads, wanting support. . . .

More subtly, with its lethargic movement and oppressive 'crowding':

> The honeysuckle, crowding round the porch,
> Hung down in heavier tufts. . . .

The infant Babe has 'from its mother caught the trick of grief' and the bark of the young apple-tree is 'nibbled round by truant sheep'. The states of a tormented mind–well known to Wordsworth–are vividly and sympathetically rendered:

> She did not look at me. Her voice was low,
> Her body was subdued. In every act
> Pertaining to her house-affairs, appeared
> The careless stillness of a thinking mind
> Self-occupied; to which all outward things
> Are like an idle matter. (793/8)

The original version, told with bitter bleakness, is later fitted with some difficulty into the framework of *The Excursion*, for this story of unrelieved and undeserved distress, of a woman suffering the torment of unfulfilled hopes, desertion, poverty, decay, despair, sickness and death, alone among unfriendly natural surroundings, hardly shows the beneficent power of Nature (under God) as promised by the Wanderer. Nor do we feel that a conclusion beginning 'The purposes of wisdom ask no more' can validly lead to the assertion that 'passing shows of Being' can have no 'dominion o'er the enlightened spirit Whose meditative sympathies repose Upon the breast of Faith'. It convinces the narrator, who turns away and walks along his road 'with happiness'–and a hardened heart, one feels. But it is not likely to convince the reflective reader. After all, the Wanderer has just told us that Margaret was such an enlightened woman 'Who in her worst distress, had ofttimes felt The unbounded might of prayer'–but she died of despair. (In any case, his own story contradictorily tells us that he 'exhorted her to place her trust In God's good love, and seek his help by prayer'–advice for which 'It seemed she did not thank me'.)

Of the remaining Books almost nothing favourable can be said (save for a few isolated passages). In style they reveal all the faults Wordsworth had once revolted against: vague personification by capital letter, awkward inversion, stilted poetic diction, and much latinised language quite inappropriate for a pedlar. Their 'philosophy' is inconsistent to the point of farce, and moreover the examples intended to prove or illustrate various statements hardly ever do so. Thus, Books IV and V repeatedly state that humble and rustic life is the best soil for virtue (cf. IV 365/9, 826/31 and V, 424/7, 828/37). Book VI gives examples, taken by the Pastor from his gravestones. His case would in any event be ruined by the highly selective nature of his evidence ('Still less, far less, am I inclined to treat Of Man degraded in his Maker's sight By the deformities of brutish vice'). But as it happens, even the selected stories he does tell could mostly have been used with equal effect by the sceptical Solitary they are supposed to be convincing. For instance, we hear the tale of a jilted young man who falls ill and is restored to health by botanising. So far, no doubt, this tends to show the power of Nature to effect a change of heart and cure illness. But what happens then? He catches fever and dies! The next story purports to show the Rewards of Perseverance through the tale of a man who spent twenty lonely years seeking 'precious ore' and finally struck it rich. The result? He takes to drink, and dies! Could not this equally well have illustrated the rewards of Avarice or Inebriety? Or there is the tale of Ellen, seduced by a country youth, left pregnant, turned out by her parents, treated with great cruelty by her employers (likewise country folk), cast into deeper misery by the death of her child, and finally stricken with such despair that she dies. And what might that illustrate? God's *mercy*, in taking her to himself when she 'can endure no more'! And so one could go on instancing stories of people dying in misery, with unfulfilled hopes or ambitions—all of them seeming rather to confirm the Solitary's point about the predominance of evil than the Wanderer's about the beneficence of Nature and Religion. It is as if somewhere in Wordsworth lingered a gremlin with that stubborn regard for fact that used to characterise him in less complacent days. But since little or nothing of that virtue escapes into the *texture* of the work to lighten its ponderous tedium, no credit can accrue to the poet from this confusion.

It is necessary to conclude by saying that the growing predominance of the inferior Wordsworthian voice was not simply the result of ageing. Rather, ageing coincided with a retreat from conflict into the comfort of a protective shell, so that a poetry based on 'public' attitudes supplanted that rooted deep in his own nature. The difference between the personal and the political sonnets of c.1800–1805 sufficiently confirms this. True, the latter are not so robot-like in rhythm, so cliché-ridden in diction as the later *Ecclesiastical Sonnets*. But how ill their Henry-Fifthery compares with the pure presentation of some contemporary but more personal sonnets. *To the Men of Kent* (1803), for example, is hectoring ('Now is the time to prove your hardiment!'), archaic in expression ('ye', 'yore', 'parley'), unempirical (could the French really 'ken the glittering lance, And hear you shouting forth your brave intent' from across the Channel?), and very vaguely uplifting in sense (How did the battle against the Normans –who won–confirm 'the charters that were yours before'?). *Composed Upon Westminster Bridge*, on the other hand, though written at much the same time, speaks with the voice that 'is of the deep'. Like most of Wordsworth's finest work, it springs not from a sense of duty but from solitary personal experience, from some moment when inner and outer worlds interact and 'those phantoms' of the void are in fact endued 'with a frame of outward life'. For obvious reasons, this usually happens in a natural setting. In this case, conditions were such that an urban scene could at once create and express that unexpurgated harmony of grandeur that is peculiarly Wordsworth's. This scene, moreover, had the advantage of not tempting him to metaphysical interpretation while still allowing a subtle humanising (in the hinted image of a sleeping woman, wearing 'the beauty of the morning; silent, bare'). A pun in 'calm' makes the river–which 'glideth at his own sweet will'–a psychological image. Background conflict comes in implicitly through what is denied (in 'smokeless' and 'Never did sun. . . . ") which brings to mind the normal bustle, the sense of stress and constricted busyness, which contrasts so strongly with the sense of comprehensive, suspended animation rendered here. Such poems, 'Wakening a sort of thought in sense', make 'that green which late was grey'; and we live, at least while reading them, more finely than before. For in his best period, like Coleridge, he is a reviser, rather than confirmer of habitual structures of apprehension.

IV

COLERIDGE

As we have seen, Coleridge's development approximated to that of Wordsworth and Blake. Like them, he was deeply affected by the social and psychological climate brought about by the French Revolution and its aftermath. Like them, too, he found it emotionally bracing–eventually too bracing to be borne–but intellectually relaxing (to judge by the directly political poetry: witness *Religious Musings* or the political sonnets of *Sibylline Leaves*). Yet a closer view reveals his distinctive contribution to be quite different from theirs. At his best, he communicates subtler shades of feeling–particularly guilt-feeling–organised more unconsciously, and therefore even less paraphrasable, than anything in the work of his two great contemporaries. No doubt the non-discursive mode of this writing and the non-rational nature of its content, too, were responsible for his greater need for supernatural settings to mediate his vision.

Unhappily, it is probably true to say of Coleridge that of all the great romantics he wrote fewest really worthwhile poems. These seem to derive from a visionary system almost as mystical as Blake's (Carlyle said he had discovered 'the sublime secret of believing by the Reason what the Understanding had been obliged to fling out as incredible'), and many critics of the sentimental sort have assumed that this metaphysical background is what gives these poems their profound validity. But nothing can be validated by a system whose validity is itself in question–in this case, indeed, a system which cannot be rationally validated. Thus any validity the poems have must be in inverse proportion to their *dependence* on the metaphysical system they ostensibly derive from. It must, in fact, be obliquely empirical. The poems must refer to, or embody, or clarify, or vivify, or subtilise, or extend what the reader has already experienced–at least in embryo–in the world or himself. Then, they can be said to give valid knowledge, by acquaintance, even though they may be correctly styled non-rational and subjective artefacts. What

Coleridge's best poems give such knowledge of is indicated by the critical theory he evolved at roughly the time of writing.

In that period, Coleridge had based his theory on psychological principles. He demonstrated that deep human desires and needs have the status of facts, just as much as objects or social conventions do, and that poetry may be justified if it conforms to the nature of the mind, regardless of whether it also conforms to external facts. He named his son after the philosopher-psychologist Hartley; and in framing his conceptions of Imagination and Fancy at first followed Hartley's distinction between Delirium (a mere associative disordering or reordering of recollected experience) and Mania (a systematic delusion, where elements of experience are creatively *used* to support the system). At this time, Fancy was for Coleridge analogous to delirium, Imagination to mania. We might interpret this by saying he assumed a creative principle in Imagination, a drive or obsession which compelled the external and superficial into some unity expressive of inner facts.

However, Coleridge came to want to maintain that these facts were also *truths*: valid expressions of something other and greater than either themselves or the external world which imaged them. Hence his deviation into mystical idealism, where he has been followed by most romantic critics, who thus ignore an important justification of romantic poetry-that it gives both apparitions from the human psyche, disposed aesthetically as objects for contemplation, and an 'education of the senses to see nature in expressive form' (Suzanne Langer, *Problems of Art* (1957), p. 73). It is in this later period that he fully develops his distinction between Reason (which becomes associated with Imagination) and Understanding (which becomes associated with Fancy). Since Understanding is roughly what most people mean by 'reason', and Reason what they mean by 'intuition' or 'faith', Carlyle's irritation is understandable. It was to justify an assumption that such intuition necessarily gives knowledge more true and real than any other that Coleridge developed a Germanic metaphysic almost as elaborate as Blake's–and, like his, more convincing in brilliant flashes than for any steady illumination.

The change of outlook, together with its relationship to changing conditions, is compactly summarised by Salingar (*Pelican Guide*, pp. 188, 189):

The prevailing attitude of Coleridge's formative years—not without fluctuations—was an emotional pantheism. He declared later that pantheism had appealed only to his head; but in 1802 he wrote that 'strong feeling and an active intellect conjoined' will at first lead a philosopher almost inevitably to Spinoza, and as late as 1826 he noted that he required a deliberate effort to resist his old pantheistic 'habit of feeling'. In the 1790s a nature-worship like Wordsworth's appealed to his heart as well as his head. It seconded his political creed, which might be described as a compound of Milton, Godwin, and Rousseau; it supported him emotionally after 1798, when his hopes in the French Revolution broke down; and it held together his favourite themes of speculation. He was both a student of 'facts of mind' in the Neoplatonic mystics and a disciple of the enlightenment descended from Locke and Hartley, believing with them that the contents of the mind are formed from sense-impressions combined by association, and even maintaining 'the corporeality of *thought*—namely that it is motion'. Coleridge's pantheism gave house-room to these unlikely partners. For his associationism (or 'necessitarianism') meant for Coleridge the Pantisocrat that evil was the product of civilisation and private property; while his Neoplatonic faith was a faith that 'fraternized' by revealing that all men were 'Parts and proportions of one wonderous whole'.

His new outlook, though yet to undergo many, and sometimes bewildering, changes of detail, was in essentials a reversal of the old. In 1803, with the renewal of the Napoleonic War, Coleridge emerged as a nationalist and a disciple of Burke, holding that government must be founded on property and inequality. At the same time, he returned to Anglican orthodoxy—or, rather, to a prolonged reinterpretation of Protestantism in the light of Plato and of Kant. By the end of 1803, similarly, he was repudiating Wordsworth's nature-worship and rejecting Hartley's theory of the mind, or severely limiting its application, mainly because he had now come to locate the source of moral evil in submission to the senses, in 'the streamy nature of the associative faculty', especially with people like himself, 'who are most reverie-ish and streamy'.

This theoretical development is indirectly reflected in the development of his creative work. His best poems—all written

in the period of conflict, between 1797 and 1803 - work by
constant spiritualisation of the physical. His poetic practice, that
is to say, tallies at its most vital with his critical perception at its
sharpest. Outer nature is organised to embody an inner intuitive
reality that could not otherwise have been convincingly represented at all, and outer conflicts give images for inner ones and
sometimes generalise them, referring the private individual to
society or principles.

Before this period, Coleridge's poetry is pre-romantic in its
use of language even though its content may be revolutionary.
The early poems contain, as it were symbolically, an imitation
from Ossian:

> The stream with languid murmur creeps,
>   In Lumin's *flowery* vale:
> Beneath the dew the lily weeps,
>   Slow-waving to the gale. . . .

And hard by it lies a poem on the French Revolution, *To A Young
Lady*, recording the poet's early enthusiasm, in aureate diction:

> When slumb'ring Freedom roused by high Disdain
> With giant Fury burst her triple chain! . . .
>
> Red from the Tyrant's wound I shook the lance,
> And strode in joy the reeking plains of France! . . .

But this was written after the Terror had begun, and already
doubts were creeping in, though as yet without sufficient penetration to cause the poet to collaborate with language creatively
instead of just using what had been left lying around:

> Fall'n is the Oppressor, friendless, ghastly, low,
> And my heart aches tho' Mercy struck the blow.
> With wearied thought once more I seek the shade,
> Where peaceful Virtue weaves the Myrtle braid. . . .

On these early poems, taken as a whole, Coleridge's own
Preface makes the correct comment: 'My poems have been
rightly charged with a profusion of double epithets, and a
general turgidness. . . (a) glitter both of thought and diction.'

This is not to deny them a number of original and effective epithets, an occasional Wordsworthian daring (notably in the much, and unjustly satirised poem *To a Young Ass*), and any amount of good intentions. (Witness, in that very bad metaphysical poem, *Religious Musings*, the long passage of social protest beginning 'O ye numberless/Ye, whom oppression's ruffian gluttony/Drives from the feast of life. . . . ") What they lack are the volcanic power and molten transfusions of the great poems of conflict.

To compare this last passage with the anti-war passage in *Fears in Solitude*, written four years later (1798) is to see clearly a progression both in thought and diction, though the latter is still far from being a great poem. But there is more effort to get at reality, and less yielding to the temptation to avoid it by rhetoric:

> (All read of war in)
> Terms which we trundle smoothly o'er our tongues
> Like mere abstractions, empty sounds to which
> We join no feeling and attach no form!
> As if the soldier died without a wound;
> As if the fibres of this godlike frame
> Were gored without a pang; as if the wretch
> Who fell in battle, doing bloody deeds,
> Passed off to Heaven, translated and not killed;
> As though he had no wife to pine for him,
> No God to judge him! (114/123)

That this harder thinking has been forced upon him by circumstances is suggested by *France, an Ode* (1798) which records the conflict produced by his disillusionment with the French Revolution after the invasion of the Swiss Republic:

> When France in wrath her giant-limbs upreared,
>   And with that oath, which smote air, earth, and sea,
>   Stamped her strong foot and said she would be free
> Bear witness for me, how I hoped and feared! . . .
>
> And when to whelm the disenchanted nation,
>   Like fiends embattled by a wizard's wand,
>   The Monarchs marched in evil day,
>   And Britain joined the dire array. . . .

Yet still my voice, unaltered, sang defeat
  To all that braved the tyrant-quelling lance,
And shame too long delayed and vain retreat!
For ne'er, O Liberty! with partial aim
I dimmed thy light or damped thy holy flame;
  But blessed the pæans of delivered France,
And hung my head and wept at Britain's name. ....

'And soon,' I said, 'shall Wisdom teach her lore
In the low huts of them that toil and groan!
And, conquering by her happiness alone,
  Shall France compel the nations to be free,
Till Love and Joy look round, and call the Earth their own.

Forgive me, Freedom! O forgive those dreams!
  I hear thy voice, I hear thy loud lament,
From bleak Helvetia's icy cavern sent. .... (22/66)

Liberty, it seemed, was not to be found amidst the dust and struggle, but in Nature:

                    – on that sea-cliff's verge,
  Whose pines, scarce travelled by the breeze above
Had made one murmur with the distant surge!
Yes, while I stood and gazed, my temples bare,
And shot my being through earth, sea, and air,
  Possessing all things with intensest love,
    O Liberty! my spirit felt thee there. (99/105)

At this time, Coleridge felt there lived 'nor form nor feeling' in his soul 'unborrowed from' the natural scenery of his country (*Fears in Solitude*, 1798). By the time of *Dejection* (1802) he recognised that 'we receive but what we give/And in our life alone does nature live'. It was more realistic to acknowledge nature as the borrower, but it marked the end of his creative period, for his was not a talent for realism with a background of orthodoxy. In this work (written first, in longer form, as a verse letter to Sara Hutchinson) he laments not only the loss of love, joy and early idealism but also the loss of imagination. Like Wordsworth, whose Immortality Ode was written at much the same period, he finds that philosophy must take the place of spontaneous response, but he does not pretend that such 'abstruse research' is really preferable. Given his premises, he was obviously right on this point. Believing as he did not only in the desirability of apprehending the manifold world as One (an attitude which robbed him of Wordsworth's sense of locality) but also in the need for an increase of consciousness in order to apprehend oneself as a whole man, he could hardly have been satisfied with increased consciousness of abstraction if it were accompanied by decreased consciousness of sensation, as it was:

> And still I gaze – and with how blank an eye!
> And those thin clouds above, in flakes and bars,
> That give away their motion to the stars;
> Those stars that glide behind them or between,
> Now sparkling, now bedimmed, but always seen;
> Yon crescent Moon as fixed as if it grew
> In its own cloudless, starless lake of blue;
> I see them all so excellently fair,
> I see, not feel, how beautiful they are!   (II)

Like Wordsworth he recognises the diminution of the visionary gleam, and more clearly than Wordsworth sees the cause:

> Though I should gaze for ever
> On that green light that lingers in the west:
> I may not hope from outward forms to win
> The passion and the life, whose fountains are within. (III)

In stanza VII the poet's own despair, though perhaps mainly due to frustrated love, is generalised in an image of the wind as a poet telling of 'the groans of trampled men, with smarting wounds', but the stanza ends, as it began, more personally, with an image of insecurity: the child that 'hath lost her way'. Not a great deal of foresight would have been required to prophesy a turning for support to political and religious orthodoxy.

Coleridge had always tended to mar his work by forcing it to teach a sublime doctrine of some sort, but after his conversion this tendency becomes more marked, in the small body of poetry he wrote. These works try to explain what can only be presented (as a psychological fact) and to justify what should provide its own justification. Oddly, the 'religious' element fades from these few later poems, though they become more churchly. They are more moralistic perhaps–but religion and morality, though historically linked by governmental use of the one as a sanction for the other, are essentially different. What comes to be lacking is the force that derives from those subliminal sources in the subconscious from which, so the psychologists tell us, much of religion springs.

This tendency of Coleridge's to teach may be partly to blame for the many elaborate interpretations that have been offered–by Wilson Knight, Middleton Murry and others, and, more soberly, by Humphry House–of the 'big three': *The Ancient Mariner, Kubla Khan,* and *Christabel.* The poems *can* be tortured to fit most of these interpretations. But to criticise this way is to treat dream-symbolism as if it were conscious allegory instead of volcanic eruption. The poems attract interpreters precisely because they do not interpret themselves, and this fact itself is sufficient to cast doubt on the validity of the approach. Coleridge is also partly to blame, in the case of *The Ancient Mariner,* for yielding to the outcries of critics and adding the prose paraphrase that attempts to give a neat moral coherence to what is, in fact, a statement akin to those of dream (though at the same time he rightly protested that the poem already had too much morality. Certainly the conclusion does cheapen the work; it is too superficial a summing-up). Obviously, no rational morality could honestly be derived from a poem in which those who didn't kill the albatross were more severely punished than the man who did.

The fact is that the 'big three' are all poems of dream or reverie, showing forth instinctive attempts to forge a new, and richer unity of being from experiences of guilt and failure. The nature of those experiences is expressed in *The Pains of Sleep:*

> A lurid light, a trampling throng,
> Sense of intolerable wrong,
> And whom I scorned, those only strong.
> Thirst of revenge, the powerless will
> Still baffled, and yet burning still!
> Desire with loathing strangely mixed
> On wild and hateful objects fixed.

> Fantastic passions! maddening brawl!
> And shame and terror over all!
> Deeds to be hid which were not hid,
> Which all confused I could not know
> Whether I suffered, or I did:
> For all seemed guilt, remorse or woe.

A justification of the method is given by the conclusion of *Phantom or Fact* (one of the pieces of Prose in Rhyme):

> AUTHOR.
> Call it a *moment's* work (and such it seems),
> This Tale's a Fragment from the Life of Dreams;
> But say, that years matured the silent strife,
> And 'tis a record from the Dream of Life.

The unfinished *Christabel* perhaps hardly warrants analysis, in view of limitations of space. Its innovation of stressed verse is interesting but the narrative shows signs of Coleridge's tendency to tamper with his vision *not* in order to clarify what was really in it but to allegorise, by coercion if necessary. Moreover, the trappings seem to have been searched for in the pages of the Gothic novel, and the Jekyll-and-Hyde antithesis is just a shade too tidy to embody the actual struggles and transformations in the psyche, even when they have been grasped and controlled. Coleridge has avoided Blake's confusion at the cost of losing complexity.

The Ancient Mariner, however, renders a fine picture of the sickness of a personality–conveyed in deathly images of ice and drought and spectres–struggling towards harmony, with the aid of a springing of natural beauty and vitality, but ending sadder as well as wiser. Yet even so general an outline falsifies. It is something to be passed through, so that the poem can be grasped as a 'virtual' experience–lifelike as the mirror-world but, like that, demanding only absorbed contemplation. It is an abstract of the total response a true reading might provoke–but won't provoke if the poem is read *for* the abstract. To take one stanza as an example:

> The fair breeze blew, the white foam flew,
> The furrow followed free:

We were the first that ever burst
Into that silent sea. (103/6)

No doubt you could interpret this. The breeze might stand for man's generous impulses, or the word of God, the furrow for the straight and narrow path of virtue, or the ploughing of the waste. For the 'silent sea' one could refer to the 'sunless sea' of *Kubla Khan* and suggest that it stood for death (The next stanza begins 'Down dropt the breeze'). And any number of players can join in. But is this sort of thing any substitute for sensibility? What really needs registering first, surely, is the sense of speed and space and freshness in lines one and two, the sense of break-through in the third (through the fog, and into a new world), the sense of wonder and adventure in the pause between the third and fourth lines, and the sense of stillness and potentiality in the last line. In the larger context, of course, this last turns out to be illusory, and the 'silent sea' does become a symbol of some sort of death. But starting with that idea one is apt to miss the aesthetic experience–and this sort of poem is not intended to *mean* but to *show forth*. It is worth mentioning, too, that the sequence from hope and adventure to disillusion is analogous to the poet's ideological progress. Not that the two stanzas are *about* that; it is just something that contributed to 'the silent strife' to which the poem gave expressive form.

The value of such romantic poems obviously lies not in their conclusions but in their tuning up of the personality (bad ones, of course, debilitate it like drugs); their symbolism is akin to that of dreams. Images take on a numinous significance from the associations of their context and then fade again into plain images or even literal references to the common world. The Albatross has this numinous significance when it first appears white through the fog:

As if it had been a Christian soul,

and when:

In mist or cloud, on mast or shroud,
It perched for vespers nine;
Whiles all the night, through fog–smoke white,
Glimmered the white Moon-shine. (75/8)

But in between these stanzas it has simply been a companionable bird (a fact which gives more, not less, force to the non-realistic connotations):

> And a good south wind sprung up behind;
> The Albatross did follow,
> And every day, for food or play,
> Came to the mariners' hollow! (71/4)

Dead, it becomes a symbol of the burden of sin and guilt-an effect perhaps subconsciously prepared for by the slightly sinister overtones of 'shroud', 'fog-smoke', 'glimmered' in the stanza above.

The hypnotic effect of the ballad rhythm and the repetition of phrases aid this fading and resurgence of significance. Moreover, this is a story so that, though some parts may be mere narrative filling, in other parts significance may come from sequence.

The opening in a normal bourgeois world makes an immediate contrast with the remainder of the poem, and the humorous treatment of the Wedding Guest suggests that the neurotic world to be presented is the less superficial:

> The Wedding-Guest stood still,
>   And listens like a three years child.
> The Mariner hath his will.
>
> The Wedding-Guest sat on a stone;
>   He cannot choose but hear.... (14/18)
>
> The Wedding-Guest here beat his breast,
>   For he heard the loud bassoon. (31/2)

Then with a splendid image of guilt and terror-which gives an anthropomorphic aura to the ship and to the storm (and therefore all the other weather)-the narrative passes into a different realm:

> With sloping masts and dipping prow,
> As who pursued with yell and blow
> Still treads the shadow of his foe
> And forward bends his head,
> The ship drove fast.... (45/9)

The implications of this early image are underlined by a similar one in Part VI, when the Mariner is about to return to the

Wedding-Guest world. Indeed a very acute critic might have foreseen Coleridge's reversion to 'England' and 'Church' before Coleridge did:

> Oh! dream of joy! is this indeed
> The lighthouse top I see?
> Is this the hill? is this the kirk?
> Is this mine own countree? (464/7)

He is leaving behind his nightmare:

> Like one, that on a lonesome road
> Doth walk in fear and dread,
> And having once turned round walks on
> And turns no more his head;
> Because he knows, a frightful fiend
> Doth close behind him tread. (446/51)

But at the end he still has to repeat the experience compulsively, like a child learning to face reality through the repetition of some gruesome game.

During the course of this round voyage, the reader is constantly reminded – though only by emotively weighted analogy – of both aspects of the romantic conflict. In Part II the fickle behaviour of the mariners is reminiscent, but not consciously symbolic of the Mob, or public opinion:

> Ah, wretch! said they, the bird to slay,
> That made the breeze to blow! . . . (95/6)

> 'Twas right, said they, such birds to slay,
> That bring the fog and mist. (101/2)

Since this last line is immediately followed by 'The fair breeze blew. . . ' with its sense of freedom, and then the disillusioned stanza ('Down dropt the breeze. . . ') and the dominance of a '*bloody* Sun', it is difficult not to think of the Albatross as something akin to a Spirit of Liberty or the Revolutionary Spirit. But this external suggestion modulates – under the glare of that bloody sun (formerly 'the glorious Sun') – into an image of internal paradox and dilemma:

> Water, water, everywhere,
> And all the boards did shrink;

> Water, water, everywhere,
> Nor any drop to drink.
>
> The very deep did rot.... (119/123)

This sort of pattern is repeated with variations, for the progress of the *story* is much more direct than that of the real *subject*, which proceeds in circling eddies within the great circle of the narrative as a whole. The two go in gear, so to speak, but at very different speeds (and even so, one fault of the ballad – as compared with the border ballads it is related to – is a certain lack of pace. Incident proliferates out of proportion to development – because the subject does *not* develop as much as has been thought). In Part III joy at the sight of a sail in the mist (like the wings of an albatross?) relapses into disillusion when it turns out to be a ship of death:

> Are those *her* ribs through which the Sun
> Did peer as through a grate?
> And is that Woman all her crew?
> Is that a DEATH? and are there two?
> Is DEATH that Woman's mate? (185/9)

Here is 'The Nightmare Life-in-Death', the inner horror so often personified by romantic poets as a Fatal Woman. But the ambiguous suggestions of 'Sun' and the imprisoning 'grate' conjure up hints of the outer conflict; so the Woman also suggests the Ideal that has turned deadly. Thus in one and the same stanza the inner conflict is rendered, and accounted for, and shown to be generally relevant (not the product of a unique, personal neurosis). In Parts IV and V, however, natural beauty taps a spring of vitality which turns out not to be altogether transitory (though more suffering does ensue, it goes with genuine progress). This turning point is, however, slightly marred by an intrusive explicitness:

> O happy living things! no tongue
> Their beauty might declare:
> A spring of love gushed from my heart,
> And I blessed them unaware.
> Sure my kind saint took pity on me,
> And I blessed them unaware. (282/7)

Like the concluding moral, this is not only too explicit for the context but also too superficial. The extended image of the storm (with the moon at its edge) which follows is much better, in suggesting concretely the release from a sense of sin and passive despair and the realisation, as Blake tersely states it, that Energy is Eternal Delight.

Kubla Khan has been so bedevilled by interpretation that it seems necessary to try to recover a primal innocence and go through it stanza by stanza, as if at a first reading, to see unsubtly what happens. Humphry House says it is a poem about writing poetry (thus reducing its status); Wilson Knight says it is about Life, Death, Eternity and Sex (thus leaving nothing it is not about, and inflating its status). For the latter, the river's flowing into the cavern is the symbol of a cosmic copulation between Life and Death. Strangely, this *is* the inflation of a small truth. There are signs of sexual sublimation in the poem. Even so, the poem is not an *account* of sexual sublimation but an *example* of it–and in itself that is not very interesting. Reading it afresh, however, we shall find it enacting something akin to the ambivalence found in *The Ancient Mariner*.

The first few lines seem to set up a tension between secular and sacred, artificial and natural. A 'pleasure-dome' is decreed beside a 'sacred river', and is contrasted with 'caverns measureless to man' and a sinister-sounding 'sunless sea'. Carl R. Woodring, in a recent article in *Essays in Criticism* ('Coleridge and the Khan', October 1959) produces evidence that for Coleridge pleasure-domes had bad associations of tyranny and license, drawn from the Empress Catherine's ice-palace and what Purchas–his chief source–called the Khan's 'house of pleasure'. The third stanza of *Separation*, written in the torment of love, to Sara Hutchinson brings these fragments from the outer conflict into relation with inner feelings:

> Is not true love of higher price
>   Than outward form, though fair to see,
>   Wealth's glittering Fairy-dome of ice,
>   Or echo of proud ancestry?

This may assure us of being on the right track so far. A feeling confirmed by the grandiose measurements of the Khan's grounds (already put in their place by the 'measureless' caverns). Yet the succeeding lines bring in a hint of pathos; in the menaced gardens, the 'sunny spots of greenery' surrounded by ancient forests. A sense of civilisation *threatened* works against the sense of frivolity *rebuked*.

In the second stanza both worlds are intersected by a chasm which is at once savage, holy, enchanted, and violent, seething (like the mind of a man in conflict) with 'ceaseless turmoil'. The river goes from the sunny world of fragile civilisation, through this 'turmoil', and finally sinks into the 'lifeless ocean'. This is like the passing of life into death, or torment into sleep, or love into despair, or sexual pleasure into relaxation, or several other things, but to tie it to any one of them would be un-warranted. In view of the implications of 'decree', and the concluding lines of the stanza,

> And 'mid this tumult Kubla heard from far
> Ancestral voices prophesying war,

the strongest association would seem to be with ideas of the overthrow of tyranny (though it seems inseparable from ideas of the overthrow of the civilised by the primitive, and of conscious control by passion).

In stanza three there is a *mingled* measure of fountains and caves, and a combination of sun and pleasure with caves of ice ('a miracle of rare device'). So far the poem is one to be apprehended rather than interpreted. It seems to shape subconscious impulses and conflicts into a model of peace and harmony built from war and turmoil without shirking or denying the part played by princely power. Only in the last lines of the poem is there an approach to a discursive mode of statement. They imply the *need* for bardic inspiration in order to achieve in the self what Kubla Khan achieved in the world: 'That sunny dome! those caves of ice!'. Since the poem itself exemplifies such an achieve-ment, this statement of need represents a slight weakness – the more so in that the concluding lines are more limited in their application than they should be, by their rather aesthetic view-point.

However, the general success of this poem and *The Ancient Mariner* is due to their expressing a very sensitive and sophisticated awareness in language of a primitive kind. That is to say, language used as it is used in uncivilised cultures, where ideas have to be conveyed indirectly through sappy metaphor because concrete words have not yet dried out into portable abstractions—ideas, in fact, mediated in the form of models for dealing with analogous situations, and making up for want of precision by density of suggestion

Dejection and *Frost at Midnight*, the two other masterpieces of Coleridge's great period, are not really of this sort. They do not draw the reader into a self-contained inner world where the rules of the outer world don't apply and objects only seem familiar. Not that they start from ideas, like much metaphysical or augustan poetry; but they are undeniably less akin to mania than the 'big three' and therefore less fully Imaginative in Coleridge's sense of the word. They do, however, have virtues the others lack: clear thought-content, a discussable conscious theme, and a greater range of diction, from the conversational to the meditative; in addition of course to suggestions of mood and attitude. *Dejection*, as we have seen, is notable for its intelligent honesty. *Frost At Midnight*, if rather naive in its theme (the effect of the countryside on young Hartley) is remarkable for Coleridge's *conscious* insight into his own nature and for the wonderful evocation of meditative stillness, a haven from conflict, which begins and ends the poem. This is the tranquil ecstasy of the commonplace which seems hardly to have been appreciated before the time of romantic conflict. Cowper found it beside his evening fire, Keats evoked it at the beginning of *Hyperion*, Wordsworth knew it on Westminster Bridge. Here Coleridge finds it at first indoors:

> My cradled infant slumbers peacefully.
> 'Tis calm indeed! so calm, that it disturbs
> And vexes meditation with its strange
> And extreme silentness. Sea, hill, and wood,
> This populous village! Sea, and hill, and wood
> With all the numberless goings-on of life,

> Inaudible as dreams! The thin blue flame
> Lies on my low-burnt fire, and quivers not;
> Only that film, which fluttered on the grate,
> Still flutters there, the sole unquiet thing.
> Methinks, its motion in this hush of nature
> Gives it dim sympathies with me who live. (7/18)

And finally he finds it outside—a movement matching the extension of the poet's interest.

> Therefore all seasons shall be sweet to thee,
> Whether the summer clothe the general earth
> With greenness, or the redbreast sit and sing
> Betwixt the tufts of snow on the bare branch
> Of mossy apple-tree, while the nigh thatch
> Smokes in the sun-thaw; whether the eve-drops fall
> Heard only in the trances of the blast,
> Or if the secret ministry of frost
> Shall hang them up in silent icicles,
> Quietly shining to the quiet Moon. (65/74)

To compare this with any of his rhetorical work is to perceive that in literature as in love sincerity is not enough. These passages are triumphs of technique as well as feeling; and though Coleridge himself would probably have classed *Frost at Midnight* and *Dejection* as poems of Fancy we are not thereby committed to rating them below the poems of Imagination, for the distinction is not necessarily one of quality, as he thought, but only one of kind.

But what all these poems have in common to distinguish them from the ruck of his work is an abstention from pulpiteering and verbal histrionics. On private themes deriving in part from public conflicts he is essentially a great romantic; on public themes evading private conflicts, a Victorian post-romantic.

V

SHELLEY

Of all the romantics Shelley is the one who most obviously possessed the quality of genius. Not even Coleridge can match the quickness and grasp of his intellect, the capacity for learning

languages rapidly, for assimilating and placing scientific principles
and discoveries. Yet no poet has been more criticised for 'falsity'
and 'lack of grasp'.

The paradox is more apparent than real, for these words apply
differently to imaginative fictions and discursive statements
and in each application–to his prose and to his poetry–there is,
in fact, a great deal of truth. Most of Shelley's poetry was intended
to serve the end of liberty in human society. Inevitably therefore
it gravitated towards propaganda-poetry, which is inferior in
kind to poetry of shared experience because it is much more
likely to become associated with fantasy-thinking rather than
reality-thinking, to become persuasive without giving any
genuine basis for the persuasion. To counter this gravitational
pull it needs hard thinking. On principle, however–the principle
of abhorring didactic poetry–Shelley reserved social thinking for
his prose works.

Let this opportunity be conceded to me (he writes in the Preface to
Prometheus Unbound) of acknowledging that I have what a Scotch
philosopher characteristically terms, 'a passion for reforming the
world:' what passion incited him to write and publish his book, he
omits to explain. For my part I had rather be damned with Plato and
Lord Bacon, than go to Heaven with Paley and Malthus. But it is a
mistake to suppose that I dedicate my poetical compositions solely to
the direct enforcement of reform, or that I consider them in any degree
as containing a reasoned system on the theory of human life. Didactic
poetry is my abhorrence; nothing can be equally well expressed in
prose that is not tedious and supererogatory in verse. My purpose has
hitherto been simply to familiarise the highly refined imagination of
the more select classes of poetical readers with beautiful idealisms of
moral excellence.

These somewhat inconsistent good intentions encouraged the
growth of poetic vices–vices which disappear when Shelley
ceases to concern himself with 'the more select classes' with
'highly refined' imaginations, and is not content to present
idealisms unstiffened by reasoning in the verse itself. They
disappear, in fact, when he writes *The Masque of Anarchy*, in
street-ballad form, for the man in the street.

Three vices in particular were encouraged by this determination to exclude reasoning in favour of idealisation. Firstly, the growth of an already strong tendency to abstraction:

Real flesh and blood ... I do not deal in. ... You might as well go to a gin-shop for a leg of mutton as expect anything human or earthly from me.

(Letter to John Gisborne, Oct. 22, 1821)

Secondly, the proliferation of imagery to an excessive degree. After all, it is much easier to know when to stop if you are illustrating and enforcing some reasoned, developing theme than if you are dealing with something as amorphous as beautiful idealisms. As R. D. Havens says:

The very abundance of these images is their weakness. One may be elaborated through a series of lines and followed by another, which perhaps has a simile within a metaphor, until, although Shelley holds firmly to his thought, the reader is lost. The confusion is often greater because the figures are more elusive or more difficult to understand than the matters they are supposed to illustrate. They are never homely....

'Shelley the Artist', *The Major English Romantic Poets* (1957), ed. Thorpe, Baker & Weaver, p. 176

Thirdly, and most important, this lack of some objective check encouraged the growth of extremism, leading at times to almost hysterical shrillness. The lack of a moderating influence on them allows his conflicts to bring about oversharp contrasts which are aesthetically unpleasing as well as implausible.

The root of conflict, typically, lies in an attraction both to materialism and to idealism. At first, Shelley inclines strongly to materialism, and is considerably influenced by Godwin; later he inclines more to a Berkleyan position, and finds Plato preferable to Godwin. But at no time is he without a fairly strong contrary inclination, so that though his emphasis may change the same oppositions recur throughout his work. In literary terms, we find a tendency to transfer personal conflict into contrasts between what *Is* in the world and what *Might Be*, if his subject is political or social in the main. If it is mainly personal (these categories are rarely quite exclusive), then it takes the form of tension between *Body* and *Spirit*. If philosophical–or rather, metaphysical–between the notion of Nature as *Necessity*, neutral and indifferent, and Nature as a *Spirit of Love*.

Such schematisation inevitably over-simplifies the truth. Shelley's poetry cannot be divorced from his philosophy, nor his philosophy from his politics. His metaphysic confirmed him in a belief that the revolution of force, which had failed, must be succeeded by a revolution of love; and on the other hand a concern with politics led to a more general concern with Good and Evil (especially after his political concern had become poetic instead of practical–if secret billposting and sending off messages in balloons and floating bottles can be called practical). The connection with poetry, and with the conflicts of Body/Spirit and Is/Might Be, is clearly stated in the *Defence of Poetry*:

> The cultivation of poetry is never more to be desired than at periods when, from an excess of the selfish and calculating principle, the accumulation of the materials of external life exceed the quantity of the power of assimilating them to the internal laws of human nature. The body has then become too unwieldy for that which animates it.

Critics have therefore been tempted into assessing and interpreting the poetry in terms of ideas. In fact, though Shelley's metaphysic does develop as his verse improves, there is little reason to think that this is a case of cause and effect, while the very diversity of symbolic interpretation indicates a danger in the method. For one critic, *Asia* is Love or Beauty, for another, Nature, for a third, a reincarnation of the ideal mate of *Alastor*: a derivative of Plato's fable of the once-spherical beings. Similarly, *The Witch of Atlas* may be Urania, Intellectual Beauty, Truth, Nature or the Life Force, though from a line in *Mont Blanc* one would expect her to be 'the witch Poesy'. Again, the image of a woman in a bark is now Hope and Love, now the Soul and Body on the Stream of Life, now Art inspired by Passion, and sometimes a sex-symbol.

None the less, ideas cannot be ignored in Shelley. The interpretations mentioned are noticeably grouped around a central core, and to that extent are aids to understanding the poem, though not to feeling and evaluating it. Since the experience

Shelley's poems offer is often insubstantial, there is a real difficulty in moving from secondary *interpretation* to primary *apprehension*—from *Asia* as Love (an abstraction from the work) to *Asia* as Asia: a presented figure having certain qualities. Shelley makes it difficult *not* to take the poetry as philosophy or politics in disguise, the protests in his prefaces being a sign that he was himself uneasy about his poetic success. Indeed there is other evidence that he was aware of a tendency to thinness, to rhythms that are brainwaves rather than pulse-beats, to sympathy (mental feeling parallel to) rather than empathy (physical feeling with). For instance, in a letter to Godwin, Dec. 11, 1817, he writes:

I am formed, if for anything not in common with the herd of mankind, to apprehend minute and remote distinctions of feeling, whether relative to external nature or the living beings that surround us, and to communicate the conceptions which result from considering either the moral or the material universe as a whole. . . . Yet after all I cannot but be conscious, in much of what I write, of an absence of that tranquillity which is the attribute and accompaniment of power.

Throughout, Shelley's real subject is the related conflicts in the state and in the soul. Thus there are two lines of attack, which often converge and usually imply each other: the personal (concerned with the inner world) and the social (with the outer), but the same metaphysic, the same emotions and, commonly, the same images attach to both in all periods.

Hughes points out in *The Nascent Mind of Shelley* that there is a tendency for poems dealing with conflict in the state to be Godwinian, while those dealing with conflict in the soul tend to be Platonic. But as Shelley does not regard these as independent conflicts, the true development of his thought can best be considered as a gradual–though never completely satisfactory–unifying of Reason and Idealism (Godwin and Plato, so to speak) in his theory of the One and the Many, the influence of a formally rejected Christianity being apparent in his coming to regard the One not only as good, but also as a Spirit of Love animating multifarious Nature.

The difficulty was to reconcile deterministic Necessity with the Free Will required for turning contemporary society into an ideal world. 'Reason' turns out to be an illusory key. True, you might say – and Shelley did say – that man's will is part of Necessity and man is rational; but such a solution is faulty (apart from its inadequate psychology) because it depends on ambiguous usage. Necessity, as the deterministic system of natural laws, can be identified with Reason because, in one sense, reason is order and predictability. So can Free Will, because it may involve independent rational thinking – but this is in quite another sense. Now, man is being said to be rational precisely because he is *not* taken to be subject to a remorseless Order. Moreover, on purely rational grounds, it is not easy to suggest a motive for the sacrifices demanded on behalf of future generations, and almost impossible to show that they will be made of necessity. Again, how does one account for the evil of men who are not governed by, but governing the monarchy, the Church, or other allegedly perverting institutions?

So more and more Shelley comes to substitute an ambiguous Nature for an ambiguous Reason. Nature becomes a Spirit working through matter and by physical laws towards the Good. Though far from clear and consistent, the conception seems to be based on a half-conscious analogy with a human being, in whom the mind may be thought to 'work through' and guide a body which (though not entirely different from the mind) is yet subject to physical laws. As Ryle has demonstrated in *The Concept of Mind*, this idea is not sound even for people, let alone for 'nature', but it would account for Shelley's belief that all matter is alive and feeling (*Queen Mab*) and that mind is a sort of electricity, material enough to persist after death as part of the 'collective energy' of the world (*Essay on Christianity*). Behind the conception is, no doubt, Plato's *spiritus mundi*, however, and the similar oriental ideas which affected Shelley's platonism. At any rate, he came to believe that men must suffer not a Godwinian argument but a change of heart.

The Spirit could not be prayed to, since it was impersonal, but man could become in harmony with it and thus aid Necessity, or he could be out of harmony with it – like kings and priests – and thus hamper Necessity. Poetry might help in harmonising.

But Shelley never denied the need for a long, hard, persuasive political struggle, and in his prose works he put forward a sober socialist policy, economic as well as political. The moral cataclysm leading immediately to the millenium, which features so often in his verse, is part of a poetic metaphysic derived *from*, but not part *of* a social programme.

For convenience, three periods may be distinguished. In the first (*c.* 1816/19), there is separation. In *Queen Mab* materialism and idealism are each taken to be the whole truth, in different parts of the poem, and theoretic contradiction is accompanied by a confused poetry which protests too much.

In the second period (*c.* 1816/19), there is division. Materialism is taken to apply to the physical, idealism to the mental realm. Thus in *The Revolt of Islam* the tyrant is pitied because his mind is taken to be independent of him, determined on a different plane. Shelley seems to believe in two separate realities, material and spiritual, connected only by 'inconstant visitation'. In many of the lyrics of this period, the body is in a world of suffering while the spirit is in some other realm where 'music and moonlight and feeling are one'. Dreams, visions, paradox, and prophecy provide a means of literary unification. Since this is rarely matched by unification of sensibility–and there is no unity of idea–poems appearing to deal with a double reality in fact either fall between two stools or tacitly abandon one reality (usually the 'outer' one).

In the third period (*c.* 1819/22), there is fusion: at any rate, in *The Masque of Anarchy* and *Peter Bell the Third*, and perhaps in the unfinished *Triumph of Life*. The algolagnia and ambivalence (being for and against the same things) disappear as the poet works towards an ability to face facts dispassionately before passionately transmuting them. To some slight extent this ability may be directly related to the fact that Shelley's metaphysic has become somewhat more coherent. Since the Ideal is supposed to manifest itself in matter, and particularly in man, there is less temptation to deal in insubstantial and unsubstantiated emotion for its own 'spiritual' sake, or to seek a different, more 'real' reality than the mundane one. Plato and Godwin have been at least verbally reconciled in a 'Spirit of Nature', seen as a Life-Force which works through death; as a Becoming which permits perfectibility. Idealism (the 'life', so to speak) and necessity (the 'force') have been made one. However, since the coherence is philosophically fragile, as Shelley must have known, it seems likely that the main benefit of it was indirect. Relieved of a metaphysical burden he was able to see reality rather from the viewpoint of the Many than the One, to take not a God's-eye but a man's-eye view of life, when in 1819 circumstances encouraged closer commitment.

When the poet ceases to be looking inward at himself, or upward to the One, and looks instead outward at the suffering Many, he feels it to be obvious:

that the conflict of body and spirit is to be resolved by spiritual effort for material welfare: for example, by passive resistance on behalf of reform,

that the conflict of nature as an indifferent system or a beneficent force is resolved by taking man's beneficence and capacity for self-determinism as the natural way of altering the direction of necessity,

that, in short, the spiritual is complementary to practical effort to bring what is nearer to what might be.

Thus the conflicts disappear in practice–if not in philosophical theory–and the poet being at one with himself and dealing with the real world (rather than a metaphysical world whose difficulties were largely the rationalised projection of his own conflicts) achieves a new credibility and solidity in his poetry.

In *Queen Mab* (1812/13), a work of Shelley's youth, are embedded the seeds of all his later poetry. The conflict consciously dealt with is that of feelings aroused by the state of the world as it was and those aroused by a Godwinian vision of what it might be, the possible millenium. Paradoxically less conscious is the metaphysical clash between materialism and idealism–a clash related to an emotional desire to have things both ways. Nature is at one moment determined down to the smallest particle, at the next is a deity, or at least a moral agent. God is denied as a fiction and at the same time condemned as 'vengeful and almighty'. In addition there are the obvious contradictions of moral feelings and laws of reason, of atheism and death 'full of hope', and of form and subject (a rationalistic and political harangue delivered by a fairy to a disembodied soul). The texture, too, is far from unified; echoes of the picturesque or the horror novel alternate with more respectable influences, and occasionally with originality. The most impressive passages of the poem are those most Shelleyan, on whirling gulfs and vastnesses, radiance and music. They are not, however, integral with the thought (a term more suitable than 'poetic experience' for this propaganda poem). The directly political writing is rhetorical in the worst sense. The king, for instance:

> Heeds not the shriek of penury; he smiles
> At the deep curses which the destitute
> Mutter in secret, and a sullen joy
> Pervades his bloodless heart when thousands groan
> But for those morsels which his wantonness
> Wastes in unjoyous revelry, to save
> All that they love from famine: when he hears
> The tale of horror, to some ready-made face
> Of hypocritical assent he turns
> Smothering the glow of shame, that, spite of him,
> Flushes his bloated cheek. (III, 34/44)

The picture of the millenium is equally extravagant. Even the globe co-operates by shifting its axis, so that the tropics extend to the pole: a supposition supported by a note pointing out that contemporary science had already perceived the beginning of such a shift. More surprising, and less supportable, is a change in the nature of living things ('The lion now forgets to roar for blood'). This provides an excellent example of the minimising effect of extravagance, for when the same change is extended to the human species one feels it is just about as plausible (although one knows it is much more so). War, religion, marriage and other evils are seen as things of the past, and 'Dawning love' is no longer checked by 'dull and selfish chastity, That virtue of the cheaply virtuous'.

Queen Mab is, however, of great value for the critic since it shows in graphic form how much of Shelley's metaphysic is related to the contemporary social situation, how constantly all three conflicts take on political colouring, and how much of his irreligion springs from the Church-State oppression-the poet being obviously of a thoroughly enthusiastic, religious temperament at heart.

Mont Blanc and the *Hymn to Intellectual Beauty*, the most important of the shorter poems of this period, both derive their tension from the 'Nature' conflict. On the whole, the Wordsworthian position is affirmed, but at the same time an element of personal experience shadows the affirmation. The two finest lines, in either poem, carry a very different implication:

> Power dwells apart in its tranquillity
> Remote, serene and inaccessible

and the following lines on Mont Blanc's deathdealing glaciers reinforce the impression of a Nature-like some rulers-indifferent and even hostile to her subjects.

Alastor, a psychological allegory of the pursuit of the ideal, is concerned mainly with the conflict of body and spirit, dealing with the romantic conflict's inner aspect. Social implications, however, invest the background. The Introduction, indeed, condemns Alastor for his 'self-centred seclusion'. However, it also points out that such turning from the struggle for the sake of an ideal is preferable to the state of those who stay in the world but do not attempt to reform it, the 'morally dead' who constitute 'together with their own, the lasting misery of the world'. It is this preference, no doubt, which permits a tone of whole-hearted admiration to attach to Alastor, unmitigated by the element of satire the Introduction would lead one to expect. The Introduction itself certainly emphasises the need for *human* sympathy with 'fellow beings' as the right middle course between Alastor's fault and that of the majority. But no middle course is represented by the poem itself. The verse is typically fluent, the imagery intangible, the narrative dream-like-all appropriate enough for the inner world of a fervid visionary. But the dream-woman is indistinguishable from the emancipated female played by Cythna in the *Revolt of Islam* (in stanzas XXXIII–XXXVII, 6). The sensuality of the ideal in the first poem and the idealising of the sensual in the later one are related flaws, indicating a passing over from one field to another without full awareness. In the one case, the Word becomes too fleshly for its poetic environment, in the other the Flesh becomes too wordy. A clear technical indication of Shelley's undue identification with Alastor is that fact that the texture of the verse rendering his dream is no more dream-like than that of the rest of the narrative (whose events incidentally are so implausible that they hardly *could* make a contrast with dream whatever the texture of the verse). Alastor, in fact, is Shelley in a state of guilt. Consequently, the typical romantic compensations crop up, higgledy-piggledy. The poem begins with an echo of Wordsworth, an apostrophe to Nature as the comforting mother. The poet is then an Aeolian Harp awaiting the breath of the 'Great Parent'. And the remainder concerns Alastor as outcast seeking the ideal. Significantly, he does not find it. He dies alone on a mountain. But this is not a saving touch of sardonic realism, for the mountain is obviously symbolic and the tone suggests that a fruitless search ending in death and doing nobody any good is somehow triumphant.

Marrianne's Dream, has puzzled critics. If, however, it is taken to be dealing, unlike *Alastor*, primarily with the outer aspect of the romantic conflict, it becomes as clear as a dream can reasonably be expected to be. Its structure, in fact, is based on the history of the preceding forty years.

It opens with the social conflict of what is and what might be, in symbolic terms. Custom (the black anchor) thwarts joy. Then an effort to reach the ideal (the high white cities) is followed by Tyranny's reaction by fire, and a counter-attack to put out the fire ('These towers are Nature's own, and she to save them has sent forth a sea'). Finally, there is a millenium in another world. Like the *Revolt of Islam*, the most important poem of Shelley's middle period, this follows the contemporary sequence of the years 1780 to 1815: heavy custom, enthusiasm for reform, reaching fever-point with the French Revolution, then the English Reaction, and finally the struggle towards a distant Freedom. *Ozymandias* (1717) acts as a pendant to the *Revolt of Islam*, by putting tyranny in the perspective of time.

The *Revolt* itself aspires to fuse both aspects of the romantic conflict. Its *Introduction* states that it is 'a series of pictures illustrating the growth and progress of the individual mind aspiring after excellence' and then goes on to relate the individual mind to the French Revolution and the reaction in England. While condemning the excesses of the French, which had so shocked the Lake poets, Shelley maintains that they were incidental and temporary defects, and recommends familiarity with nature as the most beneficial and corrective part of a poet's education.

The difficulty of this aspiration is obvious, and the only form likely to be successful would seem to be that of allegory. But since he was averse from didactic poetry, Shelley rejected that form, preferring to aim rather at conveying the enthusiasm of a vision derived from his ideas than the ideas themselves. The result is sometimes magnificent, always fascinating–far more so than any pre-romantic poem, though many are aesthetically 'better' by attempting less–yet as a whole it fails, for want of the fusion aspired to. The first stanza of the first canto may fairly stand as paradigm:

> When the last hope of trampled France had failed
> Like a brief dream of unremaining glory,
> From visions of despair I rose, and scaled
> The peak of an aerial promontory
> Whose caverned base with the vexed surge was hoary;
> And saw the golden dawn break forth and waken
> Each cloud and every wave:–but transitory
> The calm: for sudden, the firm earth was shaken
> As if by the last wreck its frame were overtaken.

This gives in a concise yet evocative way the progress of Liberty to date: Revolution (line 2), Dictatorship and defeat (1 and 3), hope of Freedom, as brief as that of Europe in 1815 (6 and 7), followed by Repression (8 and 9). The modulation in the third line from the outer world of the first two lines to that world as it affected the inner world of the writer ingeniously prepares for the use of nature as the common measure of man and society. The 'golden dawn' obviously refers mainly to the outer world which the watcher is looking back on. The transitory 'calm', however, applies equally to the state of society and of the individual (previously thrown into despair by the failing 'outer' glory). Yet isn't 'trampled' just a little hackneyed? Why 'unremaining' after 'failed' and 'brief'? If it's a 'peak' surely it *must* be 'aerial'? 'Golden dawn', too, is cliché, and wakening light is not necessarily calming. Presumably the surge would still be 'vexed' when gilded. And all in all the stanza seems a little arbitrary, particularly when one comes to the final earthquake. Nature is not *naturally* illustrating the theme; it is being manipulated and made to. And is not the effect of doing two things at once rather to weaken each than give depth to both?

Such questions and doubts, occurring constantly, point to a looseness in the texture which matches blurred thinking and feeling throughout: marks of conflicts not really resolved either emotionally or intellectually but masked by sleight of hand.

In the long run, the same criticisms are to be directed at the *Revolt of Islam* as at *Rosalind and Helen*, a lesser poem of this period, dealing with the same themes on a purely personal level: its tyranny referring to the taking of Shelley's children. The incest and algolagnia of the former poem recur in the tearing apart of the sister and the burning of her lover-brother, and echoes of the horror novel abound. The whole is a phantasmagoria in which are displayed in turn the images and themes so often met with before.

During these first two periods, Shelley's *idées fixes* come round and round like a stage army, and the verse is at once forced and over fluent. Only in the third–the easy conversation in *Julian and Maddalo* being the first sign–is the poetry condensed. Not, of course, that it always is, or that it's never great when it isn't. *Adonais* must be considered a great poem of its kind, but its kind is the lesser kind of passionate transcendence–lesser because its only evidence is strength of feeling. It asserts its 'truth' instead of reaching her the hard way, Donne's way:

> On a huge hill
> Cragged and steep, Truth stands; and he that will
> Reach her, about must and about must goe
> And what the hilles suddennes resists winne soe.

In *Adonais*, conflict is transcended by soaring spiritual elevation. But this is in the nature of an injection; its effects are not likely to be permanent.

Probably the high-water mark of Shelley's transcendent poetry – that which does not depend on the evidence of the senses or on reasoning, which abjures physical texture in the verse – is the spendid exhortation to passive resistance at the end of *Prometheus Unbound*:

> To suffer woes which Hope thinks infinite
> To forgive wrongs darker than death or night
>   To defy Power which seems omnipotent;
> To love, and bear; to hope till Hope creates
> From its own wreck the thing it contemplates,
>   Neither to change, nor flatter, nor repent;
>   This, like thy glory, Titan, is to be
>   Good, great and joyous, beautiful and free;
>   This is alone Life, Joy, Empire and Victory.

Here, the secondary political symbolism of the poem (given in some detail by Cameron PMLA (1943) vol. XL, pp. 366–493 fuses finely with the psychological and metaphysical explorations which are its main concern. This tactful subordination of one element to another permits a rare combination of scope and homogeneity. Despite its cosmic range and political symbolism, the poem is an acknowledgedly inner landscape, a vision of what man might be if bodily and environmental frustrations were overcome by the spirit. Consequently, though there are many inferior passages, there is no general sense of confusion or unreality, and the poet can, as it were, step forward out of the play without incongruity in order to point the moral this inner world holds for the outer. After all, that was the play's *raison d'être*; its unity is implicitly based on contrast. Thus, the *ideal* of Prometheus (admitted to be ideal, though not incredible) sharpens the point of such a comment on the *fact* of men as they are:

> In each human heart terror survives
> The ruin it has gorged: the loftiest fear
> All that they would disdain to think were true:
> Hypocrisy and custom make their minds

The fanes of many a worship now outworn.
They dare not devise good for man's estate,
And yet they know not that they do not dare.
The good want power, but to weep barren tears,
The powerful goodness want: worse need for them,
The wise want love, and those who love want wisdom:
And all best things are thus confused to ill.

(Act I, 618/28)

Of the three other dreams of this period, all of which, unlike *Prometheus Unbound*, are primarily outer-directed, *Hellas* and *The Cenci* are lesser works.

In the story of the Cenci, Shelley found a model of tyranny, injustice and pernicious priestcraft that also provided a fitting vehicle for incest and algolagnia. Fitting, because all the sadism came from the tyrants or from orthodox religion. The corollary was obvious. Unfortunately, though the picture *was* factual, Shelley does not make it sound so. The verse is often diluted, Shakespeare or, worse, concentrated Monk Lewis: like the larger part of this:

that wretched Beatrice
Men speak of, whom her father sometimes hales
From hall to hall by the entangled hair;
At others, pens up naked in damp cells
Where scaly reptiles crawl, and starves her there
Till she will eat strange flesh. (Act III, 1, 43/8)

Hellas is an improvement. Indeed there is some approach to a tragic vision in the last stanzas, and this is related to the fact that the play springs from a realistic grasp of current events. The first part is mainly concerned with versifying – and very well – the feeling and accurate prose analysis of the Introduction, which anticipates the policy England was in fact forced to adopt in 1827. The remainder, however, is devoted to a mystical statement of Shelley's fully developed metaphysic (the One now having care for 'the meanest'). Such a metaphysical solution to the preceding political problems makes a queer mixture, on which Mahmud's is the appropriate comment:

What meanest thou? thy words stream like a tempest
Of dazzling mist within my brain.

Oedipus Tyrannus or Swellfoot the Tyrant, however, is a unity, though it exists on a different level, bearing much the same relationship to *Hellas* and *The Cenci* as *The Witch of Atlas* bears to *Adonais* and *Epipsychidion*. It is comedy, but as concrete as that was gossamer. Its subject, the gouty king's attempted divorce, keeps the metaphysician at bay. Thus anchored to earth, the proper place for attacks on society, the poetry gains immensely in solidity and impact.

The poems of 1819, the year in which Peterloo and the Six Acts directed Shelley's attention to the need for immediate, practical reform, bear this out. *The Masque of Anarchy* is his one completely successful serious work of any length, and *Peter Bell the Third* his one completely successful comic one.

The latter is, indeed, a test case. Ostensibly about Wordsworth and his poetry, it offers ample scope for metaphysics. But it is about the later Wordsworth, when

> His eyes turned up, his mouth turned down;
>   His accent caught a nasal twang;
> He oiled his hair; there might be heard
> The grace of God in every word. (I, II)

and that inevitably caused the poem to gravitate to the only possible subject for the times, the condition of England. *Peter Bell the Third* becomes, in fact, a gayer *Masque*.

The outward sign of its inward grace is the ease with which throughout 153 stanzas it deals with fantasy and fact, with the early admired and later detested Wordsworth, with Grasmere and London, without ever getting out of key. Its literary criticism of Wordsworth and Coleridge is beyond praise, but its real subject is contemporary England:

> Hell is a city much like London....

> There is a Castles, and a Canning,
>   A Cobbett and a Castlereagh;
> All sorts of caitiff corpses planning
> All sorts of cozening, for trepanning
>   Corpses less corrupt than they....

> There is a Chancery Court, a king;
>   A manufacturing mob, a set
> Of thieves who by themselves are sent
> Similar thieves to represent;
>   An army and a public debt....
>
> There is great talk of revolution,
>   And great chance of despotism,
> German soldiers–camps–confusion–
> Tumults–lotteries–rage–delusion–
>   Gin–suicide–and Methodism. (III, I/VI)

From the one bodily and two spiritual escapes from the current situation, the poem goes on to taxes, jobbery, profiteering, and that contemporary morality–for which Byron too had such contempt–which makes 'all that is divine in women Grow cruel, courteous, smooth, inhuman,/Crucified 'twixt a smile and whimper'. Nor is this simply negative satire. Behind the picture of what is, loom the Godwinian positives for the future: passive resistance, forgiveness, and anarchical equality, contrasting with this hell where 'All (*not now only the governors*) are damnable and damned'. Shelley has come to realise–and let the realisation appear in his verse–that the problems of injustice are not simple, since human nature, his own included, is at fault as well as the nature of society. Both aspects of the romantic conflict are associated in poetry of wide range:

> The rich are damned, beyond all care
>   To taunt and starve and trample on
> The weak and wretched; and the poor
> Damn their broken hearts to endure
>   Stripe on stripe with groan on groan;
>
> Sometimes the poor are damned indeed
>   To take,–not means for being blessed–
> But Cobbett's snuff, revenge; that weed
> From which the worms that it doth feed
>   Squeeze less than they before possessed:–

> And some few, like we know who,
>   Damned – but God alone knows why –
> To believe their minds are given
> To make this ugly Hell a Heaven,
>   In which faith they live and die. (IV, xviii/xx)

All this leads, as so often in this poem, to a nodal stanza which gathers up what has gone before in imagery typically Shelleyan but of increased density. Tyranny and selfishness, it is felt, produce Care in tyrant and tyrannised alike. From this it can be deduced that liberalism and selflessness would change present care into future joy. Nature-as-Love which man must harmonise himself with, though it follows laws of Necessity, can be attained by spiritual effort; but if he chooses to be materialistic, subject to the lower deterministic nature, he will be perverted and miserable. Such – or something similar – is the background of ideas, but the stanza itself is profound comedy not because of the validity of these ideas but because the weight of thought and heartsearching acts as ballast, preventing emotional wallowing:

> All are damned – they breathe an air
>   Thick, infected, joy-dispelling;
> Each pursues what seems most fair,
> Mining like moles through mind, and there
> Scoop palace-caverns vast, where Care
>   In thronèd state is ever dwelling. (IV, xxiii)

This is sound psychology. Depth of conflict has led to profundity of implication. Compare the same vision as expressed in a neo-augustan manner by Peacock, who felt no conflict and therefore was wittily shallow:

> This world is a well-furnished table
> Where guests are promiscuously set:
> We all fare as well as we're able
> And scramble for what we can get.

> *(Melincourt)*

The Masque of Anarchy, similarly, is freighted by hard thought, deep feeling, and a sense of purpose. Its street-ballad form and clipped 'unShelleyan' rhythm help in compressing and condensing:

> Next came Fraud, and he had on
> Like Eldon, an ermined gown;
> His big tears, for he wept well,
> Turned to millstones as they fell;
> And the little children who
> Round his feet played to and fro
> Thinking every tear a gem
> Had their brains knocked out by them. (IV/V)

With the abstractions Fraud, Murder and Anarchy tellingly embodied in figures of contemporary reality, it is not difficult to accept the millenial stanzas on Hope (XXII–XXXIII). The remainder of the poem justifies that acceptance, for Shelley completes the subjective vision by an objective picture.

The aspects under which Is and Might Be are seen are respectively those of Slavery (XXXIX–LI) and Freedom (LIII–LXI), and in both idealistic feeling is combined with hard thought. Thus Freedom is not a vague aspiration, a sense of longing, but for the labourer Bread

> And a comely table spread,
> From his daily labour come,
> To a neat and happy home.
>
> Thou art clothes and fire and food
> For the trampled multitude. . . .
>
> To the rich thou art a check
> When his foot is on the neck
> Of his victim; thou dost make
> That he treads upon a snake.
>
> Thou art Justice–ne'er for gold
> May thy righteous laws be sold
> As laws are in England:–thou
> Shield'st alike the high and low. . . .
>
> Thou art Peace–never by thee
> Would blood and treasure wasted be
> As tyrants wasted them, when all
> Leagued to quench thy flame in Gaul.

Shelley has obviously travelled far from the rhetorical idealism and misty verse of *Queen Mab*. But the difference in quality is not due to any fundamental change in his beliefs. The *Masque* is not a better poem because his metaphysic is more unified, but because the conflicts that were shaped by society have been resolved and fused there.

This is not so true of *The Triumph of Life*, which deals primarily with the imperfections of the individual, the follies of the body and the uncontrolled ego which defeat the spirit. Consequently it is more obscure than the *Masque*, though it shares its technical firmness and unflinching gaze:

> And much I grieved to think how power and will
> In opposition rule our mortal clay,
>
> And why God made irreconcilable
> Good and the means of good. ...

In adumbrating a need to recapture the unity of body and spirit possessed in childhood, it remains well aware that the heart hardens, the pleasures of sense fade, and the will falters, so that one is likely to be left with a life neither of the body nor the spirit but only with the 'death' of experience. A feeling given memorable expression in a tensely sculpted stanza:

> The marble brow of youth was cleft
> With Care; and in those eyes where once hope shone
> Desire, like a lioness bereft
> Of her last cub, glared ere it died. (523/6)

Yet for all its merits, the poem is not quite a satisfactory work of art. Nor is this simply because it is unfinished. The broken line which concludes it is, in fact, as good an ending as it could have had: 'Then, what is life?' (After all, such metaphysical questions have no answer.) When society was his subject he could be sure. Here, where it was not, all his new-found technical firmness could not prevent a wavering, an occasional blurring of the thematic line.

VI

BYRON

This should have been a noble creature: he
Hath all the energy which would have made
A goodly frame of glorious elements,
Had they been wisely mingled; as it is
It is an awful chaos—Light and Darkness,
And mind and dust, and passions and pure thoughts
Mix'd, and contending without end or order.

(Act III, Sc. 1, 160/6)

So wrote Byron, with considerable insight, of his *alter ego*, Manfred, who may be taken as the type figure of his middle period. The contrast of 'passions and pure thoughts', however, is typical rather of his first, and most personal, period.

In no poet is conflict more obvious than in Byron. He loved Liberty and died for it in Greece, yet despised the common people; he hated England, yet resented exile; he was a Romantic who attacked his kind and praised Pope; he hated war-mongering, but was obviously attracted to war; he was a libertine, yet longed for a settled life as an English peer, reconciled with his wife; he was a sceptic who rebelled even against his own beliefs and yet believed in his rebellion. One feels that he had a *need* to feel remorse—to prove his guilt in order to be forgiven. Robson states the case admirably:

Whatever view we take of Byron's own character, there can be no doubt that much of the cult of Byron, in his own time and later, was merely the gratification, in fantasy, of numerous petty egotisms; the magnifying to heroic proportions of one's own easy angers, tears, and surrenders; the indulgence of *saeva indignatio*; and that sense of injured merit which provides so many occasions for the release of a vindicated self-pity. Which of us cannot see himself as the hero-victim of that *besoin de fatalité* which M. du Bos declares to be the dominant force in Byron's life? And who does not also see, in his more veracious moments, that this vision is but an illusory enlargement of his own pettiness? But to see that constantly; and yet to be unable to resist the recurrent temptation thus to indulge oneself; and to have also the power to give truly classical expression to both sides of that state of mind and soul–this is Byron's own case, . . . and it is a very unusual one.

(Byron as Poet, (1957), pp. 29/30)

In Byron's case, the personal factors of his ancestry, his maternal upbringing in a Calvinist society and his lameness, may well largely account for such a need and for the conflict behind it. Certainly it might be said, as a generalisation, that where Shelley starts from the faults of society, Byron starts from those of the individual. Shelley is the poet of the suffering reformer, Byron of the suffering ego (and Keats, from the start more objective, of the sorrow of life in general). But like all generalisations this would not be entirely true. In his last period, indeed, it would cover only a small part of the truth, for Byron's development is a clear illustration of the effect of 'period', since it takes the form of a movement from the personal to the social and political. As his conflicts are projected and impersonalised, his poetry acquires unity and force. When the impulse from without is insufficient he easily degenerates into fustian: his energy and passion lack the control given by *direction*.

What chiefly give direction are a hatred of Britain[1] and its Cant, and a more generalised hatred of Tyranny. Whether these in fact spring from principle or merely an emotional reaction to personal circumstances is hardly relevant, and, in any case, probably impossible to determine, for the threads are inextricably tangled. Thus, to take one instance, Byron's attraction to foreign women seems to be partly a reaction against all things English, partly the result of his marriage, and partly the prudery and hypocrisy of English morals (which are connected with the marriage system, and indirectly with the whole detested structure of society). What *is* relevant is that his themes become increasingly 'outward', his conflicts resolved in satire.

---

[1] Witness, for instance, the legacy for Allegra–on condition that she did not marry an Englishman, or this letter, typical of many, 'I defy all of you, and your climate to boot to make me mad. But if I ever do really become a Bedlamite, and wear a strait-waistcoat, let me be brought back among you; your people will then be proper company' (August 24th, 1819, *Byron, A Self-Portrait* (1950), ed. Quennell, vol. II, p. 485).

It is highly significant that Byron's last, and best, period coincides with his positive action in Italy and Greece. The pre-romantics owe their indecision to the fact that their dissatisfaction with late augustan society had not vent or direction. To a lesser extent this seems to apply to the romantics. Though their reaction against society does give an outlet to their romanticism, it is none the less cranky, limited or distorted while they remain imprisoned in egotism. In Byron's case, the complaints and vagaries of the early letters make a startling contrast to the practical energy of the later. Committed, Byron is happier and more competent. Witness, for instance, his Diary for January and February 1821, or his letter on street fighting:

I advised them (*i.e. the Italian patriots*) to attack in detail, and in different parties, in different *places* (though at the *same* time), so as to divide the attention of the troops, who though few, yet being discip-lined, would beat any body of people (not trained) in a regular fight –unless dispersed in small parties, and distracted with different assaults. Offered to let them assemble here if they choose. It is a strongish post–narrow street, commanded from within, and tenable walls.

(Jan. 8th, 1821, *Byron, A Self-Portrait* (1950), ed. Quennell vol. II, p. 557)

Byron saw realistically enough the probable outcome, but was prepared for sacrifices:

They mean to *insurrect* here, and are to honour me with a call thereupon–I shall not fall back; though I don't think them in force or heart sufficient to make much of it. But *onward*!–It is now time to act, and what signifies *self*, if a single spark of that which would be worthy of the past can be bequeathed unquenchedly to the future? It is not one man, nor a million, but the *spirit* of liberty which must be spread.

(Jan. 9th, 1821, Quennell, vol. II, p. 560)

This vigour seems reasonable evidence that the apathy and ennui constantly referred to elsewhere were not innate in Byron's nature, but due to frustration and dissatisfaction with the world around him. Hence, the need for rhetorical passion, as a release, when his attention was not directed outward to the field of action. Hence, too, the greater objectivity and high spirits of his poetry, after 1820–'Difficulties are the hotbeds of high spirits, and

Freedom the mother of the few virtues incident to human nature'
(Quennell, vol. II, p. 558).

The following schematic outline of Byron's poetic development may serve as a useful framework for more detailed analysis:

In the *First period* (c. 1807-15) Byron is more concerned with
himself than with society, but he has not found himself. The
conflicts are there, unrealised, making poems with little in
common and written in imitative styles, sub-augustan or picturesque. Fundamentally any criticism of society is *self*-justifying.
(The 'street-ballad' poem 'O well done, Lord Eldon!' is, however, an exception).

In the *Middle Period* (c. 1815-18) the conflicts are recognised
to have at least this in common: that they belong to the same
person. That implies a common core, and the verse no longer
needs to be imitative. It is now a medium for penetrating to the
heart of his own personality. Meanwhile the diverging halves
of the conflicts produce tension and thought; and with thought
comes a scepticism about any possible solution of conflict in the
individual so long as there is cant and oppression in society. Thus
Byron moves into the last period, when he projects his contradictions back on to society and there attacks them. Fantasy is subject
to fact, and the poetry assimilates the real earthly world.

In the *Last period* (c. 1818-24), then, the core is found in an
inner fire of antagonism to society, the cause of personal conflict.
All paths have led to satire, and Byron's thwarted warrior instincts
have full play.

To put it another way: in the *first* period, Byron's heroes are
in retreat, defeated by their conflicts, and assuming the false
personality of borrowed styles in lieu of self-knowledge. In the
second period, they are on the defensive. Self-knowledge leads to
nihilism, and the poetry becomes ambivalent–against and for the
same things, since Byron has no positives. In the *third* period, they
are attacking, and the verse–formerly a two-edged weapon of
weakness–has now a single cutting edge. Rhythm is no longer
sacrificed to arithmetic as in the first, metrical, period, the
dramatic does not become theatrical, and the sentiment is never
sentimental.

In the first period, then, there is a general division of style, into sub-augustan and pre-romantic, but this is by no means the only sign of disunity. For instance, Byron, though misanthropic in *Hours of Idleness*, is not consistently so. Diatribe against mankind is contradicted by deep friendship for men (as in *Epitaph for a Friend* or *The Cornelian*). Again the conflicts tend to be compartmented. *Gloom* (the 'pre-romantic' form of the later *Bitterness*) will predominate in an Ossianic or Gothic poem, while *Humour* is self-contained elsewhere. Thus, *On Leaving Newstead Abbey* is a Gothic poem prefaced by a quotation from Ossian and containing some Ossianic cadences, whereas the *Epitaph on John Adams of Southwell* (A Carrier, who Died of Drunkenness) has no trace of the gloom one might expect to be attendant on the theme of mortality. It is plain English fun:

> John Adams lies here, of the parish of Southwell
> A *Carrier* who *carried* his can to his mouth well;
> He *carried* so much, and he *carried* so fast
> He could *carry* no more–so was *carried* at last;
> For the liquor he drank, being too much for one,
> He could not *carry* off–so he's now carri-on
>
> (*Occasional Pieces*)

The seeds of his gift for satire are evident in this period (1807–15) in such poems as the sub-augustan *To Woman*, and there is some powerful writing in *English Bards and Scotch Reviewers*, despite its unaugustan prolixity. It contains the devastating couplet on Wordsworth (which anticipates the battering of the renegade Lake poets in *Don Juan*), and also Byron's first attack on social injustice:

> The midnight orgy and the mazy dance,
> The smile of beauty, and the flush of wine,
> For fops, fools, gamesters, knaves, and lords combine;
> Each to humour–Comus all allows;
> Champagne, dice, music–or your neighbour's spouse.
> Talk not to us, ye starving sons of trade!
> Of piteous ruin which ourselves have made
> In Plenty's sunshine Fortune's minions bask
> Nor think of poverty, except 'en masque'. (647/55)

Here at least is part of the explanation of Byron's self-disgust and guilt of this period, for not only was he himself addicted to the midnight orgy-and for that matter his neighbour's spouse-but also he had a considerable tincture of aristocratic hauteur, as the letters reveal:

> ... and then, if I can't persuade some wealthy dowdy to ennoble the dirty puddle of her mercantile blood-why-I should leave England and all its clouds for the East again.
>
> (To Augusta Leigh, Aug. 30th, 1811. Quennell, vol. I, p. 111)

> As for Democracy, it is the worst of the whole; for what (in fact) is democracy? An Aristocracy of Blackguards.[1]
>
> (May 1st, 1821. vol. II, p. 605)

The main rebellion of this period is against what Byron feels to be the dominant form of poetry, Romanticism. But it is significant that what he actually attacks (*v. To A Lady* or *To Romance*) is *pre*-romanticism of Sensibility and Melancholy. Here is an interesting example both of the influence of period and of Byron's lack of direction. Thinking himself a neo-classic poet attacking romanticism, he is actually a romantic attacking precisely the pre-romanticism he himself indulged in (and without realising the conflict).

In all these early lyrics there is the personal element of romanticism, but it is all too personal. Thus the Restraint/Liberty conflict in the *Epistle to a Friend* is a sheer egotism of stern self-pity:

> But if, in some succeeding year
> When Britain's 'May is in the sere'
> Thou hear'st of one whose deepening crimes
> Suit with the sablest of the times,
> Of one, whom love nor pity sways,
> Nor hope of fame, nor good men's praise,
> One, who in stern ambition's pride
> Perchance not blood shall turn aside,

---

[1]Against this must be set his realisation that people are much affected by their circumstances, and his desire for equality: 'The greater the equality, the more impartially evil is distributed, and becomes lighter by the division among so many - therefore, a Republic!' (Feb. 18th, 1814, Quennell, vol. I, p. 245).

> One rank'd in some recording page
> With the worst anarchs of the age,
> Him wilt thou *know* and *knowing* pause,
> Nor with the *effect* forget the cause.

A clear modelling of the spoilt-child hero-villain of the middle period; the falsity at the heart showing clearly in the literary echoes (of *Hamlet* and *Macbeth*), in the movement, and in the puff pastry of the language: there is nothing to bite on.

Robson well states the predicament:

There is today a prejudice against poetry which expresses only vague emotion; but it should be noted that in Byron's verse, while the emotion may be vague, the statement of it is explicit. And here of course is the unsatisfactoriness of this kind of poetry. Byronism is better expressed in music; there is something about words which is alien to it, their obstinate tendency to particularize. The Byronic mood at its most intense consists of desire and sadness in their simplest, their most general character; to specify what the sadness is about, or what object could satisfy the desire, can only dissipate the mood by recalling those very particulars which it was its consolation to transcend. (p. 32)

Certain of the later short poems, however–particularly *She walks in Beauty like the Night* (1815) and *So We'll Go no more A-Roving* (1817)–as Byron acquires greater self-knowledge, are effectively moving.

It is at this time (strictly, in the middle period) that Byron is moving away from the superficial egotism of *Childe Harold* I and II to more objective embodiment in cantos 3 and 4;

> 'Tis to create, and in creating live
> A being more intense, that we endow
> With form our fancy, gaining as we give
> The life we image, even as I do now.
> What am I? Nothing: but not so art thou
> Soul of my thought!
>
> (Canto 3, VI)

Here, in a nutshell, is the kernel of the achievement of the middle period. The genuine concern with realised conflicts, which leads to the discovery that the great egotist is 'Nothing', paradoxically leads also to poetry that bears the stylistic mark of genuine personality. By being concerned more with the conflicts than himself, Byron makes something, 'a being more intense', from his nothingness. That concern – histrionic though it may be – *is* itself his personality – the personality that, in the last period, attacks, from the paradoxical positive of rebellion.

But *Childe Harold* I and II shares the characteristics of the *Giaour*, the *Bride of Abydos*, the *Corsair*, and *Lara*. The narrative technique is often excellent, but the heroes are of the type drawn in the *Epistle to a Friend:* inherently noble natures thwarted by society, thereby becoming hero-villains, subject to guilt and angry pride; and the style is melodramatic. In Conrad, for instance, is painted, with some admiration, a vulgar desire for leadership and a comforting aristocratic philosophy:

> That man of loneliness and mystery
> Scarce seen to smile and seldom heard to sigh;
> Whose name appals the fiercest of his crew,
> And tints each swarthy cheek with sallower hue;
> Still sways their souls with that commanding art
> That dazzles, leads, yet chills the vulgar heart.
> What is that spell that thus his lawless train
> Confess and envy – yet oppose in vain? . . .
> Such hath it been – shall be – beneath the Sun
> The many still must labour for the one!
> 'Tis Nature's doom – but let the wretch who toils
> Accuse not, hate not *him* who wears the spoils.
> Oh! if he knew the weight of splendid chains
> How light the balance of his humbler pains! . . .
> There was a laughing Devil in his sneer,
> That rais'd emotions both of rage and fear,
> And where his frown of hatred darkly fell
> Hope withering fled, and Mercy sigh'd farewell . . .
>
> > (*The Corsair*, I, 173/226)

None the less, Conrad is not to be condemned – though the poet who wrought him in lines so pedestrian may be – he is a good man scoured by society:

> His heart was form'd for softness – warp'd to wrong
> Betray'd too early and beguil'd too long;

> Each feeling pure–as falls the dropping dew
> Within the grot–like that had hardened too.
>
> (III, 1820/33)

The really appalling thing is that the core of *fact* wrapped up in this tinselly language does convey a truth about such delinquents. The wrapping is further evidence that Byron in this period wished to disguise the truth, to be self-justifying.

The 1813 *Addition to the Preface* of *Childe Harold* sets the tone, of half-repressed and half-believed excuse:

> It had been easy to varnish over his faults, to make him do more and express less, but he never was intended as an example, further than to show, that early perversion of mind and morals leads to satiety of past pleasures and disappointment in new ones, and that even the beauties of Nature and the stimulus of travel . . . are lost on a soul so constituted, or rather misdirected.

And, indeed, the whole of the first two Cantos is kept to the surface, the conflicts are there but never explored, the sense of guilt evaded by a mock acceptance of sin (*v.* Canto 1, v). Throughout, the emphasis falls on satiety, and gloom. The sense of Time and Death does, however, give rise to an occasionally more impressive, if equally rhetorical, stanza, such as that on the skull:

> Look on its broken arch, its ruined wall
> Its chambers desolate and portals foul:
> Yes, this was once Ambition's airy hall,
> The dome of Thought, the palace of the Soul:
> Behold, through each lack-lustre eyeless hole,
> The gay recess of Wisdom and of Wit,
> And Passion's host, that never brook'd control;
> Can all that Sage or Sophist ever writ
> People this lonely tower, this tenement refit? (2, VI)

This is the actual in which all ideals end. Here is a first hint of an ability to place personal experience instead of merely exhibiting it.

Similarly Byron is better when an admixture of humour with his gloom forces him to satire, for satire necessarily stands at some little distance from the raw emotion. On the whole, however, none of the major conflicts is resolved–they are only played with–in these first two cantos. Love is offered as a solution, but love's union of body and spirit is defeated by satiety or inherent human fickleness. Death, of course, may give Liberty in place of Restraint–or it may be just a full stop. There is Nature, but Nature may be not only a comfort but an avenger, or it may be a bloodstream of which one's own corrupt nature is a globule. Finally, there is Pleasure–a solution rejected as soon as proffered:

> Then must I plunge again into the crowd
> And follow all that Peace disdains to seek? (2, xcvii)

The same qualities are evident in the remaining poems, which display similar weakness, despite one or two neat touches, such as the Romantic paradoxes of the *Giaour*, e.g.

> Faithless to him, he gave the blow,
> But true to me, I laid him low:
> Howe'er deserved her doom might be
> Her treachery was truth to me.

These look forward not only to the moral relativity of Cain but to the cleverness of *Don Juan*–whose brilliance, it must be said, cannot disguise the fact that it marks the first slight movement away from wit of intellect towards the later nineteenth-century wit of words, that empire on which the pun has not yet set.

In *Lara*, however, occur brief glimpses of reality, in unreal rhetoric: glimpses to be developed into magnificent verse in the *Age of Bronze* (1823), where rhetoric is associated with a public theme rather than personal posing. Between the two, however, come the poems and dramas of the middle period (1815–17) and the last two cantos of *Childe Harold*.

In this period, Byron's exploration–which seeks a central self where conflict may be resolvable–leads in fact to nihilism and disillusion. But the note of rhetoric and the element of pose are rarer, for the poet is no longer over-compensating a secret doubt. Disillusion is the fulfilment of doubt. Nihilism, moreover, is at least a basis for satire; therefore the hero-villain, blaming society for the discrepancy between what he seemed and what he actually was, gradually turns (probably with some assistance from Shelley), into the satirist attacking the same discrepancy in society. The satiric Byron of the last period is a disillusioned idealist, whose disillusion has made manifest a formerly latent social sense.

In this middle period there is a clearly defined 'social' path leading towards the satire of the *Age of Bronze*. Four poems are directly concerned with tyranny. The *Ode to Venice* deals with decay due to oppression–and in typically Romantic fashion turns to America, since the French Revolution has failed. *Tasso*, in effect, is a lament for captive Ferrara, the *Prophecy of Dante* (1819), for captive Ravenna, and the *Prisoner of Chillon* deals directly with the theme of Liberty/Oppression. When the theme is put thus, socially rather than personally, Byron is not divided. Consequently, since he has not yet come to fuse the personal and social, conflict plays comparatively little part. They are straight-forward indictments in narrative: telling, but without that controlled complexity and intensity necessary for poetic greatness.

The *Prophecy of Dante* (which perhaps should be in the last period) is the most interesting. Dante, as an exile, can be seen as a romantic outcast, and thus the theme of Italy's suffering can be taken at once on the personal plane (Restraint/Liberty), and the impersonal plane of a struggle between Social Oppression and Freedom.

Canto 3 gives a remarkably full picture of the romantic poet and his inspiration in the Shelleyan contrast of *Is* and *Should be* (together with echoes of Gray and Shakespeare). Moreover, it explicitly points the newly perceived relationship, for Byron, of this social conflict with the personal conflict of *Ideals*/'*Vulture Passions*':

> Must all the finer thoughts, the thrilling sense
> The electric blood with which their arteries run,
> Their body's self turned soul with the intense
> Feeling of that which *is*, and fancy of
> That which *should be*, to such a recompense
> Conduct? Shall their bright plumage on the rough
> Storm still be scattered? Yes, and it must be,

For, form'd of far too penetrable stuff,[1]
These birds of Paradise but long to flee
Back to their native mansion, soon they find
Earth's mist with their pure pinions not agree,
And die, or are degraded, for the mind
Succumbs to long infection, and despair
And vulture Passions flying close behind
Await the moment and assail and tear:
And when at length the winged wanderers stoop
Then is the Prey-birds' triumph, then they share
The spoil, o'erpowered at length by one fell swoop.
Yet some have been untouched who learnt to bear,
Some whom no Power could ever force to droop,
Who could resist themselves even, hardest care!
And task most hopeless; but some such have been.

(3, 161/82)

This may be taken as a key passage on the nature of romanticism.
The same relationship of internal and external conflict is evident-
as also is the problem of death (common to Shelley and Keats
as well as Byron)-in the next Canto where the theme is again
taken up in a Shelleyan image:

For what is Poesy but to create
From overfeeling, Good or Ill, and aim
At an external life beyond our fate,
And be the new Prometheus of new man,
Bestowing fire from heaven, and then, too late,
Finding the pleasure given repaid with pain...? (4, 11/16)

Let these highly significant extracts be linked with the conclusion
of the poem and there is a complete statement of the Romantic
position:

The age which I anticipate, no less
Shall be the Age of Beauty . . .
Sovereigns shall pause amidst the sport of war
Weaned for an hour from blood, to turn and gaze

[1]Is it too fanciful to see here, in the echo of *Hamlet* (III, 4, 36), a curious
connection with the romantic preoccupation with the tortured heart? (In
Hamlet's 'And let me wring your heart; for so I shall if it be made of penetrable
stuff'.)

On canvas or on stone; and they who mar
All beauty upon earth, compell'd to praise,
Shall feel the power of that which they destroy . . .
Oh, Power that rulest and inspirest! how
Is it that they on earth, whose earthly power
Is likest thine in heaven in outward show,
Least like to thee in attributes divine,
Tread on the universal necks that bow,
And then assure us that their rights are thine?
And how is it that they, the sons of Fame . . .
Must pass their days in penury or pain . . .
(Or) In their own souls sustain a harder proof
The inner war of Passions deep and fierce? (471/110)

Here is the hatred of contemporary oppression, cant and industrial ugliness which engenders the romantic contraries of Freedom, Truth, Beauty and Nature. Here, too, is the torment of conflict: the 'inner war' due not only to the difficulty and complexity of the task of realising the Good, but also to the ostracism resulting from a pursuit of it–enough to make a man ironic; and ironic Byron duly becomes, for this 'social' path leads to the *Vision of Judgment* and the *Age of Bronze*.

The other, 'personal', path to the last period leads through the *Siege of Corinth*, *Parisina* and cantos 3 and 4 of *Childe Harold* to *Beppo*. A branch of this track of personal exploration is *Manfred*, which links *Lara* and the *Corsair* to *Cain*. All have this in common: that they deal with 'The inner war of passions fierce and deep'. Little need be said of the first two poems. The *Siege* gives a new type of Fatal Woman, a *good* woman, and *Parisina* adds a new moral complexity, which is reflected in the oxymorons of the verse. (Witness the opening where the latent personifications of Nature serve to link Parisina and her love with the Natural, while the heaven's 'Clear obscure so softly dark and darkly pure' links Nature with the poem's moral: that the right is not always a clear and simple matter.)

But *Manfred* is more typical of the period. All the romantic characteristics are there, from perversion ('The deadliest sin to love as we have lov'd', Act II) to communion with infernal powers. Like the hero of *Alastor*, Manfred is driven to seek a solution in nature:

> My joys, my griefs, my passions, and my powers
> Made me a stranger . . .
> and with the thoughts of men
> I held but slight communion; but instead
> My joy was in the wilderness, to breathe
> The difficult air of iced mountain's top . . .
> and with time and toil,
> And terrible ordeal, and such penance
> As in itself hath power upon the air . . .
> I made
> Mine eyes familiar with Eternity
>
> (Act II, Sc. 2, 55/80)

But conflict is now faced squarely and found unresolvable—though the work is still self-dramatising rather than dramatic. Passions and Ideals are alike renounced:

> I have had those earthly visions
> And noble aspirations in my youth,
> To make my own the mind of other men,
> The enlightener of nations; and to rise
> I knew not whither—it might be to fall;
> But fall even as the mountain-cataract . . .
> But this is past,
> My thoughts mistook themselves
>
> (Act III, Sc. 1, 104/115)

(The disillusioned idealist of the satires is obviously latent here.) Similarly egotism and restraint are equally condemned. Restraint leads to puerility and ignorance, egotism to hypocrisy (Seeming/Being conflict) and destruction:

> By thy cold breast and serpent smile,
> By thy unfathom'd gulfs of guile,
> By that most seeming virtuous eye
> By thy shut soul's hypocrisy . . .
> By thy delight in other's pain
> And by *thy brotherhood of Cain,*
> I call upon thee! and compel
> Thyself to be thy proper hell   (Act I, Sc. 1, 242/51)

Only one solution offers itself, 'Oblivion, self-oblivion'. This nihilism, which knows:

> That knowledge is not happiness, and science
> But an exchange of ignorance for that
> Which is another kind of ignorance
>
> (Act II, Sc. 4, 61/3)

is preparing the way not only for *Cain* but for the *Vision of Judgment*. Indeed, there is social satire in Act III (Sc. 3)–though this is admittedly not very good, perhaps because it occurs in a personal poem; that is, in a poem dealing rather with Byron than the world.

The last and best canto of *Childe Harold* brings him finally to the grim detachment necessary for negative satire. The core, the central personality so long sought, may not be what was hoped but it is stable: the rock bottom:

> Existence may be borne, and the deep root
> Of life and sufferance makes its firm abode
> In bare and desolate bosoms. . . . (4, XXI)

Death becomes not an escape but simply an inevitable and not unwelcome end:

> All suffering doth destroy, or is destroy'd,
> Even by the sufferer–and, in each event
> Ends. (XXII)

The verse is now more often sinewy and clear, no longer aiming at a stock, period response (though it still often achieves no more).

The poet's soul *does* fall with the cataract as desiderated in *Manfred*, with

> The Hell of Waters! where they howl and hiss,
> And boil in endless torture; while the sweat
> Of their great agony, wrung out from this
> Their Phlegethon, curls round the rocks of jet
> That gird the gulf around, in pitiless horror set. (LXIX)
>
> And mounts in spray the skies, and thence again
> Returns in an unceasing shower, which round,
> With its unemptied cloud of gentle rain,
> Is an eternal April to the ground
> Making it all one emerald. (LXX)

A fine objective correlative for the peace at the heart of strife. Similarly, ruined Rome, 'An empty urn within her withered hands', objectifies the Body/Spirit conflict: it ends in emptiness.

On this core of realism, Byron is able to base himself. He becomes increasingly sceptical of the romantic consolations–Love, Nature and God–all being seen to be in fact projections of the self–where only is peace to be found, if at all:

> O Love! no habitant of earth thou art–
> An unseen seraph, we believe in thee,–
> A faith whose martyrs are the broken heart,–
> But never yet hath seen, nor e'er shall see
> The naked eye, thy form, as it should be;
> The mind hath made thee, as it peopled Heaven,
> Even with its own despairing phantasy.... (CXXI)

> Of its own beauty is the mind diseased
> And fevers into false creation: where
> Where are the forms the sculptor's soul hath seiz'd?
> In him alone. Can Nature show so fair? (CXXII)

> Nor Worth nor Beauty dwells from out the mind's
> Ideal shape of such (CXXIII)

This realisation that the actual and the ideal are both in man significantly leads to near-satire, for though men make their own values they are to a large extent moulded by the society that others' values have made, and thus have small hope of being better till it is changed:

> And thus they plod in sluggish misery
> Rotting from sire to son, and age to age,
> Proud of their trampled nature, and so die,
> Bequeathing their hereditary rage
> To the new race of inborn slaves, who wage
> War for their chains. (XCIV)

The logical consequence is, however, immediately tested: 'Can tyrants but by tyrants conquer'd be?' Moreover, the complementary fact that mankind gets the kind of society its nature deserves is also seen and applied (XCVII). France got 'drunk with blood' and by the innate folly of human nature fell into the

hands of 'vile Ambition'; and that failure has been made 'the
pretext for the eternal thrall which nips life's tree, and dooms
man's worst–his second fall'.

Yet the conclusion is not now ostentatious withdrawal, but a
battle-cry:

> Yet Freedom! yet thy banner, torn but flying
> Streams like the thunder-storm *against* the wind;
> Thy trumpet voice, though broken now and dying,
> The loudest still the Tempest leaves behind;
> Thy tree hath lost its blossoms, and the rind
> Chopp'd by the axe, looks rough and little worth,
> But the sap lasts–and still the seed we find
> Sown deep, even in the bosom of the North;
> So shall a better spring less bitter fruit bring forth.
>
> (xcviii)

Beneath the disillusion and despair is a hope, the firmer for them,
finding typically romantic expression in the symbol of seasonal
rebirth. Add Reason to the complex of Feeling just examined
and the satiric armoury is complete. This is precisely the weapon
Byron turns to. 'Our life is a false nature. . . .''

> Yet let us ponder boldly–'tis a base
> Abandonment of reason to resign
> Our right of thought–our last and only place
> Of refuge; this, at least, shall still be mine;
> Though from our birth the faculty divine
> Is chain'd and tortured–cabin'd, cribbed, confin'd
> And bred in darkness, lest the light should shine
> Too brightly on the unprepared mind,
> The beam pours in, for time and skill will couch the blind
>
> (cxxvii)

Byron's most important works all appear in his last period:
Beppo, the *Vision of Judgment*, *Don Juan*, the *Age of Bronze* and
Cain. Though the last two are perhaps nearer to the rhetorical
vein of *Childe Harold* and *Manfred* than to the colloquial satire
typical of this period, they are fully of their period in that the
rhetoric is directed 'outward' and approximates more nearly in
its rhythms to natural speech–though speech rather *to* than *in a*

gathering. Still, they too show the 'signs' mentioned by Robson in connection with the three comic works:

> There is an incidental comparison and contrast here between Byron's development and that of Shelley and Keats. In their later work, in *The Triumph of Life* and the revised *Hyperion*, there are signs, interesting to the few who are interested in literary criticism, that the acceptance of a stricter criterion of reality is associated with a need for greater technical control in the versification. (p. 47)

Personal conflicts are resolved in attack on the world of man (*Age of Bronze*) and God (*Cain*), and the hypocritical Church-State oppressors are beset on both sides.[1]

Cain is the best of Byron's 'dramas'. Like the others, it is too schematised in structure and its characters are too flat. But its myth-form has five useful results:

Firstly, it enables the conflicts to be objectified. Secondly, it limits them, not only to a few persons, but also to a small, new, and therefore uncomplicated world where their moral implications can be seen in essence and the sense of guilt and frustration arising from them be judicially weighed. Thirdly, the cosmic resolution of conflicts by the acceptance of complete moral relativity gives excellent opportunity for dramatic irony. Fourthly, the cosmic myth gives universal types of conflict in God and Lucifer, which can be easily and safely applied to the present (Tyrant/Rebel). Fifthly, it allows for the expression of opinions which would have been impossible in any other form. Thus, Byron is in the delicious position of being able to defend incest, show it as ordained by God, use the question of its sinfulness to condemn the Church by implication, and modulate into a disguised praise of rebel virtue and a statement of the relativity of moral judgements:

[1] The unity of the two worlds in Byron's mind is clearly seen, e.g. in the *Age of Bronze*, VIII, 'But lo! a Congress!'

> Who now assemble at the holy call?
> The blest alliance, which says three are all!
> An earthly trinity! which wears the shape
> Of heaven's, as a man is mimick'd by the ape
> A pious unity! in purpose one –
> To melt three fools to a Napoleon!

Adah: What!
        Must not my daughter love her brother Enoch?
Lucifer: Not as thou lovest Cain.
Adah: Oh my God!
        Shall they not love and bring forth things that love
        Out of their love? have they not drawn their milk
        Out of this bosom? was not he, their father,
        Born of the same sole womb, in the same hour
        With me? did we not love each other? and
        In multiplying our being multiply
        Things which will love each other as we love
        Them?–and as I love thee, my Cain!...
Lucifer: The sin I speak of is not of my making
        And cannot be a sin in you–whate'er
        It seem in those who will replace ye in
        Mortality.
Adah: What is the sin which is not
        Sin in itself? Can circumstance make sin
        Of virtue?–If it doth we are the slaves
        Of–
Lucifer: Higher things than ye are slaves: and higher
        Than them or ye would be so, did they not
        Prefer an independency of torture
        To the smooth agonies of adulation,
        In hymns and harpings and selfseeking prayers,
        To that which is omnipotent, because
        It is omnipotent, and not from love
        But terror and self-hope.   (Act I, Sc. 1, 365/389)

With this realisation of the relativity of accepted morality, comes a bitter questioning of all the props of Religion and Rule. In the same scene there is an attack on God, which implicitly repudiates egotism and the escape to solitude (for they lead to ennui and the creation of evil–*v*. the passage beginning

            'He is great–
      But in his greatness is no happier than
      We in our conflict...' 1446

The magnificent rhetorical satire of the *Age of Bronze*, then, is not unexpected. Nor is it surprising to find Byron's most often expressed conflicts fused for the first time. For example, that of

Society and the Ego is fused in the person of Napoleon, to whom Byron returns again and again as if obsessed. That of Gloom and Humour is merged in the bitter political satire. That of the Passions and Ideals in the satire on those members of the great British public (subjects of the magnificent bravura passage-**xiv**-on rent) who have neither:

> For what were all those country patriots born?
> To hunt – and vote – and raise the price of corn? (572/3)

That of Restraint and Liberty is resolved in satire on the tame society that sets over itself the petty tyranny of profiteers and swindlers, or the greater tyranny of kings, and in satire on the kings themselves whose freedom is seen to be a jest. And what makes it a jest? Partly human nature, and partly Time and Death, now seen not as panaceas for the tormented ego but simply as those facts which set all things in impersonal perspective:

> We – we have seen the intellectual race
> Of giants stand, like Titans, face to face....
> But where are they – the rivals! – a few feet
> Of sullen earth divide each winding sheet....
> How vain, how worse than vain, at length, appear
> The madman's wish, the Macedonian's tear!
> He wept for worlds to conquer – half the earth
> Knows not his fame, or but his death and birth,
> And desolation; while his native Greece
> Hath all of desolation, save its peace. (13/38)

Napoleon is used to show that, if morality is relative, it should be relative to something: namely, its social results – a belief which gives consistency to the immense variety of satiric brilliance in *Don Juan*.

On a lesser plane, as befitting lesser men, the jest of royal freedom can be elaborated in imagery which recalls *Beppo*:

> But where's the monarch? hath he dined? or yet
> Groans beneath Indigestion's heavy debt?
> Have revolutionary patés risen,
> And turned the royal entrails to a prison?
> Have discontented movements stirred the troops?
> Or have *no* movements followed traitorous soups? (502/7)

The same easy style casual, but pointed, is common to *Beppo*, and the more specifically political poems, the *Vision of Judgment* and *Don Juan:* the works of Byron's greatest maturity. Nihilism and hope together lead to irony, irony to objectivity. The ego is curbed by humour, and that restraint gives power with ease. All three works gain immensely from their stanza-form, an ottav rima that relieves Byron from any obligation to bear in mind the practice of Pope.

Byron's defence of Pope, and the elements they share in common, have obscured the difference of emphasis. Byron is the *romantic* satirist. The augustan satirist defends 'Nature', as Reason or Law, against irregularity. He defends the 'natural' morality of a reasonable, civilised order against indecorum and excess. He is, or pretends to be normal, and defends the norm. The romantic satirist is, and is proud of being different. He defends Nature as the spontaneous, as right feeling, and attacks civilised decorum and its props, the Church and Throne, as things of hypocrisy and artifice. The one is for, the other against, the conventional values.

Since his values are the unconventional ones Byron can be irreverent and must not be alarmingly serious. The casual, conversational style, appealing jovially to the fellow-feeling of unpretentious men, is therefore an essential tool. Pope had his audience with him in a straight fight against backsliders, and could afford to hammer home his point straight away in telling couplets. His problem was merely one of economy: to get maximum power in the minimum time. Byron needed to disarm an antagonistic audience before he could undermine its assumptions. His problem was one of salesmanship; so he needed a larger scope than the couplet could give, and a wider range of tone (including a much larger admixture of frivolity, to jolly his readers along till it was time to slip in a punch). Hence, the leisurely, genial fantasy which opens *The Vision of Judgment*, and the bland medium of jesting *bonhomie*, of aristocratic Regency recklessness, which surrounds the barbed shafts of the succeeding satirical stanzas, making palatable not only the contemptuous humour about the King and the humorous contempt for Southey but also various sharp implications about law, politics, war, love and religion. Byron's prolixity, his incapacity for linguistic concentration, for Keatsian density, has now become a necessary virtue. Even his insensitivity to shades of feeling becomes a positive merit.

None of Byron's satire, then, is pure; all of it must contain much play-wit and humour for these technical reasons. But this is especially true of poetry in which conflicts are not projected on to society, from whence, it is felt, they came. This work, non-social but comic, must humoristically evade conflict.

Roughly speaking, it may be said that the first six cantos of *Don Juan* are thus humoristic, the remaining ten satiric; and that *Beppo* and *A Vision of Judgment* are the respective forerunners. The roughness of the division is, of course, plain. The humour of Beppo contains a good deal of satire, the satire of the *Vision* some humour and play-wit. None the less, the general tone of each is strikingly different. For instance, *Beppo's* satire of English sexual morality, as compared with the natural Italian, is not only genial enough, but it imperceptibly passes through an irreverence to the moral and sentimental, which is but distantly related to satire, till it ends in pure humour about the English miss:

> 'Tis true, your budding Miss is very charming,
> But shy and awkward at first coming out,
> So much alarmed that she is quite alarming,
> All Giggle, Blush, half Pertness and half Pout;
> And glancing at *Mamma*, for fear there's harm in
> What you, she, it, or they may be about.
> The Nursery still lisps out in all they utter—
> Besides they always smell of bread and butter. (XXXIX)

Again, much of the humour is that of sheer sound: treble or strained rhyme. Some comes from neat typology:

> He was a lover of the good old school
> Who still become more constant as they cool. (XXIV)

Some comes from ingenious punning:

> Crush'd was Napoleon by the northern Thor,
> Who knocked his army down with icy hammer,

Stopp'd by the *Elements*, like a Whaler, or
A blundering novice in his new French grammar. (LXI)

Little of this is to be found in the *Vision of Judgment*. What humour there is inheres rather in the matter than the manner.

The point is put beyond doubt if one compares the most sustained passage of social satire in *Beppo* (the three ironic stanzas (XLVII–XLIX) beginning 'England! with all thy faults I love thee still') with almost any passage of similar length in the *Vision*. In the former, the tone is tolerant, the irony broad, and mostly on subjects open to all Englishmen, and the touch of acid ('Our little riots just to show we are freemen') is immediately mellowed by the following lines. Not so, with the latter poem. One needs to search for play-wit, and when found it has more often than not political or sociological overtones. The Church-State alliance, for example, is obviously implicit in stanza XXVI where the angels lead in George III:

(for by many stories
And true, we learn the angels are all Tories)

The satire itself, moreover, has a bite absent from *Beppo*. *The Vision of Judgment* is perhaps Byron's most serious poem, its apparent cheerfulness being in fact a desperate gaiety, adopted for personal and technical reasons. George III, 'this old, blind, mad, helpless, weak, poor worm', is merely a pretext for satire on contemporary society as Byron saw it. And so is most of *Don Juan*.

Something of the change of tone in *Don Juan* is to be attributed to the almost unbelievable vituperation which critics poured upon the early Cantos. Byron had every reason for attacking cant.[1] But that can be only one more tributary to the stream of

---

[1] *v.* the letter to Kinnaird, Venice Oct. 26th, 1819. (Quennell, vol. II, p. 491.) 'As to Don Juan, confess, confess—you dog and be candid—that it is the sublime of *that there* sort of writing—it may be profligate but is it not life, is it not *the thing*? Could any man have written it who has not lived in the world?—and fooled in a post-chaise?—in a hackney-coach?—in a gondola?—against a wall?—in a court-carriage?—in a vis-à-vis?—on a table?—and under it? I have written about a 100 stanzas of a 3rd Canto, but it is damned modest—The outcry has frightened me. I have such projects for the Don, but the Cant is so much stronger than the—, nowadays that the benefit of experience in a man who had well weighed the work of both monosyllables must be lost to despairing posterity.'

tendency in Byron which was bearing his genius outwards. While writing the early cantos he was philandering in Venice, while writing the later he was occupied with Italian politics and the fate of the Greek rebellion.

The first cantos, then, follow on in manner from *Beppo*. There is punning and ingenious rhyme, there is the surprise ending, the play-wit about feminine psychology ('A little still she strove, and much repented, And whispering "I will ne'er consent" consented'. 1, CXVII) and the acquirements of the English female are still contrasted with

> that useful sort of knowledge
> Which is acquired in Nature's good old college. (2, CXXXVI)

But even in the early cantos depths beyond *Beppo* are plumbed. The ridiculous rhyme lightly carries weighty implications, and the basic concern with appearance and reality, hypocrisy and self-deception masquerading in high-faluting guises, is already present in the first canto:

> What are the hopes of man? Old Egypt's King
>   Cheops erected the first Pyramid
> And largest, thinking it was just the thing
>   To keep his memory whole and mummy hid;
> But somebody or other rummaging,
>   Burglariously broke his coffin's lid.
> Let not a monument give you or me hopes
> Since not a pinch of dust remains of Cheops. (1, CCXIX)

Feelingly, but unsentimentally, it generalises the more personal reflection of the preceding stanza:

> What is the end of fame? 'tis but to fill
>   A certain portion of uncertain paper:
> Some liken it to climbing up a hill,
>   Whose summit, like all hills, is lost in vapour.
> For this men write, speak, preach, and heroes kill,
>   And bards burn what they call their 'midnight taper',
> To have, when the original is dust,
> A name, a wretched picture and worse bust.

This technique—typical of the whole poem—taken together with the new ability to 'place' the once personal conflicts (against Time, beside Death, or in Society), gives Byron immense range and flexibility. The mockery of woman, for instance, merges naturally into pity for her:

> for man to man so oft unjust,
>> Is always so to women; one sole bond
> Awaits them; treachery is all their trust;
>> Taught to conceal, their bursting hearts despond
> Over their idol, till some wealthier lust
>> Buys them in marriage – and what rests beyond?
> A thankless husband, next a faithless lover,
> Then dressing, nursing, praying, and all's over. (2, CC)

A certain clarity in the language, an absence of the blurred edges of pathos, bears witness to what may be called, for want of a better word, a dispassionate quality in the verse. Yet is not that last line more poignant than anything in Byron's previous writing from the heart? Indeed, much of its poignancy springs from the clear outline. One feels that it is both a normal and accurate picture of life for contemporary women – the point, 'Their's being an unnatural situation', being rendered more effective by its setting, the naturalism of the Haidée episode. Similarly, that episode itself – one of the peaks of romantic love-poetry – is the more effective for being set in a satire. Having been given other aspects of love ironically – and having this one given unpretentiously in Byron's colloquial ottava rima – the reader feels that the primitivistic answer – in such a stanza, for example, as that on the sleeping lover – is not cooked: this *is* natural and right, and what is contrasted with it is unnatural and wrong:

> For there it lies so tranquil, so beloved,
>> All that it hath of life with us is living;
> So gentle, stirless, helpless and unmoved,
>> And all unconscious of the joy 'tis giving;
> All it hath felt, inflicted, pass'd and proved,
>> Hushed into depths beyond the watcher's diving;
> There lies the thing we love with all its errors
> And all its charms, like death without its terrors. (2, CXCVII)

Even in these early cantos, moreover, the material of Byron's irony is often derived, directly or indirectly, from the social background: from the incongruity between Actual/Ideal (which issues in Cant); between Political Restraint/Primitive Freedom, or Orthodox/Natural Morality (morality, that is, not of dogma but the desires of man–and woman–in a free society); or, finally, between the Bitterness of one who feels, and the Laughter of one who thinks.

Stylistically speaking, it may be said that the final couplet is admirably suited to a surprise ending which underlines incongruity. The ridiculous rhyme on a serious subject serves the same purpose. Even the despotism of the rhyme scheme and the contrasting liberties of the language are in keeping. The strained rhymes, too, often emphasise an irreverence implicit in the matter. This is the only long romantic poem which is never dull, and one of the few poems of any length in this period which reconcile discordant elements without needing to blur the narrative line with symbolism.

So far as the matter is concerned, the Dedication acts as overture to the whole poem. Thus its attack on the Lake poets contains much pure humour, but the general tone is bitter and politically inspired. Passing from contemporary poet-renegades the Dedication goes on to praise Milton, as a rebel, and then mounts to the onslaught upon Castlereagh–paralleled by that on Wellington in Canto 9.

Such bitter personal attacks are, however, rare. Byron's disillusion usually sweetens and generalises even the most directly social satire. In the admirable stanzas CXXXII–IV in Canto 1, for instance, his reaction to the age merely acts as a gravitational pull giving coherence to the generality and variety of his subject matter:

> This is the patent age of new inventions
>   For killing bodies and for saving souls,
> All propagated with the best intentions;
>   Sir Humphrey Davy's lantern, by which coals
> Are safely mined for in the mode he mentions,
>   Tombuctoo travels, voyages to the Poles,
> Are ways to benefit mankind as true,
> Perhaps, as shooting them at Waterloo.

> Man's a phenomenon, one knows not what,
>   And wonderful beyond all wondrous measure;
> 'Tis pity though, in this sublime world, that
>   Pleasure's a sin, and sometimes sin's a pleasure;
> Few mortals know what end they would be at,
>   But whether glory, power, or Love, or treasure,
> The path is through perplexing ways, and when
> The goal is gain'd we die, you know,–and then–

> What then? I do not know, no more do you–

How perfectly the inconclusive colloquial phrasing–and that pause on the brink of the unknown–conveys Byron's agnosticism! And further, it keeps the romantic sublime to earth, as the clown saves tragedy from bombast.

In these first cantos, however, the gravitational pull rarely operates so obviously as in these stanzas (or those in the song *The Isles of Greece* which is directly on the Oppression/Freedom conflict). Usually it is rather glimpsed as the narrative goes by, as in the thumbnail sketch of the lawyer who

> ne'er believed in negatives, till these
> Were proved by competent false witnesses. (I, CLX)

or, more subtly, in the lines of Haidée's father:

> He loved his child, and would have wept the loss of her,
> But knew the cause no more than a philosopher. (3, XXVI)

The sense, by implication, sets up the natural against the sophisticated. The wit of the second line, linked with the sense of the first, involves the Melancholy/Mockery conflict in Byron's personality, and the treble rhyme firmly cements this union of opposites.

Sometimes there is only this relationship with the social background: that the almost cynical handling of the narrative implicitly attacks the prevailing cant. Thus, the appalling distance really existing between the actuality of human nature and the period armchair ideal of love and adventure is exposed in the shipwreck episode in Canto 2. Juan's eternal love is tempered by seasickness. He is eventually glad to eat one of the paws of his faithful spaniel. And his parting letter from Julia is used for a cannibilistic lottery. Love, the spiritual, has no power over hunger, the bodily. Or has it? Yes, indeed–and this is the unkindest cut–it saves the mate!

> his saving clause
> Was a small present made to him at Cadiz,
> By general subscription of the ladies. (LXXXI)

Behind this sardonic handling, however, lies not a cynic but a realist.

With the opening of Canto 7, the realism takes on a darker tone. Emphasis falls less on incident and banter, more on comment and satire.

> Must I restrain me through the fear of strife,
> From holding up the nothingness of life? (VII)

> Dogs, or men!–for I flatter you in saying
> That ye are dogs–your betters far–ye may
> Read or read not what I am now essaying,
> To show ye what ye are in every way. (VIII)

The same tone makes earnest the sort of punning that would formerly have been play-wit[1]; and the narrative turns from love to war. Consequently, although all the conflicts are involved, the chief concern is with that of Oppression and Freedom. Of the uneasy attraction to war in *Childe Harold* not a trace remains. Cantos 7 and 8 are perhaps the most telling attacks on it in our literature, and they bring in all Byron's preoccupations. The contrast between the real and the 'poetic' ideal–together with the bitterness and mockery aroused by it–is devastatingly resolved in satire (*v.* e.g. 8, XIII–IV). This leads to a fierce attack on war itself (*v.* 8, CXXIII) and from this Byron moves, by associative detestation, to England:

> Think how the joys of reading a Gazette
> Are purchased by all agonies and crimes:
> Or if these do not move you, don't forget
> Such doom may be your own in after-times.

[1] E.g. *v.* the question whether 'a man's name in a bulletin May make up for a bullet in his body' (7, XXI).

Meantime the Taxes, Castlereagh and Debt
  Are hints as good as sermons or as rhymes.
Read your own hearts and Ireland's present story,
Then feed her famine fat with Wellesley's glory (cxxv)

The last line, it may be mentioned, provides an interesting
example of the technical skill behind Byron's casual style, for
not only do the alliterative f's cement the paradox, but also they
make the caesura fall not after the second foot (as in the preceding
line) but after 'fat'—a word to be spat out.

The attack on England is followed by an explicit statement
of the intention of Byron's satire: unlike Shelley, he does intend
the contrasts of Is/Might Be, Oppression/Freedom to incite to
revolution:

  For I will teach, if possible, the stones
To rise against earth's tyrants. Never let it
  Be said that we still truckle unto thrones;—
But ye—our children's children! Think how we
Show'd *what things were* before the world was free! [Byron's italics]
That hour is not for us, but 'tis for you;
  And as in the great joy of your millenium,
You hardly will believe such things were true
  As now occur, I thought that I would pen you'em. (8, cxxxv–vi)

The millenium, indeed, seemed to be coming into being in
America after a successful war against tyranny. Why then was
this not so in Europe after Waterloo? Typically, the answer was
given in terms of character. America had a Washington and
Franklin who triumphed over the conflicts of the actual and ideal
in human nature. Europe had Wellington and its kings, concerned
to cant about a holy ideal in order to benefit materially.

Hence Canto 9 opens with a bitter attack on Wellington, and
thereafter the poem becomes more closely concerned with
contemporary conditions. The nihilism becomes more acute,
rebellion the only positive:

  And I will war, at least in words (and—should
  My chance so happen—deeds) with all who war

> With Thought;–and of Thought's foes by far most rude,
>> Tyrants and sycophants have been and are.
> I know not who may conquer : if I could
>> Have such a prescience, it should be no bar
> To this my plain, sworn, downright detestation
> Of every despotism in every nation.
>
> It is not that I adulate the people ...
>> I wish men to be free
> As much from mobs as kings–from you as me.
>> (9, XXIV–V)

Significantly, the love episodes of the early cantos change, firstly to the warm lust of a Russian tyrant, secondly to the cold lust of commercialised English husband-hunting, and the whole is corroded with an ironic scepticism. Any attempt at a solution of the conflicts, other than that of projecting them into the social field where they can be absorbed into the millenium (with the help of the satirist), is immediately crushed by a realistic view of human nature. Are the real and ideal the same, 'since what men think, Exists when the once thinkers are less real/Than what they thought'? If so, how very puzzling on the brink of 'what is called eternity, to stare/And know no more of what is here than there' (9, xx). And as for the ideal in the individual–Why, the world soon deals with that!

> –must make us selfish
> And shut our souls up in us like a shellfish. (XXIII)

There remains, of course, Berkeley's attempt to produce a philosophic solution:

> Nothing more true than *not* to trust your senses,
> And yet what are your other evidences?
>
> For me I know nought.... (14, X–XI)

And Religion?

> as I suffer from the shocks
> Of illness, I grow more orthodox.... (9, V)
>
> I devoutly wish'd the three were four
> On purpose to believe the more. (9, VI)

It is, however, precisely this scepticism which Byron now prizes.

He has travelled far from the days when feeling was exalted above reason.

> I may stand alone
> But would not change my *free thoughts* for a throne.
>
> (II, XC)

When Juan reaches England, the core of the satire is still political: the sins of

> That worse than *worst of foes*, the once adored
> False friend, who held out freedom to mankind,
> And now would chain them, to the very mind; –
>
> Would she be proud, or boast herself the free,
>   Who is but first of slaves? The nations are
> In prison, – but the gaoler, what is he? (10, LXVII–VIII)

What indeed? In England, Byron is, in one sense, *at home*.

Consequently, much of the later Cantos of this long and masterly poem exceeds all that has gone before, both in technique and content. The difficult stanza-form is made capable of infinitely varied effects, ranging from the Villonesque world of stanzas XIX–XXII (12) to the frosted mock-Gothic of stanzas XVII–XXII (16); or from the wellbred inanity of society (13, XXIV–V) to the easy mockery of it when Byron speaks in *propria persona* (13, XCV and CX).

The satire moves with great aplomb from the dullness of the English, 'a people famous for reflection Who like to play the fool with circumspection', to English cooking, inns, dingy towns, climate, marriage barter, morality, and politics. And threading it all run the interwoven strands of conflict, now taking the form chiefly of satire on Seeming/Being, as befitting perfidious Albion, where Juan must be advised to 'Be hypo-critical, be cautious' (11, LXXXVI).

Though this advice applies equally to love and business, it is typical of these cantos that the deadliest satire is political – witness the portrait of the sham Liberal (16, LXXI–LXXVI):

> A friend to freedom and freeholders – yet
> No less a friend to government – he held,

225

That he exactly the just medium hit
  'Twixt place and patriotism – albeit compelled
Such was his Sovereign's pleasure (though unfit,
  He added modestly, when rebels rail'd)
To hold some sinecures he wish'd abolish'd,
But that then all law would be demolish'd.

This flexibility, which can so catch the victim's very tone and rambling cadence, is turned to splendid use in the brilliant *ubi sunt* passage in Canto II (LXXVI–LXXXV). Something unique in English literature, it mingles, without any sense of incongruity, love, literature and politics, sorrow, anger and laughter. The style runs the whole gamut from the oratorical to the slangy, just as the imagery ranges from 'the world' to 'an old Opera hat'. In a sense, this passage incapsulates the essence of the poem – and the later Byron. For what unifies it is what unifies the whole created world of *Don Juan*: the earnest belief in the freedoms of body, mind, and morality – which (for good or ill) is the romantic reaction to emotional conflicts set up by the spirit of the age – and a realisation of the importance of not being earnest in expression.

In his first period, Byron's reaction had been a confused dissatisfaction with himself, in his middle period a mixture of soft sentiment, and hard cynicism. But now –

I would not be a tortoise in his screen
  Of stubborn shell, which waves and weather wear not
'Tis better on the whole to have felt and seen
  That which humanity may bear, or bear not:
'Twill teach discernment to the sensitive
And not to pour their ocean in a sieve. (14, XLIX)

The result is something very different from the common conception of a romantic (derived from the later romanticism of escape) as a dreamer above, or out of, the petty world. Byron, like Shelley, has learnt the futility of egotism and the life of the passions; and, on the other hand, the absence of any sure criteria for spiritual or moral values, except in the empirical world of society. He knows, too, as Shelley and Keats came to know, that men – and poems – are not easily perfectible. But out of the dis-illusion has come finally neither cynicism nor blind faith, but a battle against the odds. Byron's last words, spoken in delirium at Missolonghi, form a fitting pendant to his unfinished work:

Forwards, forwards, follow my example!

VII

KEATS

More than any other writer of the age, Keats seems to be a poet born. He has more gusto, more ability to focus several sense-impressions on one item so as to give a rounded, rich apprehension of it; an instinctive command of empathetic imagery and a wider range of synaesthesia give greater capacity for conveying his vision as a sensuous experience. His conflicts thus find expression at a more substantial level than those of any con-temporary poet. One other gift which seems to have an affinity with verse-form rather than prose is noted by Mr Jackson Bate:

But the really distinctive quality in Keats – and a quality his Victorian imitators rarely attained – is less the *substitution* than it is the *substantiation* of one sense by another in order to give, as it were, additional dimension and depth, as in the *moist scent* of flowers. . . .
('Keats's Style', *Major English Romantic Poets*, p. 222)

Such gifts, however, are not without a drawback. They are the gifts of a sensation-type personality; and while verse is a more obviously suitable medium for that type than for any other it cannot give transcendence to its natural limitations. At first sight, Keats might seem inescapably imprisoned in the life of sensation; he peppered his tongue before taking cold claret, and held as an ideal for the artist the amoral, aesthetic conception of 'negative capability'. Yet, on the other hand, there is evidence throughout his career – from *Sleep and Poetry* to *Lamia* or the second *Hyperion* – of a strong contrary inclination to 'philosophy' and service to mankind; and in contradiction to the doctrine of 'negative capability' he asserted the need to acquire through experience a positive ethical identity. That this was not altogether his natural bent is revealed by the poor quality of that poetry which is *directly* political or philosophical. None the less, this bent is strong enough in the end to give to his poetry an intellectual stiffening and human range that the early work, predominantly poetry of sensation, conspicuously lacks. More and more he comes to feel that he must create beauty not to escape, but to transmute ugly contemporary fact. Truth, material reality, must become beauty, and beauty must be 'truth'–acceptable even though *not* mere wish-fulfilment.

Keats's interest in social conditions has been so largely ignored[1]– or even denied–that it seems politic, if tedious, to quote some of the evidence. Haydon reports in Keats 'a fierce hatred of rank', Houghton that

he could not bear to go to an opera (*when he visited Italy, to die*) on account of the sentinels who stood constantly on the stage, and whom he at first took for parts of the scenic effect. 'We will go to Rome' he said, 'I know my end approaches and the continual visible tyranny of this government prevents me from having any peace of mind. I could not die quietly here. I will not leave even my bones in the midst of this despotism.   (*Life and Letters*, Everyman's, (1946), p. 215)[2]

Keats's own words, however, obviously provide the best evidence– and there is a good deal of it. For instance, he is writing on the 22nd April 1818:

I know nothing–I have read nothing–and I mean to follow Solomon's directions 'Get learning, get understanding'. I find earlier days are gone by–I find I can have no enjoyment in the world but by the continual drinking of knowledge. I find there is no worthy pursuit but the idea of doing some good to the world.   (P. 82)

Or again:

Women must want imagination, and they may thank God for it;

[1] An exception is C. de Witt Thorpe, whose article *Keats's Interest in Politics and World Affairs* (PMLA (1931) Vol. 46, pp. 1228/45) covers the ground fairly fully.

[2] For convenience of reference other examples will be taken from this edition. But more of similar import will be found in Forman's complete collection: *v.* particularly the long letter of Sept. 1819, ed. Forman, *Complete Works*, vol. V, 107/8.

and so may we, that a delicate being can feel happy without any sense of crime. It puzzles me, and I have no sort of logic to comfort me.

(10 June 1818, p. 91)

In a letter unfortunately too long to quote in full, he writes:

There is of a truth nothing manly or sterling in any part of the Government. . . . The motives of our worst men are interest, and of our best vanity. . . . Governors in these days, lose the title of man, in exchange for that of Diplomat or Minister. We breathe a sort of official atmosphere. . . . A man now entitled Chancellor has the same honour paid him whether he be a hog or a Lord Bacon. . . . Notwithstanding the noise the Liberals make in favour of the cause of Napoleon, I cannot but think he has done more harm to the cause of Liberty than anyone else could have done. Not that the Divine Right gentlemen have done, or intend to do any good—no, they have taken a lesson of him, and will do all the further harm he would have done, without any of the good.

(29 Oct 1818, pp. 138/9)

And shortly before his death he wrote:

I hope sincerely I shall be able to put a mite of help to the liberal side of the question before I die.

(Aug. 1819, p. 181)

In his notes on *Paradise Lost*, Bk. I, 595, he exclaims, 'How noble and collected an indignation against kings'. (See also the fierce attack on them in the first dozen lines of *Endymion*, Book III).

Nor did this quality in Keats go unrecognised—though it is comparatively rarely *directly* evident in his poetry—for an anonymous admirer, in November 1818, sent him £25 and a sonnet beginning:

> Star of high promise! Not to this dark age
> Do thy mild light and loveliness belong;
> For it is blind, intolerant and wrong,
> Dead to empyreal soarings, and the rage
> Of scoffing spirits bitter war doth wage
> With all that bold integrity of song. . . .

In Keats's own poetry, the same concern crops up: in the early *Endymion* and *Sleep and Poetry* ('Can I ever bid these joys farewell . . .?') and the late *Hyperion, A Dream* ('None can unsurp this height. . . . '). Then, of course, there are the political sonnets:

To Leigh Hunt, *To Kosciusko*, and *On the Peace*, and stanzas XIV–XVI in *Isabella*. *To Hope* expresses the same feeling:

> O let me see our land retain her soul,
> Her pride, her freedom; and not freedom's shade....
> Let me not see the patriot's high bequest,
> Great Liberty! how great in plain attire!
> With the base purple of a court oppressed.

And it is evident in the poem *To Charles Cowden Clarke*, or in the anti-militarism of the image of poppies

> So pert and useless that they bring to mind
> The scarlet coats that pester human kind
>
> *(Epistle to G. F. Mathew)*

With these examples in mind, it may not be thought over-fanciful to take such lines as these, from the first *Hyperion*, to give not only the primary narrative, but a seondary *image*, of repression:

> the brawniest in assault
> Were pent in regions of laborious breath;
> Dungeon'd in opaque element, to keep
> Their clenched teeth still clenched, and all their limbs
> Lock'd up like veins of metal, crampt and screwed
> Without a motion save of their big hearts
> Heaving in pain.   (Book II, 21/7)

And finally, we may cite towards the end of Keats's brief career his satiric mockery of the Regent in *The Cap and Bells*:

> 'I'll trounce some of the members,' cried the Prince,
> 'I'll put a mark against some rebel names,
> I'll make the Opposition-benches wince,
> I'll show them very soon, to all their shames,
> What 'tis to smother up a Prince's flames;
> That ministers should join in it, I own,
> Surprises me!—they too at these high games!
> Am I an Emperor? Do I wear a crown?
> Imperial Elfinan, go hang thyself or drown!

'I'll trounce 'em – there's the square-cut Chancellor,
His son shall never touch that bishopric,
And for the nephew of young Palfior,
I'll show him that his speeches made me sick,
And give the colonelcy to Phalaric;
The tiptoe marquis, moral and gallant,
Shall lodge in shabby taverns upon tick!
And for the Speaker's second cousin's aunt,
She shan't be maid of honour – by heaven that she shan't!'

(XVI/XVII)

It is this social concern with the miseries of the world, which will not let him rest, that puts Keats in fundamentally the same position as Shelley and Byron. A good deal more weight must be given in his case to conflicts due to the torments of unhappy love, but nevertheless, these wider concerns give to his poetry as to theirs, at its best, a depth and richness, a partial transcendence of the merely personal, and implications of generality which it would have lacked without them. Probing into personal problems he finds analogues of outside ideas and affairs. The verbal form his conflicts take is usually that of Magic and Fact, Sensuous and Spiritual Beauty, and Joy and Melancholy.

Keats's writing life was so short – a brief six years or so – that talk of periods seems almost irrelevant. Yet his development was so rapid that striking differences are in fact to be seen in poems with no more than a year or eighteen months between them. Certainly, it is true to say that the earliest work – *Endymion* and the shorter poems of that time – tends to be escapist. Joy, Sensuous Beauty and Magic are emphasised, their contraries ignored or minimised. Then with *La Belle Dame Sans Merci*, *Lamia* and *The Eve of St Agnes* a guilty ambivalence reveals itself in algolagniac undertones to these magical worlds. In each case, there is an awakening to reality but never a wholehearted rejection of the false, the Fatal Woman or the dream of youth; for Keats has not yet brought himself to accept the beauty of truth as well as the 'truth' of beauty. With *Hyperion* and the *Odes* comes a balanced complexity, a reconciliation of ideal and real. Throughout, though, there is complication by time and death, for Keats loved life and knew his time was short.

There is, of course, a great deal of fine sensuous writing and accurate observation in the earlier work. If the union of the ideal and the real in the conclusion of *Endymion*–when the Indian maid is metamorphosed into Cynthia–seems theoretical and unearned, it must be set alongside such textural gems as 'the *chuckling* linnet', the dolphins that '*bob* their noses through the brine', the fish in 'bright mail', or Venus seen

> when her lips and eyes
> Were closed in sullen moisture, and quick sighs
> Came vexed and pettish through her nostrils small.

Yet the one-sided, escapist emphasis, leads in general to overwriting, 'denoting a feverish attempt, rather than a deed accomplished' (as Keats himself put it). He is still in the realm 'Of Flora and old Pan' where life is 'A pigeon tumbling in clear summer air'–the realm he knew he must abandon, however reluctantly:

> And can I ever bid these joys farewell?
> Yes, I must pass them for a nobler life,
> Where I may find the agonies, the strife
> Of human hearts.   (*Sleep and Poetry*, 121/4)

Towards the end of *Endymion* an attitude similar to that of the *Ode to Autumn* is expressed, yet nothing could more clearly indicate change:

> ... Why, I have been a butterfly, a lord
> Of flowers, garlands, love-knots, silly posies,
> Groves, meadows, melodies and arbour roses.
> My kingdom's at its death, and just it is
> That I should die with it.   (iv, 937/41)

Not only is the statement itself somewhat more crude than that of the late poem, but the language is hackneyed, ornamental and tapestry-woven in comparison. No real pressure of sensuous and emotional urgency is felt to be backing up the statement. When Keats becomes a little less certain of 'the holiness of the heart's affections', a little less sure that 'What the Imagination seizes as Beauty must be Truth' (22 Nov. 1817. Everyman's (1946) p. 45) his poetry acquires shadow, and therefore a sense of depth and substantiality, despite the fact that it deals still in magical and legendary realms that inevitably tempt towards escapism.

In place of life as 'A pigeon tumbling in clear summer air', a sick rose opens, the romantic guilt. Magic darkens to sorcery and the dream love of Endymion is tinged with nightmare: witness Isabella's passion for 'All this wormy substance' (the decayed head of her murdered lover) or Lamia's garlands 'from vales *deflowered*'. The darkening shows too in curious ambivalences. Lamia seems 'some demon's mistress, or the demon's self'. Yet she does nothing evil. Indeed her possession of magical powers is actively beneficial to her lover. Yet one touch of fact, one sight of virtue destroys them. No sooner does Apollonius, the virtuous philosopher, look at Lamia 'like a sharp spear' than 'with a frightful scream' she vanishes. Even if we take Lamia's evil nature for granted, without evidence of it, the poem is still odd, since the predominant tone is one of attraction to the side of the unrighteous:

> And for the sage,
> Let speargrass and the spiteful thistle wage
> War on his temples! Do not all charms fly
> At the mere touch of cold Philosophy?
>
> (Pt. II, 227/30)

However, the new ambivalance leads here and there to genuine complexity of perception. Thus there is a new awareness of the close relationship between joy and melancholy (here, a little more sinisterly, referred to as bliss and pain):

> A virgin purest lipped, yet in the lore
> Of love deep learned to the red heart's core:
> Not one hour old, yet of sciential brain
> To unperplex bliss from its neighbour pain;
> Define their pettish limits, and estrange
> Their points of contact and swift counterchange.
>
> (Pt. I, 189/94)

or

> for all his love, in self-despite,
> Against his better self, he took delight
> Luxurious in her sorrows, soft and new.
>
> (Pt. II, 72/4)

The conflict of joy and melancholy is again inherent in *The Eve of St Agnes* where the banquet and the consummated love contrast effectively with the dusty corridors and icy halls of the castle: a contrast more emphatic in the original version, which the publisher toned down. In the printed version, for instance, stanza xxv ends:

> O leave me not in this eternal woe
> For if thou diest I know not where to go.

In George Keats's MS these lines read:

> See, while she speaks, his arms encroaching slow
> Have zon'd her, heart to heart–loud, loud the dark winds
> blow.

Then followed the two stanzas referred to by Woodhouse in a letter to Taylor (20 Sept. 1819), which are now missing, but evidently gave more plainly that contrast of warm passion within and cold storm without which is now implied in the single stanza following the U-certificate substituted couplet:

> Ethereal, flushed, and like a throbbing star
> Seen mid the sapphire heaven's deep repose,
> Into her dream he melted, as the rose
> Blendeth its odour with the violet–
> Solution sweet: meanwhile the frost wind blows
> Like Love's alarum pattering the sharp sleet
> Against the window-panes; St Agnes' moon hath set.
> (xxxvi)[1]

Similarly, the conflict of sensuous and spiritual beauty is involved in the contrast of virgin purity ('on her hair a glory like a saint') and the watched undressing, which modulates into the romantic union of the lovers. This *corrective* element in the poem persists to the end, for it concludes, not with a paean of rejoicing at the successful elopement, as might have been expected, but with a sudden shift of perspective, as if a telescope had been turned round. We suddenly see it all in the perspective of time and death. The lovers, the dream over, 'have gone: ay ages long ago' out into the storm of life and age, while old Angela and the beadsman,

[1] Fuller details are given in M. R. Ridley's *Keats's Craftsmanship* (1933).

who were throughout remote from youth, love, warmth or luxury, have died neglected.

All this makes the realism of *Teignmouth* less surprising than it might have been. This verse-letter recognises the inescapably ugly fact in the beauty of nature and rejects something of the magic nature usually had for the romantics:

> The rocks were silent; the wide sea did wave
> An untumultuous fringe of silver foam
> Along the flat brown sand; I was at home
> And should have been most happy – but I saw
> Too far into the sea, where every maw
> The greater on the less feeds evermore –
> But I saw too distinct into the core
> Of an eternal fierce destruction
> And so from happiness I was far gone.

This rare, and rather clumsy statement of sad sensuous fact is superseded later, in the first *Hyperion*, by an attempt to reconcile the ruthless aspect of nature with a feeling that *on the whole* natural life is good and worthwhile. In verse which is far superior (despite unassimilated Miltonic and Elizabethan elements) it tries to fuse truth and beauty, fact and magic. Oceanus's speech expresses an evolutionary view: individual lives may be short and sad, but Life is beautiful since it presents a spectacle of constant improvement:

> We fall by course of Nature's law, not force
> Of thunder or of Jove. . . .
> And first, as thou wast not the first of powers,
> So art thou not the last; it cannot be:
> Thou art not the beginning nor the end. (ii, 181/190)

Beauty is now found not by tactful turning of a blind eye but by dominating the truth:

> Now comes the pain of truth, to whom 'tis pain;
> O folly! for to bear all naked truths,
> And to envisage circumstance all calm,
> That is the top of sovereignty. . . .
> So on our heels a fresh perfection treads,
> A power more strong in beauty, born of us
> And fated to excel us. . . . (ii, 202/14)

It is significant that Apollo, the 'beauty born of us' is born with great pain and effort from a world of childlike innocence into a world of thought and experience. It is 'Knowledge enormous' that 'makes a god' of him.

The blank verse is now attuned to a great compass, from the opening stillness (where the implicit image of a mountain aptly conveys Saturn's fallen grandeur, his massive and frozen loneliness) to the roaring vowels in the passage which introduces Hyperion full of fiery wrath. Worth noting too is the skilful use of negatives to enforce a sense of subtraction:

> Forest on forest hung about his head
> Like cloud on cloud. No stir of air was there,
> Not so much life as on a summer's day
> Robs not one light seed from the feather'd grass,
> But where the dead leaf fell there did it rest....
>   Upon the sodden ground
> His old right hand lay nerveless, listless, dead,
> Unsceptred, and his realmless eyes were closed.
>
> (Bk. I, 6/19)

.   .   .   .

> His flaming robes stream'd out beyond his heels
> And gave a roar, as if of earthly fire....
>   On he flared
> From stately nave to nave, from vault to vault.
>
> (Bk. I, 214/18)

However, the poem does have certain faults– of which the one Keats gives as his reason for leaving it unfinished (that it was too Miltonic) is surely the least. Though it doesn't avoid the conflicts and contradictions of experience it is still an ambivalent work. There is more emotional sympathy with Hyperion (the world of sense, as it were) than the Apollonian theme can bear. Like Milton's Satan, for Blake, he is the unintentional hero. Moreover, the myth is confused. The Old Gods seem to represent, firstly, Keats's own unaccepting self (censured more severely in the second version, *Hyperion, A Dream*[1]), secondly, the old order, moribund but persistent:

> Scarce images of life, one here, one there. . . .
>   like a dismal cirque
> Of Druid stones, upon a forlorn moor
> When the chill rain begins at shut of eve
> In dull November.   (Bk. II, 33/7)

and thirdly, the present oppressed 'O'erwhelmed and spurned and battered' (Bk. I). In a word, not only are the repression and the progress by the same new gods, but the same old gods must be given at once sympathy and condemnation, so that the structure collapses owing to internal strain.

Changes in the second version indicate a desire to emphasise more the relation of beauty and truth to the world of suffering humanity. Saturn is made more peevish and defeatist, and Moneta is made wiser than Mnemosyne and more admonitory (as the new name implies). The minor verbal changes are not very important, and are fully dealt with in the notes to de Selincourt's edition. On the whole, they seem to be for the better–and no doubt would have been better still if Keats had revised this version as he did the first. English is 'kept up' more and the work is less rhetorical. But the really important difference lies in the new Induction of some 300 lines.

Brian Wicker, in *Essays in Criticism* (January 1957) maintained that this addition was obscure and selfcontradictory, and that Keats did not agree with Moneta. However, he shares Middleton Murry's view (expressed in *Keats and Shakespeare*) that lines 188/210 should be omitted. Since it is their omission which makes the piece obscure and self-contradictory, there seems good reason to agree with de Selincourt that Keats meant to revise, not omit them. At any rate, the general drift of the Induction seems pretty clear, and the verse itself to be a fitting vehicle for the wrestling of intellectual energy and creative power which Coleridge thought of as characteristically Shakesperian.

[1] Also called *The Fall of Hyperion*: but the first version was also intended to have had that title on completion.

The key to it, as de Selincourt points out, is to be found in *Sleep and Poetry*. Garden, temple and shrine represent three stages in the poet's development: the stages of nature and self-indulgent art, of knowledge and social concern, and finally of a hardly-achieved vision of reality in which truth and beauty are seen honestly and yet as ultimately one. Keats is recording a conviction that he has narrowly escaped the spiritual death of being an escapist poet, a Dreamer. In his newfound humility he admits that even a non-escapist, a *real* poet, is inferior to those who actually work for mankind, but pleads that such a poet is not useless; he is 'a sage,/A humanist, physician to all men'. In a word, Keats has become more urgently aware of the danger of the worse aspect of romanticism, and has resolved to reject it in favour of the better, calling on Apollo to strike down

> all mock lyrists, large self-worshippers
> And careless Hectorers in proud bad verse.

The better sort of romantic will make an immense effort to attain a state of serenity where he is able to face reality, the harshness of nature and yet find it beautiful. This fits in with the original intention of showing that the new gods were to be preferred. Saturn lived in a dream of sense, whereas the little we saw of Apollo indicated a new awakening. In the revised version, Keats seems to take Apollo's place; through painful effort, with the help of Moneta, he comes 'To see as a god sees'. Unhappily, this version, too, was left unfinished, probably owing to illness, so we have only the Odes–particularly the *Ode to Autumn*–to show that he *could* 'usurp those heights . . .'

Jackson Bate aptly speaks of them as miniature dramas in each of which the poet seeks 'to identify himself with an object that can lift himself beyond a world of flux. In each there is a gradual disengagement, an inability to follow completely the implications of sympathetic absorption, and a return back (implicit in the *Grecian Urn*, more obvious in the *Nightingale*) to the world of process and the claims of the human heart' (*Major English Romantic Poets*, p. 227). This is true, but more needs to be said, however briefly.

The *Ode To A Nightingale*, had it been written two hundred years earlier, would almost certainly have been an ode to the Holy Spirit, for it expresses a yearning to be translated to a better and more blissful world. So this nightingale is a theological rather than an ornithological one, and the poem is typically romantic in that use of Nature. It had considerable advantages. Christian vocabulary had become very hackneyed with centuries of use and could no longer express experience freshly. Again, no sectarian or theistic associations in the mind of poet or audience, no stock responses, were likely to be stimulated by the new vocabulary. The psychological experience had a chance of coming through embodied but pure. Moreover, it permitted Keats the more easily to admit his yearning to be wishful-thinking and to win through finally to an acceptance of fact in place of magic–'win through' implying assimilation, not merely repression of the wish. What matters, of course, is not the 'thought', the right moral conclusion but the experience one lives through in the company of a richly-endowed personality become, at last, fully articulate. A great variety of responses is ordered, not as a complicated theory, but as a rendering of psychological fact.

The first stanza starts with heartache and ends with an anticipation of 'summer'–after crossing Lethe. In the second, a rich pagan sensuousness is used to attain ghostliness. The third contrasts the world of reality 'Where palsy shakes a few, sad, last grey hairs, Where youth grows pale, and spectre-thin and dies' with the Nightingale's world. Then, in the fourth stanza, magic is seen as a solution, a way of escape from this world 'Where but to think is to be full of sorrow'. Or, to put it another way, Dreamers' poetry, and not drink or drugs, is desiderated. In the fifth stanza, natural reality is coloured with the mood of the visitation of 'Poesy' but fades to the memory of a murmur, and the sixth stanza *half* wishes for death, but ends with the realistic acknowledgement that this would not bring with it the eternal beauty and joy of the 'immortal Bird' (thought of as a species, unchanging, in contrast to man):

> Still would'st thou sing, and I have ears in vain–
> To thy high requiem become a sod.

In the seventh stanza the poet's feeling of alienation is beautifully evoked through the picture of Ruth 'in tears amid the alien corn' and leads naturally into a renewed wish for magical escape-but this time so blatantly magical ('Charming magic casements, opening on the foam/Of perilous seas in fairy lands forlorn') that one is prepared for the rejection of the last stanza 'Adieu! the fancy cannot cheat so well As she is famed to do, deceiving elf' (a bad flaw-but what else rhymes with *self*?). At the end, we are back where we started-with a question, not a conclusion-but sadder and wiser:

> Was it a vision, or a waking dream?
> Fled is that music:-Do I wake or sleep?

The *Ode on A Grecian Urn* is about another desired world-now clearly known to be unattainable from the start. The main conflict is now that of Truth and Beauty, not Magic and Fact. Such knowledge results in wistfulness, turning to affirmation, perhaps a little too aggressively, at the end. Again the desired world is contrasted with the real world, but mostly by implication. So, though the poem is not ironic it lives in the neighbourhood of irony. The paradoxes too-of soundless sound, timeless time, stationary growth and so forth-are allied to wit, though not witty. (The reason the poem can't be really ironic and witty is that the poet hasn't chosen a side. He feels deeply about both Beauty and Truth, the main conflict involved in the piece.) Nevertheless, much of the flavour of the poem is due to the sweetness of what is said combined with the acridness of what is implied-the unarcadian, unideal world, where love fades and beauty is mortal, and often far from true. The limitations and unrealism of the eternal are conceded in the last lines of the second stanza. It follows that 'Beauty' in the much-discussed conclusion of the poem must be akin to that in 'A thing of beauty is a joy for ever' or 'What the imagination seizes as Beauty must be Truth'-the essence of the wished-for world. A world desired because timeless and thus free from age and death and failing love. Beauty, in fact, is a sort of imaginary magic-and 'Truth' is fact, the empirical world where he will *not* love for ever nor she be fair. This is the world of *actual*, sensuous beauty. The final lines assert a reconciliation between

these worlds, but it carries conviction only in so far as 'Art' is the
answer. As a rule for life it won't do. Indeed the note of affirmation in the last line seems to indicate a *wish* that this were 'all
Ye know on earth, and all ye need to know', the real *belief* having
been already given in the phrase 'a friend to man': a work of art
is an impersonal beauty surviving our death to console other men
'in midst of other woe'; a momentary way of living out of time
(like Eliot's moment of ecstasy,)[1] This is true, but obviously not
all one needs to know for living well. Furthermore, the general
tenor of the poem belies the conclusion. Not only is it tinged
with nostalgia throughout, but stanzas three and four suggest that
the timeless world has its pathos too. Implicitly they recognise
that any intense joy or melancholy depends on one's sense of their
evanescence, on time and death, in fact. These therefore can be
accepted (and will be in the *Ode to Autumn*) as subsidiary goods
rather than necessary evils, and the Urn can be stigmatised as
'*Cold* Pastoral'. The recognition, admittedly, is somewhat masked
by a little cheating in stanza three, when the frozen lovers of the
cold pastoral are spoken of as 'warm' and 'panting'. The repeti-
tions and exclamation-marks in this area perhaps signalise an
attempt to overcompensate ('More happy love! more happy,
happy love!'). Like the conclusion, it protests a shade too much,
and marks thereby a lapse in an otherwise brilliant piece of
funambulism.

In the *Ode to Melancholy* the Joy/Melancholy conflict is
obviously primary, as the title indicates. The two are shown to be
inseparable, in passages of remarkable psychological insight
memorably phrased (though this is not so fine a poem as the other
odes). The first stanza instances again a latent wit, in the conscious
exaggeration, the sophisticated overuse of horror-novel vocabulary, and in the last lines shows awareness of a masochistic
element in melancholy, a *desired* anguish. The second stanza urges
the melancholic to go to Nature, but *not* to comfort his melan-
choly-to glut it. Why? Because melancholy 'dwells with

---

[1] If we take 'ye' to be the Urn, as some critics argue, we have an absurdity on
our hands. Urns don't *need* to know anything. But 'ye' as the reader, suddenly
turned upon, is acceptable dramatic rhetoric.

Beauty' (it does so because beauty 'must die' and this is sad); therefore it also dwells with Joy, similarly evanescent. The following lines in the third stanza imply–rightly–that you *must* have an opposite for the full appreciation of anything:

> Ay, in the very temple of Delight
> Veiled Melancholy has her sovran shrine,
> Though seen of none save him whose strenuous tongue
> Can burst Joy's grape against his palate fine.

The energy of the last clause, prepares the reader for the logically odd but psychologically honest sense of impressive achievement in becoming subject to Melancholy:

> His soul shall taste the sadness of her might,
> And be among her cloudy trophies hung.

After all, Moneta represented life on a richer level than that signified by the pigeon 'tumbling in clear summer air'.

Such criticism, thematic rather than textural, is somewhat unsatisfactory for works like these, which are characterised by constant verbal felicities. Considerations of space, however, forbid close criticism throughout. But the *Ode to Autumn*, as the culmination of Keats's sadly brief career, warrants fuller treatment, which may serve as token payment.

In this ode all the conflicts–the literary expressions of the one major division in living experience–are reconciled in a rendering of reality which is at once sensitive and sensuous. No mention is made of magic, fact, truth, beauty, joy, melancholy, time or death but all these are implicit, and so is all they stand for. Nor is there any statement of their inseparability for anyone living at full potential, but in this poem, itself living at full potential, their inseparability is enacted.

Each stanza embodies one thing more than another, so that the poem is progressive, not merely repetitive, in its richness. But each stanza also contains some hint of the other aspects embodied elsewhere. The first stanza suggests the atmosphere of morning, early autumn, and ripeness, but 'conspiring' and 'think' (for after all the bees are wrong in thinking 'warm days will never cease') prepare for a decline and enhance the total impression that there is no further to go, since this is perfection. The middle stanza calls up an idea of afternoon, mid-autumn, and reaping, the time of garnering but also of destroying. The 'twined flowers' are emblems of beauty that must die. Sparing some swaths implies cutting others; and 'careless' suggests Nature's ruthless inevitability as well as freedom from care. The last stanza evokes the mood of evening, late autumn, and remembrance, but contains hints of its opposite, spring, and of the earlier ripeness (in 'bloom' and the singing hedge-crickets, for instance).

This variety in unity is reflected texturally in the evolutionary abundance of the style. The opening lines brilliantly use assonance and alliteration to suggest bountiful maturity, and the unobtrusive humanisation anticipates the economical, fullscale personification of Autumn in the next stanza:

> Season of mists and mellow fruitfulness,
>   Close bosom-friend of the maturing sun;
>   Conspiring with him. . . .

Then evocations of weight, touch, taste and muscular tension give body to the mellowness. ('To *bend* with apples', '*mossed* cottage-trees', 'fill all fruit'–nearly a tongue-twister, giving a packed effect, '*plump* the hazel shells', '*sweet* kernel', 'clammy'.)

'Store' in the opening line of the second stanza picks up these suggestions, but gives them a slightly sinister overtone (of fruits *picked*, as it were). Autumn's hair 'soft-lifted by the winnowing wind' makes a lovely feminine picture, but 'winnowing' finely reminds one of the necessary ruthlessness of the season, of what the maturity is for–a reminder repeated in 'thy hook' and 'the last oozings hours by hours' (where, again, sound substantiates sense). The air of lotus-eating languor, given by 'sitting careless,' or 'drowsed with the fume of poppies,' is countered by the firm step of 'sometimes like a gleaner thou dost keep/Steady thy laden head across a brook'. This is only a *respite*.

So the last stanza begins bravely with 'Where are the songs of Spring? . . . . Think not of them, thou hast thy music too'. But it turns out to be 'wailful' or premonitory of winter. In this stanza all the implications of the preceding ones are fulfilled, sad or sweet, all the conflicts woven into one seamless experience.

Suppose 'full-grown lambs' had been 'sheep'? We should have lost the sense of time passing, of another season, of ripe maturity–and of readiness for the knife. No wonder they 'loud bleat from hilly bourn'; it wouldn't have done, poetically, for them to munch or nibble! Such marvellously simple complexity is characteristic of the whole stanza. After sound, the songs of spring, sight is invoked:

> While barred clouds bloom the soft-dying day,
> And touch the stubble-plains with rosy hue.

A sort of magic and beauty is here fused with hard fact and cold truth. A sense of aftermath is evoked by stubble-plains, of foreboding by 'barred' (the shades of winter's prison-house are closing in) and 'dying', but all this is tempered by the tenderness of 'soft', by the reminiscence of summer and health in 'rosy' and by the early-autumnal ripeness of 'bloom' which transposes 'barred' into a less melancholy key. Joy and melancholy are balanced in 'mourn' and 'sing' and are fused (with each other and with evanescent beauty) in the redbreast's whistling. Time and death, ecstasy and despair are fleetingly imaged by one tactful brushstroke in the small gnats, 'borne aloft,/Or sinking as the light wind lives or dies'–the wind that earlier soft-lifted Autumn's hair and more harshly winnowed.

This harmony of myth and nature, melancholy happiness, full yet fated beauty–a harmony so far beyond anything compassed by the pre-romantics–is surely due first to previous conflict and consequent wrestling with experience, a disinclination to rest content with stereotypes and stock responses, and finally to acceptance of facts as well as ideals. The signature to his masterpiece is the *beauty* seen in what must have been then to Keats a terrible symbol: the fact that the 'gathering swallows twitter in the skies'.

CONCLUSION

THIS study has attempted to define and account for English romanticism by relating the species to its environment, using the concepts of conflict and mutation to illuminate its growth and quality. *Part I* considered the outward, and more neglected, aspect of the complex forcing-process that promoted romanticism, and *Part II* considered the more immediate aspect as it revealed itself, differently, in various poets–their differences being a mark of that individuality which is paradoxically the sign of a common romanticism.

Perhaps too much has been attempted in one short book–and no doubt specialists in various fields will be rightly scandalised–yet much has been omitted too. Nothing has been said of one great failing: the romantics' neglect of the poetry of the Town–so brilliantly exploited by Baudelaire, Auden and Eliot to image certain labyrinthine complexities of experience which the country cannot: after all, to give Cowper an unintended emphasis, 'Man made the Town . . .'. The factor of literary influence, too, has been little considered, not because it was supposed unimportant but because others have fully covered the ground. However, receptivity to certain influences–as has been indicated–is itself part of the spirit of the age, and thus in no way conflicts with this account of romanticism.

On the other hand, it is hoped that some fresh light has been thrown on the limitation and lack of development in the pre-romantics, as compared with that scope and movement from disharmony to organic unity which characterises the work of the later romantics, at their best–a development coinciding with an increased infiltration of the real into the ideal and a greater collaboration with their linguistic medium.

Certain further points seem to follow from the analyses of *Part II*. Firstly, romantic poetry obviously can be profitably studied in relation to the background of ideas and events, but it should not be studied *for* them. There is no kernel to be extracted from the poetry. Secondly, ages of great romantic poetry will evidently be rare since it depends on a combination of several circumstances, and on a state of mind which cannot long be sustained. (Seemingly, it must find release or security, often in a return to rigid orthodoxy.) But ages of escapist romanticism—like that of the Victorians—may well be longer and more frequent. Thirdly, romantic poetry will necessarily have shortcomings, the virtues of energy, depth, originality and daring being inseparable from the complementary vices of extravagance and strain. Without their extremism the romantics would have been not better, but different. Finally, since romantic extravagance is fundamentally neither psychical nor philosophical, but psychological, the poetry cannot in the end be judged by its metaphysics. Its confusions are simply confusions, not revelations. What one does get is something qualitative: the quality of their effort. The poetry does not give a creed for Life, but *is* a verbalised mode of living (at the expense, as it were, of one more richly endowed)—at its rare best, a mode wherein destructive energies are converted to illumination, conflicts to alliances.

BOOKLIST

ONLY the works of authors actually quoted or considered are listed (but all titles and authors occuring in the text are indexed). For those who may wish to pursue various aspects of the subject further a comprehensive bibliography of the period is handily available in the *Pelican Guide to English Literature*, vol. 5 1957. London publication unless otherwise noted.

Abrams, M. H. *The Mirror and the Lamp.* New York, 1953

Bate, Jackson. *Keats's Style* (in *Major English Romantic Poetry*, ed. Thorpe, Baker and Weaver). Illinois, 1957

Bateson, F. W. *English Poetry, A Critical Introduction.* 1950
    Wordsworth, A Reinterpretation. 1954

Beattie, J. *The Minstrel.* 1771

Beckford, W. *Vathek.* 1786

Blake, W. *The Poetry and Prose of William Blake*, ed. Keynes, one-volume Nonesuch, 1948

Brooke, A. Stopford. *Naturalism in English Poetry.* 1920

Burns, R. *Poetry and Prose*, ed. Dewar. Oxford, 1929

Bush, D. *Science and Poetry.* New York, 1950

Byron, G. G. *Poems*, ed. E. H. Coleridge. 1898/1904
    Letters and Journals, ed. Prothers. 1898/1901
    Byron, a Self-portrait, ed. Quennell. 1950

Chatterton, T. *Poems*, ed. Roberts. 1906
    Rowley Poems, ed. Hare. Oxford, 1911

Cleland, J. *Memoirs of a Woman of Pleasure* (Fanny Hill). 1749
    Memoirs of a Coxcomb. 1751

Cobban, A. *The Debate on the French Revolution.* 1950

Coleridge, S. T. *Poetical Works*, ed. E. H. Coleridge. 1912

Combe, W. *Tours of Dr. Syntax.* 1809

Cowper, W. *Poems*, ed. Bailey. 1905
    Letters, ed. Frazer. 1912

Crabbe, G. *The Poetical Works*, ed. A. J. & R. M. Carlyle. 1932

Dacre, C. *Zofloya, or the Moor.* 1806

Davie, D. *The Late Augustans.* 1958

Fairchild, H. N. *Religious Trends in English Poetry* (III). New York, 1949

Foakes, R. A. *The Romantic Assertion.* 1958

Gibbon, E. *Autobiography* (1796), ed. Smeaton. 1948

Gilpin, W. *Observations on the River Wye, relative chiefly to Picturesque Beauty.* 1783

Godwin, W. *Political Justice* (3rd Edn., 1798), ed. Priestley. Toronto, 1946
  Caleb Williams. 1794
  St. Leon. 1799

Graham, W. *The Politics of the Greater Romantic Poets*, PMLA 36. Menasha, Wisconsin, 1921

Hart, B. *The Psychology of Insanity*. Cambridge, 1946

Havens, R. D. *Shelley the Artist* (in *Major English Romantic Poetry*, ed. Thorpe, Baker & Weaver). Illinois, 1957

Haydon, B. *Autobiography & Memoirs*, ed. Huxley. 1926

Hazlitt, W. *Complete Works*, ed. Howe. 1932

House, H. *Coleridge*. 1953

Huchon, R. *George Crabbe and his Times* (tr. Clarke). 1907

Hughes, A. M. D. *The Nascent Mind of Shelley*. Oxford, 1947

Hussey, C. *The Picturesque*. 1927

Johnstone, C. *Chrysal or the Adventures of a Guinea*. 1760/5

Jones, J. *The Egotistical Sublime*. 1954

Keats, J. *Complete Works*, ed. Buxton Forman. 1900/1
  Life and Letters, ed. Houghton. 1946

Knight, G. W. *The Starlit Dome*. 1941

Lamb, C. *Letters*, ed. Ainger. 1897

Langer, S. *Problems of Art*. 1957

Leavis, F. R. *Revaluation*. 1936

Lewis, M. *The Monk*. 1796

Lowes, J. L. *The Road to Xanadu*. 1930

Malthus, T. *An Essay on the Principles of Population*. 1798

Maturin, C. *Melmoth the Wanderer*. 1820

Murry, M. *Keats and Shakespeare*. Oxford, 1925

Newman, J. H. *Apologia*, ed. Ward. Oxford, 1913
  Porochial and Plain Sermons. 1869/70

Orwell, G. *1984*. 1949

Paine, T. *The Rights of Man*, ed. Holyoake. 1494

Pettet, E. C. *On the Poetry of Keats*. Cambridge, 1957

Pope, A. *Essay on Man*. 1732/4

Radcliffe, A. *The Romance of the Forest* (1791), ed. Rose. 1904

Ridley, M. R. *Keat's Craftsmanship*. Oxford, 1933

Robinson, Crabb H. *Diaries*, ed. Sadler. 1869

Robson, W. W. *Byron as Poet*. Oxford, 1957

Rogers, S. *Recollections of the Table Talk*, ed. Bishop. 1952

Russell, B. *History of Western Philosophy*. 1946

Ryle, G. *The Concept of Mind*. 1949

Salingar, L. G. *Coleridge: Poet and Philosopher* (in *Pelican Guide to English Literature*, 5). 1957

Selincourt, E. de. *Coleridge's 'Dejection: an Ode'* (containing the original version) *Essays and Studies*, xxii. 1937

Shelley, M. *Frankenstein*. 1818

Shelley, P. B. *Complete Works*, ed. Ingpen & Peck. 1926/1930

Smart, C. *Poems*, ed. Callan. 1949
        Jubilate Agno, ed. Bond. 1954

Smith, Logan Pearsall. *All Trivia*. 1933

Stephen, J. K. *Lapsus Calami*. 1891

Sterne, L. *Sentimental Journey*. 1768

Thorpe, C. de Witt. *Keats's Interest in Politics and World Affairs*, PMLA 46. 1931

Tieghem, J. Van. *Romantisme dans le Litterature Européenne*. Paris, 1948

Walpole, H. *The Castle of Otranto* (1764), ed. Henderson. 1930
        Letters, ed. Toynbee. Oxford, 1918

Ward, W. S. *Some Aspects of the Conservative Attitude toward Poetry in England 1798-1820*, PMLA 60. Menasha, Wisconsin, 1945

Wicker, B. *The Disputed Lines in 'The Fall of Hyperion'* (in *Essays in Criticism*, Jan. 1957). 1957

Willey, B. *The Eighteenth Century Background*. 1940

Winkler, R. O. C. *Wordsworth's Poetry* (in *Pelican Guide to English Literature*, 5). 1957

Witcutt, W. P. *Blake, a Psychological Study*. 1946

Woodring, C. R. *Coleridge and the Khan* (in *Essays in Criticism*, Oct. 1959)

Wordsworth, W. *Poetical Works*, ed. de Selincourt. Oxford, 1940/49
        Early Letters, ed. de Selincourt. Oxford, 1935

INDEX

INDEX

INDEX

INDEX

INDEX